VIRGINIA WOOLF'S MYTHIC METHOD

CLASSICAL MEMORIES/MODERN IDENTITIES
Paul Allen Miller and Richard H. Armstrong, Series Editors

VIRGINIA WOOLF'S MYTHIC METHOD

~

Amy C. Smith

THE OHIO STATE UNIVERSITY PRESS
COLUMBUS

Copyright © 2022 by The Ohio State University.
All rights reserved.

Library of Congress Cataloging-in-Publication Data
Names: Smith, Amy C., 1978– author.
Title: Virginia Woolf's mythic method / Amy C. Smith.
Other titles: Classical memories/modern identities.
Description: Columbus : The Ohio State University Press, [2022] | Series: Classical memories/modern identities | Includes bibliographical references and index. | Summary: "Through close readings of Mrs. Dalloway, To the Lighthouse, and Between the Acts, Smith argues that Virginia Woolf crafts a paratactic mythic method in her fiction that expresses critical views about the role of rational materialism in social structures"—Provided by publisher.
Identifiers: LCCN 2021044626 | ISBN 9780814215135 (cloth) | ISBN 0814215130 (cloth) | ISBN 9780814281918 (ebook) | ISBN 0814281915 (ebook)
Subjects: LCSH: Woolf, Virginia, 1882–1941—Criticism and interpretation. | Woolf, Virginia, 1882–1941—Political and social views. | Woolf, Virginia, 1882–1941. Mrs. Dalloway. | Woolf, Virginia, 1882–1941. To the lighthouse. | Woolf, Virginia, 1882–1941. Between the acts. | Myth in literature. | Modernism (Literature) | English fiction—20th century—History and criticism.
Classification: LCC PR6045.O72 Z876525 2022 | DDC 823/.912—dc23/eng/20211206
LC record available at https://lccn.loc.gov/2021044626

Other identifiers: ISBN 9780814258200 (paper) | ISBN 0814258204 (paper)

Cover design by Susan Zucker
Text composition by Stuart Rodriguez
Type set in Minion Pro

CONTENTS

List of Abbreviations		vii
Acknowledgments		ix
INTRODUCTION	A Paratactic Method	1
CHAPTER 1	Clarissa's Eleusinian Desires	25
CHAPTER 2	Septimus's Dionysian Sacrifice	51
CHAPTER 3	Peter Walsh's Primitivist Odyssey	69
CHAPTER 4	The Goddess in the Lighthouse	91
CHAPTER 5	Harmonious Discord in *Between the Acts*	119
Bibliography		137
Index		153

ABBREVIATIONS

The following abbreviations used for frequently cited books by Virginia Woolf occur throughout the book.

BTA — *Between the Acts*. 1941. Reprinted with introduction and annotation by Melba Cuddy-Keane. Orlando: Harvest-Harcourt, 2008. Page references are to the 2008 edition.

JR — *Jacob's Room*. 1922. Reprinted with introduction and annotation by Vara Neverow. Orlando: Houghton Mifflin Harcourt, 2008. Page references are to the 2008 edition.

MOB — *Moments of Being*. Edited by Jeanne Shulkind. London: University of Sussex Press, 1976; second revised edition, San Diego: Harcourt Brace, 1985.

MD — *Mrs. Dalloway*. 1925. Reprinted with introduction and annotation by Bonnie Kime Scott. Orlando: Harvest-Harcourt, 2005. Page references are to the 2005 edition.

RO — *A Room of One's Own*. 1929. Reprinted with introduction and annotation by Susan Gubar. Orlando: Harvest-Harcourt, 2005. Page references are to the 2005 edition.

TG — *Three Guineas*. 1938. Reprinted with introduction and annotation by Jane Marcus. Orlando: Harcourt, 2006. Page references are to the 2006 edition.

TTL — *To the Lighthouse*. 1927. Reprinted with introduction and annotation by Mark Hussey. Orlando: Harvest-Harcourt, 2005. Page references are to the 2005 edition.

ACKNOWLEDGMENTS

This book has been a long time in the making and has been helped along by many kind friends and teachers, too many to name here. Several friends have read parts of this book and offered helpful advice that significantly strengthened the arguments. In particular, I would like to thank Vara Neverow, Jeannette McVicker, Julie Wilhelm, Shilo McGiff, Vicki Tromanhauser, Ben Hagen, Drew Shannon, Kristina Groover, and Alison Heney. Betty Chen, Casey Ford, and William Brewer have grown from students to colleagues, and their careful attention to the text has improved the clarity of the writing.

Along the way I have been blessed with many wonderful mentors and teachers including Zoja Pavlovskis-Petit, Luiza Moreira, Gisela Brinker-Gabler, Marilyn Gaddis-Rose, Fred Garber, Bat-Ami Bar-On, Leon Goldstein, Ernie Alleva, Vicky Spelman, and Richard Bernstein. Henry Carrigan and David Hall encouraged me to publish this book, and I thank them deeply for believing in my potential very early in my career.

At Lamar University, I have found an engaging and warm community of colleagues who have shown appreciation for my work, contributing to my well-being and to my professional development. In particular, I would like to thank Adrienne Blackwell-Starnes, Jim Sanderson, Sara Hillin, Brenda Nichols, Steve Zani, and Melissa Hudler. Completion of this project was aided significantly by a half-year leave and a research enhancement grant from Lamar University.

An earlier version of chapter one was published in *Woolf Studies Annual* 17 (2011). Parts of chapter two and of chapter three were published in *Virginia Woolf Miscellany* 70 (fall 2006) and the *Lamar Journal of the Humanities* 35:1 (2010). My thanks to the editors of these three journals for allowing me to reprint revised material from those articles.

I have been blessed with a warm, loving family who valued education and independent thought. My parents and sister have been consistently loving and supportive of me during this project, as well as providing me with the solid foundation to be able to undertake work of this sort at all.

Andrew Wolin and Marcy Lewis have, for many years, been my closest and best examples of how to live and think. Our shared efforts to live philosophically, and the many lessons I have learned along the way, enrich every day of my life and inform everything I do.

Finally, I would like to thank my husband, Richard, for bearing the burden of writing most closely with me. Your intellectual rigor pushes me to think and write better, and your nurturing support gives me the courage to do so.

INTRODUCTION

A Paratactic Method

In his 1923 review of James Joyce's *Ulysses*, T. S. Eliot formulated his influential modernist "mythical method," a theory that for a long time dominated modernist studies of myth. Eliot praises Joyce for shaping the jumble of modern life into a meaningful order through mythic parallels. In that essay Eliot may be inaccurately projecting his own idée fixe on to *Ulysses*, since his description of the method more accurately fits *The Waste Land*. While Eliot's theory has often served as a paradigm for how modernist authors used myth, I argue that Virginia Woolf developed her own original method of incorporating myth into modernist literature. Her method's divergence from Eliot's shows in the absence of Woolf in many studies of myth in modernism, including Michael Bell's classic *Literature, Modernism, and Myth*, which includes chapters on all the major male modernists as well as Latin American Boom authors and postmodern writers, but none on Woolf.

Inspired by the structure of archaic oral literature, Woolf's mythic method reflects her feminist vision of the modern world. Eliot's mythic method was, in his own words, "a way of controlling, of ordering, of giving a shape and a significance to the immense panorama of futility and anarchy which is contemporary history," an impulse that Jean Mills characterizes as the search for "a reaffirmation of masculine hierarchies in mythic structures" following the destruction of World War I.[1] Despite her friendship with Eliot, the problems that concern Woolf stem not from a failure of control and order but from an excess of the masculine hierarchies that Eliot mourned. Woolf dreads not the anarchy of contemporary history but the oily craving for power and domination that the modern world evinces. In contrast to Eliot, who believes that classicism is the "goal toward which all good literature strives," Woolf's literary goals are not classical at all but rather archaic.[2] Rather than seeing myth as a straightforward unifying force with the role "of controlling, of ordering" reality, her careful practice of translating Greek tragedies led her to view myth as a powerfully disordered and disordering influence and to prioritize the indeterminate style of oral literature.

In this study I combine the long, though recently neglected, scholarly conversation about myth in Woolf's fiction with more recent conversations regarding Woolf's treatment of social and political issues; the influence of Jane Harrison's scholarship and Woolf's reading in Greek on her intellectual and political views; and Woolf's preference for indeterminacy in narrative structures. As early as 1956, with Joseph Blotner's study of the Homeric *Hymn to Demeter* and the Oedipal conflict in *To the Lighthouse*, scholars began analyzing Woolf's use of Greek myth. This topic gained prominence in the 1970s, '80s, and '90s with feminist analyses of Woolf's allusions to Greek and Egyptian goddesses, but it has been relatively neglected as an area of critical inquiry in recent years.[3] Over the last twenty years, attention has turned to Woolf's treatment of social and political issues in her fiction and nonfiction, building on feminist scholarship to address issues of empire, race, the British class

---

1. Eliot, "Ulysses, Order, and Myth," 478; Mills, *Spirit of Modernist Classicism*, 64. Jane Marcus also addresses this topic in *Languages of Patriarchy*.

2. Eliot, "Ulysses, Order, and Myth," 477. Regarding Eliot's Classicism, Viorica Patea writes that "the diverse, heterogeneous nature of [Eliot's] fragments is subsumed by a universal unifying principle. . . . In his classical view, the universal alone is a safeguard for human integrity and solidarity." Patea, "Poetics of Mythical Method," 106.

3. Blotner, "Mythic Patterns." The following is a small sample of some of the later feminist interpretations of Woolf's use of myth: Madeline Moore examines Woolf's incorporation of Harrison's Mother and Maiden in *The Voyage Out* in "Some Female Versions of Pastoral." Vara Neverow analyzes the Great Goddess in *Jacob's Room* in "The Return of the Great Goddess." Evelyn Haller traces the references to Egyptian religion, specifically the rituals of Isis, Osiris, and Horus in *Between the Acts* in "Isis Unveiled." Eileen Barrett reads La Trobe's play in *Between the Acts* as a matriarchal play and detects Persephone's rape and the Mother Goddess in the novel in "Matriarchal Myth on a Patriarchal Stage." Lisa Tyler analyzes references to Demeter and Persephone in *The Voyage Out*, *To the Lighthouse*, and *Mrs. Dalloway* in "Mother-Daughter Passion and Rapture." See also Anne G. Hoffman, "Demeter and Poseidon" and Jean O. Love, *Worlds in Consciousness*.

system, fascism, war, and many other topics.[4] A third track of scholarship, which has lately seen a resurgence, examines how Harrison's scholarship and Woolf's own reading of Greek literature and philosophy influenced Woolf's intellectual and political views, but it largely does not address the position and function of myth in the artistic expression of these views.[5] Finally, a range of scholars examine Woolf's refusal to settle meanings or resolve inconsistencies within her fiction.[6] Woolf's strategies for incorporating myth in her fiction have not generally been part of these important conversations, yet I will argue in this book that Woolf often explores these ideas through a particular type of allusion to Greek myth. I aim to bring together these areas of Woolf studies, reviving the study of myth in Woolf's work by showing that Woolf's mythic method is a primary aesthetic vehicle for expressing critical views about the role of modern epistemological and metaphysical assumptions in social structures.

The study of myth in modernist literature may feel passé today, but this is likely due to the past influence of Eliot in literary studies, which led to an unfortunate association of modernism with orthodoxy that has since been rejected.[7] It should be no surprise, then, that the study of myth and modernism, once a prominent area of inquiry in modernist literary studies inflected

---

4. The following is again a necessarily incomplete list of such works, but provides another small sample: Merry Pawlowski, *Virginia Woolf and Fascism*; Berenice Carroll, "'To Crush Him in Our Own Country'"; Christine Froula, *Virginia Woolf and the Bloomsbury Avant-Garde*; Alex Zwerdling, *Virginia Woolf and the Real World*; Mark Hussey, *Virginia Woolf and War*; Jeanette McVicker, "'Six Essays on London Life'"; Nicholas Crawford, "Orientalizing Elizabeth"; Jed Esty, *A Shrinking Island*; Eileen Barrett, "Septimus and Shadrack"; Kathy Phillips, *Virginia Woolf against Empire*; Steve Ellis, *British Writers and the Approach of World War II*; and Janice Ho, *Nation and Citizenship in the Twentieth-Century British Novel*.

5. Recent works include Jean Mills, *Virginia Woolf, Jane Ellen Harrison, and the Spirit of Modernist Classicism*; Emily Dalgarno, *Virginia Woolf and the Migrations of Language*; and Theodore Koulouris, *Hellenism and Loss in the Work of Virginia Woolf*. There is a long tradition of scholarship about the influence of Jane Harrison and the role of Greek in Woolf's fiction. See, for instance, Rowena Fowler, "Moments and Metamorphoses"; Angeliki Spiropoulou, "'On Not Knowing Greek'"; Annabel Robinson, "Something Odd at Work"; Yopie Prins, *Ladies' Greek: Victorian Translations of Tragedy*; and Sandra Shattuck, "The Stage of Scholarship: Crossing the Bridge from Harrison to Woolf."

6. On this topic, see Molly Hite, *Woolf's Ambiguities*; Anna Snaith, *Public and Private Negotiations*; Susan Lanser, *Fictions of Authority*; Koulouris, *Hellenism and Loss*; Vicki Mahaffey, *Modernist Literature: Challenging Fictions*; Anne Fernald, *Feminism and the Reader*; and Madelyn Detloff, *Persistence of Modernism*, among others.

7. Mao and Walkowitz, *Bad Modernisms*, 6. As James Nikopoulos writes, Eliot's formulation of a mythic method in his review of *Ulysses* "has been the starting point for discussions, not just of the classical legacy in early twentieth century literature, but for discussions of modernism as a whole . . . [it] conditioned how we think of modernity, of myth." Nikopoulos, "Wisdom of Myth," 292.

through Eliot's theory, has come to feel irrelevant in contemporary modernist studies. But shifting away from Eliot need not mean shifting away from the study of myth in modernism. Exploring other modernist mythic methods, such as Woolf's, can reveal both the variety of ways myth functions for modernists and its enduring significance for understanding modernism.

I characterize Woolf's mythic method as paratactic, and I believe that her paratactic method best fits our contemporary understanding of modernism, which emphasizes the disruption of hierarchy, fragmentation, and reader's active construction of meaning out of these fragments. Susan Stanford Friedman identifies parataxis as a distinguishing feature of modernist writing and art, "developed to disrupt and fragment conventional sequencing, causality, and perspective. . . . [It is] the opposite of hierarchical relationships of syntactic units."[8] The modernist aesthetic exemplified by Woolf and Joyce has long provoked scholars to theorize the narrative structures of their fiction, prompting labels of stream of consciousness, free indirect discourse, cubism, bricolage, and fragmentation, among others. Recent discussions in this vein almost invariably emphasize the political and epistemological implications of such aesthetic strategies. In *The Concept of Modernism*, Astradur Eysteinnson argues that fragmentation is a crucial modernist tool for countering totalizing synthesis and instrumental reason.[9] Vicki Mahaffey writes that by frustrating readers' wish to passively receive a text's authorized meaning, fragmentary modernist literature trains readers in more ethical, because more actively responsible, interpretive practices.[10] More recently and writing specifically about Woolf, Molly Hite argues that by removing tonal cues Woolf withholds authorially sanctioned opinions and forces readers to decide how to understand and assign values to elements of fiction.[11] The paratactic mythic method that Woolf develops in her fiction reflects more accurately than Eliot's "controlling and ordering" mythic method this view of modernist aesthetic innovations and anti-establishment political commitments while it reminds us of modernist artists' persistent interest in the ancients.

In developing her mythic method Woolf found inspiration in the style of preclassical oral literature, which she encountered directly through her early reading of the *Odyssey* in Greek and indirectly through Harrison's scholarship on preclassical Greek religion. In contrast to the syntactic storytelling common in written literature, which tells the reader a story by providing the

---

8. Friedman, "Definitional Excursions," 494–95. Similarly, Franco Morretti describes James Joyce's style in *Ulysses* as paratactic. Moretti, *Modern Epic*, 135.

9. Eysteinnson, *Concept of Modernism*.

10. Mahaffey, *Modernist Literature: Challenging Fictions*.

11. Hite, *Woolf's Ambiguities*.

logical connections between events and ideas, indicating the sequence and cause of events through subordination and coordination, paratactic storytelling presents the ideas and events of a story one after another without providing the logical connections that order these items. While syntaxis directs readers toward meaning, creating the illusion that the written text and world are unified and readable, and its pushier cousin hypotaxis—from the Greek *to place under*—insists on hierarchy through subordination, parataxis—from the Greek *to place side by side*—presents ideas and events in equilibrium, asking the reader to participate in making the meaning of a story by filling in their relationships. Parataxis thus engages the reader in more active reading, or listening, practices and counteracts the numbing effects of hegemonic discourse. The performance/composition of oral epic, in which the poet radically alters the story in different performances, illustrates the dynamic participatory relationship of storyteller and audience and the empowerment of the audience as co-composer, enabled by parataxis. In *Regarding Penelope*, Nancy Felson, sounding like Mahaffey in a very different context, describes this effect in the *Odyssey*, arguing that "the indeterminacies of multiple voices contend in a poetic tug-of-war in which the listeners take as active a role as does the performing poet, who indeed anticipates their diverse responses as he weaves his verse."[12] By presenting conflicting perspectives on characters and refusing to prioritize any one of these, the epic maintains interpretive openness and challenges readers' interpretations and moral judgments, at times even making Penelope's villainous suitors sympathetic.

While on the surface Woolf's writing, with its long sentences full of subordinating clauses and semicolons, may not strike us as classically paratactic, she frequently employs asyndetic parataxis, which omits coordinating conjunctions. "I came, I saw, I conquered," from Plutarch's *Life of Caesar*, illustrates the asyndetic mode. In place of coordinating conjunctions, Woolf famously uses the semicolon. Consider this early passage from *Mrs. Dalloway*:

> How fresh, how calm, stiller than this of course, the air was in the early morning; like the flap of a wave; the kiss of a wave; chill and sharp and yet *(for a girl of eighteen as she then was)* solemn, feeling as she did, standing there at the open window, that something awful was about to happen; looking at the flowers, at the trees with the smoke winding off them and the rooks rising, falling; standing and looking until Peter Walsh said, "Musing among the vegetables?"—*was that it?*—"I prefer men to cauliflowers"—*was*

---

12. Felson, *Regarding Penelope*, xiii. Besides Mahaffey, Felson's emphasis on indeterminacy also resembles Hite's claim that Woolf removes tonal cues in *Woolf's Ambiguities*.

> *that it?* He must have said it at breakfast one morning when she had gone out on to the terrace—Peter Walsh. He would be back from India one of these days, June or July, she forgot which, for his letters were awfully dull; it was his sayings one remembered; his eyes, his pocket-knife, his smile, his grumpiness and, when millions of things had utterly vanished—*how strange it was!*—a few sayings like this about cabbages. (3–4, emphasis mine)

This passage incorporates three instances of interruptive embedding, both as parenthetical asides and as interjected questions or exclamations (the repeated "was that it?" and "how strange it was!"), another feature of parataxis that Woolf employs to great effect throughout her work to illustrate the meanderings of thought. Notably, Woolf often leaves out subordinating conjunctions like *because*, a feature of hypotaxis that directs readers toward an interpretation by marking the hierarchical relationship between clauses within a sentence. This passage does not make it obvious to me as a reader what I am supposed to take from these sentences, which elements matter more than others, and how these seemingly random moments are related to one another. I am left with plenty of space to create meaning as a reader, much like the audience member/co-composer of an oral epic.

Woolf develops this paratactic narrative method in "Kew Gardens" and "The Mark on the Wall," and she provides her first sustained example of it in *Jacob's Room*, where she felt she had now finally "found out how to begin (at age 40) to say something in [her] own voice" (July 26, 1922: *Diary 2*, 186).[13] Woolf's "new form for a new novel" involved a narrative with "no scaffolding; scarcely a brick to be seen; all crepuscular" (January 26, 1920: *Diary 2*, 13–14). In that novel, she incorporates several techniques to refuse providing unilateral meaning for readers, coaxing readers into gazing at her contiguous fragments and arranging them into meaning. The most widely noted is the removal of scaffolding, which leaves readers to "decipher the work independently . . . piece together the fragmented events."[14] Woolf also pushes back against readers' somnambulant compulsion to read as they are told to through her use of spatial gaps and ellipses.[15] Her method becomes particularly intense in chapter four, which features frequent use of ellipses to diffuse meaning,

---

13. Hereafter, citations to Woolf's diaries will occur parenthetically in text.
14. Neverow, Introduction to *Jacob's Room*, lvi, lxxxv.
15. Regarding Woolf's spatial gaps, Edward Bishop notes, "The text instead of providing an answer for us asks us to speculate on our own. The gap is for us to fill in." Bishop attests that the editions that regularize or remove these gaps "direct and foreclose the reader's response, rather than engage it. *Jacob's Room* is a novel full of fissures, ruptures, gaps, and chasms, and the intent of the novel is . . . to make us aware of these spaces." Bishop, "Mind the Gap," 37, 41.

perhaps suggesting, as Timmy Durrant thinks, "there are things that can't be said" (*JR*, 49).[16] When Timmy and Jacob have "a tremendous argument," the narrator obscures the conversation through ellipses and the rapid juxtaposition of seemingly unrelated paragraphs about cats, the coast of Cornwall, and pokers. Are we to read these interjections as the content of Jacob and Timmy's argument? Are we to read them as unrelated thoughts of the narrator, or as obscure commentary on Jacob and Timmy's argument? Why does the narrator not show us the argument?

The reading experience that these structures produce, which recurs throughout the novel, bears the marks of parataxis. The narrative method Woolf develops in *Jacob's Room* cannot be separated from the role of Greek in her intellectual life, particularly her reading of Greek plays and the influence of Harrison. But, despite the role of Greek myth in *Jacob's Room*, Woolf only fully develops her paratactic *mythic* method in *Mrs. Dalloway*, and so this study begins there.

Lurking beneath the surface of apparently straightforward, ordered classical representations of Olympian myth, the oral pre-Olympian religion that Harrison studied shares this indeterminate structure. Figures slip in and out of each other's stories; there are multiple, contradictory stories concerning a particular character; figures resemble each other to such an extent that it is not always possible to differentiate them; multiple deities may derive from one earlier ancestor whose aspects they share. Myth is not singular, linear narrative. There is not one authoritative source that could provide the real events and traits of a mythic character because local stories and sources supposedly concerning the same figure contradict one another. Regional figures merge and disperse in untold patterns, while stories change over time. The deities that Woolf emphasizes in her fiction—various aspects of Harrison's Great Goddess and the god most closely associated with her, Dionysus—embody this aesthetic especially clearly because they appear in archaic and preclassical oral literature formed in a diverse archipelago with a history of syncretism. Dionysus is an ambivalent god, at once the terrifying one who imprisons people in madness and the gentle liberator.[17] Persephone appears simultaneously as a lovely young maiden and the terrifying queen of the Underworld; the Sirens and the Great Goddess, figures that Woolf employs repeatedly throughout her work, share this paradoxical nature as well.[18] Even the classical Greek literature

---

16. Page references are to the 2008 edition.
17. On this topic, see Alain Daniélou, *Shiva and Dionysus*; H. S. Versnel, *Inconsistencies in Greek and Roman Religion I*; and Walter F. Otto, *Dionysus: Myth and Cult*.
18. Jung and Kerényi, *Science of Mythology*. See Kerényi's essay on the *Kore* in this collection.

that Woolf could read in Greek, primarily the tragedies of Sophocles, Aeschylus, and Euripides, of which she read several, reflects the indeterminacy of its archaic source material. In some cases, the tragedians introduce additional ambivalence into the archaic figures they dramatize. This paradoxical slipperiness motivates Woolf's turn to myth as a tool with which to carve out a space for thinking beyond binary categories and their manifestations in political and social life, an aim shared by her friend and mentor, Jane Harrison.

Rowena Fowler also describes Woolf's writing as employing a "mythical method," but she means by that term something very different than I do. Fowler characterizes Woolf's mythic method as one "of Greek correspondences invoked in a spirit of celebration, tragedy and irony," and gives as examples "Mrs. Ramsay as Demeter, Septimus Smith/Evans as the dead soldier of the Anthology, and doctors Holmes and Bradshaw as the Erinyes, or Kindly Ones."[19] While Fowler's scholarship is always illuminating, on this point I disagree. As I illustrate throughout this study, Woolf's method explicitly resists the one-to-one correspondences between characters and figures from myth that Fowler draws. The nature of archaic myth informs Woolf's method in ways that extend far beyond celebration, tragedy, and irony.

Woolf knew well the political implications of reading Greek as a woman who had been excluded from the elite educational institutions that conferred so-called knowledge of Greek.[20] Emily Dalgarno and Anne Fernald both argue that studying the Greeks enabled Woolf to radically challenge patriarchal epistemology and militarism.[21] Fernald, Mills, Fowler, Theodore Koulouris, and several others have rightly connected Woolf's fragmentary modernist aesthetic to the insights about knowledge, mastery, and loss that she gleaned by reading Greek and from Harrison's study of vase fragments. Studying Greek helped Woolf develop an awareness of the political potential of maintaining the openness of the fragment, an acceptance of, as Fernald puts it, "being in the midst of shards of civilization too varied to organize."[22] This capacity

---

19. Fowler, "Moments and Metamorphoses," 233.

20. As Christine Kenyon Jones and Anna Snaith have shown, Woolf took courses in Greek, as well as many other subjects, at King's College Ladies' Department. She also received years of tutoring in Greek from Clara Pater and Janet Case, and knew Greek well enough to translate the *Agamemnon*. Despite this training, which would seem to qualify as knowledge of Greek, "proper" study of Greek at Oxford or Cambridge functioned as a mark of membership in an elite boys' club. Christine Kenyon Jones and Anna Snaith, "Tilting at Universities."

21. Fernald, *Feminism and the Reader*, 27–28.

22. Fernald, 35. Greek became particularly important in Woolf's early intellectual development, as Rowena Fowler documents. She composed essays, including "Magic Greek," a prose sketch called "A Vision of Greece," a story fragment, a dialogue, and a review called "The Perfect Language," before writing "On Not Knowing Greek." Fowler, "Moments and Metamorphoses," 217–18.

enabled Woolf to avoid the compulsion to mold these fragments to "shor[e] against [the] ruins" of the futility and anarchy of modern society, and "set . . . in order" that "arid plain."[23] While Harrison's predilection for the fragment in her analysis of Greek art plays a role, since parataxis underlies both ancient and modernist *narrative* styles and highlights the influence of archaic myth on Woolf's aesthetic, I prefer parataxis over other more visual metaphors to describe Woolf's mythic method.

In seeking to correct the Scylla of Eliot's vision of modernist myth as a literary tool to return traditional order to modern life, we should be careful to avoid the Charybdis that Charles Altieri warns against in the New Modernist Studies, that by overemphasizing modernist subversion, we strip modernism of its ability to "model significant attitudes and modes of thinking."[24] While Woolf does not turn to myth to shore against the ruins of modern society, what she offers goes beyond mere subversion and critique of Enlightenment epistemology. Rather, she envisions new modes of thought and social life inspired by archaic material and by the community-oriented social structures that Harrison associates it with. Over and over in the chapters that follow we shall see that Woolf draws on archaic myth to envision possible futures for her country, for local communities, for interpersonal relationships, and for individuals, that do not return to the safe yet stifling old order.

Both Woolf's vision of making space for those marginalized by conventional power structures, and Eliot's traditionalist response to the breakdown of social values after World War I, reflect the theories of myth that influence them. Eliot's choice of J. G. Frazer's *The Golden Bough* as one of the three forces that make possible his mythic method stands in contrast to Woolf's preference for Harrison's perspective on ritual and myth. Frazer's overarching message about the ritual killing of the king in ancient societies emphasizes the maintenance of power and order in a threatening universe; it is both a story about the symbolic power of the exceptional individual to stem the tide of chaos and a reification of that symbolism. In contrast, Harrison's ritual theory, the primary theoretical influence on Woolf's view of myth, emphasizes collectivity and undermines the patriarchal narrative of the exceptional individual who must be sacrificed to secure order and cosmos. Harrison's portrait of archaic peoples decentralizes power and celebrates the emergence of inspiration and goodwill from the community. In this contrast we see two very different responses to the heroic nationalist ideology and ensuing destruction associated with World War I.

---

23. Eliot, *Waste Land*, lines 425–33.
24. Altieri, "Afterword," 769.

Finally, while Eliot imagines that Joyce pursues his method by "manipulating a continuous parallel between contemporaneity and antiquity," it is not clear that Woolf shares this conservative view of humanity as timeless and unchanging in its nature.[25] Her strategic revisions of archaic material demonstrate that, in her view, the human situation of her time differs from the context in which the myths were composed, and these stories are useful for moderns not because they bring us back to the order they supposedly embodied but because their paratactic nature makes them malleable enough to meet specifically modern needs.

Woolf attempts to recover Greek for her own purposes in *Jacob's Room*, where she works to kill the Greek Master in the college so that she may wrest Greek from its institutionalized educational setting by highlighting the groundlessness of male identification with and fantasies about Greece. To undermine male academia's claim on Greek, Woolf portrays academic study of Greek by privileged young men at Cambridge satirically, emphasizing its masculine hierarchies, dominance, order, certainty, and authority. The classics professor Sopwith, in whose room gather young men modeled on the Cambridge Apostles, advocates particularly troubling ideals of masculinity that Woolf links to Victorian Hellenism. This male academic conception of ancient Greek philosophy and culture reinforces Jacob's misogyny.

Though the narrator tells us that Jacob and Timmy's spoken Greek would neither be intelligent to a present-day Greek person nor correct in the eyes of a classics professor, and that Jacob never listened to Aeschylus, Jacob believes that probably "'we are the only people in the world who know what the Greeks meant'" (*JR*, 77). Woolf's evisceration of male academic claims to know Greek in "On Not Knowing Greek" renders Jacob's statement highly ironic. Indeed, the narrator makes clear that Greek fills a very different role for Jacob than the purely intellectual. Jacob's "love of Greek" serves as his "miracle," a remedy for the mundane contemporary world of "sallow, hollow, fruitless London days" (77–78). Likewise, once in Greece, Jacob writes to Bonamy that coming to Greece is "the only chance I can see of protecting oneself from civilization," an assertion that stands in stark contrast to Bonamy's "rational" reaction (154). In this moment, Greece moves from a cultural marker of rational, Western civilization to a cultural marker of the irrational outside to civilization. In short, Jacob has become Nietzschean. Jacob's change reflects a larger shift in Western views of the ancient Greeks, from the pre-Nietzschean view of ancient Greek culture as supremely rational and beautiful, characterized by sculptures of the

---

25. On Woolf's attitude to historical continuity, see Michael Whitworth, "Virginia Woolf, Modernism and Modernity."

human form, to a Romantic and even primitivist view of ancient Greek culture as nonrational.

Undermining the academic perversion of Greek intellectual heritage to envision a more inclusive study of Greek, one that could welcome women who studied outside the academy and working-class people like those to whom Woolf taught Greek myth at Morley College, *Jacob's Room* laid the foundation for Woolf's developing mythic method in later novels. By decoupling Greek from misogyny and elitism, Woolf created space for her counterhegemonic feminist approach to Greek myth and literature. Woolf takes great care to decenter patriarchal elements of Greek myth, including the myth of the exceptional individual hero. While those around him project heroism and exceptionalism onto Jacob, he is decidedly ordinary. By drawing this contrast, Woolf demonstrates the ideological interpellation, here as a mythicization, of individuals into cultural scripts and works to satirize this process. While Woolf's paratactic mythic method becomes fully developed in her next novel, *Mrs. Dalloway,* she begins in *Jacob's Room* to destabilize Greek allusions, creating the space for a feminist Greek modeled on her own reading and Harrison's vision of prepatriarchal Greek religion.

Woolf found myth particularly helpful for her literary engagement with contemporary social problems for two main reasons. First, her adaptation and revision of Greek myth lay bare the epistemological and metaphysical foundations of Woolf's political vision because the paratactic structures of both archaic myth and Woolf's mythic method parallel her approach to social and political challenges. This structure is intersectional and disordering, undermining linear models of rational thought exemplified in Mr. Ramsay's infamous vision of gaining knowledge as plodding sequentially through the alphabet. A woman who wrote toward the end of her life, "thinking is my fighting" (May 15, 1940: *Diary* 5, 281), Woolf sees contemporary sociopolitical problems as a network of mutually reinforcing structures that stem from an incorrect and damaging worldview.

Three Guineas demonstrates the extent to which the struggle for women's financial independence, the expansion of women's education, resistance to the capitalist system, and the abolition of war are both causally and ideologically interdependent for Woolf. In that work, Woolf clearly does not conceive of any one of these political issues as more important than all others, but rather argues that they cannot be addressed in isolation. This becomes most obvious when she argues to the pacifist organization that they must support women's financial independence and education, a cause they do not consider integral to their own antiwar struggle, to reach their goals. But it is just as telling that in a publication so focused on feminism, Woolf does not turn away from questions of war and economics, going so far as to occasionally subordinate the advancement of women to the abolition of war and the fair treatment of working men. Woolf did not artificially impose boundaries between the serious problems affecting humanity, nor did she prioritize some within a hierarchical ordering. Her political views, like her aesthetic values, reveal a consistent concern with the dehumanizing effects of such ways of organizing thought and human beings. She consistently refuses to present individual social or political issues as simple and straightforward, easy to understand and easy to solve.

Woolf's understanding of politics shares much with parataxis as it manifests in modernist literature and in archaic myth. Thus, the paratactic nature of mythic thinking and oral literature, learned through long study of Greek and from Harrison's work, is reflected not only in her aesthetic vision but also in her political vision. Woolf presents this intersectional and disordering approach to sociopolitical issues in fiction and she often codes it in images, symbols, and themes adapted from Greek religion. To grasp the full force of the rational materialist underpinnings of these social problems, we must read Woolf's fiction with attention both to the archaic myth she references and to her paratactic method of incorporating myth into her fiction.

Rational materialism is the term I use throughout this study to indicate the metaphysical claim that everything, including the mysteries of human consciousness and life, has a material cause, and the epistemological claim that everything can be explained rationally and that anything that falls outside this sphere is mere superstition. Rational materialism combines the underlying assumptions of rationalist epistemology and materialist metaphysics, dominant views in nineteenth- and twentieth-century thought. Rationalism asserts that reason, rather than sense perception, spiritual experience, or intuition, is the only reliable source of knowledge about the world. Materialism connotes different things in philosophy but for my purposes here refers to the doctrine that all phenomena, including human consciousness and life, are ultimately reducible to material causes. These beliefs take various forms, and in this project, I have some particularly pernicious versions in mind, associated with positivism, scientism, and physicalism. In essence, rational materialism refers to the view that anything that cannot be explained through science and found to have a material cause is nonsense and not to be taken seriously. That would include symbolic structures such as religion, literature, art, and myth, as well as emotion, intuition, and spiritual experience; in short, perceptions and experiences that are taken to be subjective rather than objective. This overconfidence in reason and science, the inappropriate application of scientific thinking to all areas of life, gained dominance in the nineteenth century.

Woolf probably began thinking through these questions by wrestling with her parents' philosophical views and the consequences of those views within their marriage, as Mark Gaipa persuasively argues.[26] Leslie and Julia Stephen were famous agnostics in the late nineteenth century and Leslie Stephen elaborated a Darwinian theory of ethics, emblematizing the Victorian spread of scientific discourse to nonscientific areas of life, in *The Science of Ethics*. Stephen, ordained as a priest in the Anglican Church in 1859, left the church in 1875 and became a major figure in the growing agnostic movement. Gaipa demonstrates that, in the "Time Passes" section of *To the Lighthouse*, Woolf comes to terms with the materialist philosophy that permeated her parents' marriage and the competing philosophy of spiritualism that they rejected.

In this book I extend Gaipa's analysis of Woolf's response to this very personal intellectual history, but I wish to avoid reproducing the many excellent biographical readings of Woolf's work that exist. I argue instead that since Woolf had some exposure to philosophy, these intellectual currents motivate her paratactic mythic presentation of sociopolitical realities.[27] A growing number of Woolf scholars recognize the link between Woolf's critique of rational materialism and her view of social problems. Much of this scholarship explores Woolf's ecological critiques of what Justyna Kostkowska terms the "Cartesian tenets of modern science," a logic that some take to underlie civilization's oppression of the individual.[28] Likewise, Kristina Groover characterizes Woolf's fiction, particularly *To the Lighthouse*, as a rejection of "extreme rationality" in contrast to which, for Mrs. Ramsay, "truth emerges . . . from embodied, relational lives."[29] Like these critics, I believe that Woolf's understanding of social and political realities grew out of a sensitivity to the lived experience of certain metaphysical and epistemological assumptions.

Because I am particularly concerned with the social implications of rational materialism, my use of the concept extends beyond metaphysics and epistemology to rationalization, a concept that sociologists have located at the heart of modernity and have tied to concrete social phenomena. Rationalization involves replacing traditional values, ways of thinking, and social structures with ways of organizing human life that supposedly derive from rationality. At the turn of the century, Max Weber illustrated the process of rationalization through the development of institutionalized rational economic objectives—

---

26. Gaipa, "An Agnostic's Daughter's Apology."
27. For a discussion of the role of philosophy in Woolf's novels, see Banfield, *Phantom Table*.
28. Kostkowska, "Scissors and Silks," 197. See also Elizabeth G. Lambert, "Proportion Is in the Mind of the Beholder."
29. Groover, "Body and Soul," 222

the capitalist accumulation of wealth—out of the Calvinist religious concerns that they ultimately replace; in the process, the world becomes disenchanted and *devoid* of value, meaning, and individual freedom.[30] In 1944, Max Horkheimer and Theodor Adorno extended Weber's critique of the effects of rationalization by analyzing the ways that attempts during the Enlightenment to eradicate superstition and myth ultimately led to greater irrationality in the forms of early twentieth-century outbursts of fascism, anti-Semitism, and rampant nationalism.[31] To Horkheimer and Adorno's list of political manifestations of the modern drive to rationality, I would add the many social issues Woolf addresses through myth in her fiction. Thus, for these sociologists and for Woolf, effectively addressing the problems of modernity requires recognizing the underlying cause, the misguided utopian wish for a purely rational, masculinist world. The disenchantment of the world, as Weber conceived it, leads to an inevitable imbalance.

Despite Weber's influential theory, the mythic has never disappeared from the modern world, and it saturates the lives of Woolf's modern characters.[32] For many of her characters, like Septimus Warren Smith and Lily Briscoe, mythic experience competes uncomfortably with modern liberalism and rationalism. Others, like Mrs. Ramsay, Clarissa Dalloway, and Peter Walsh, find ways to subordinate myth to the modern social order. But in no case does Woolf present the modern world as mythless. In this, she shares much with the Polish philosopher, Leszek Kołakowski. In *The Presence of Myth*, Kołakowski explores the enduring counterbalance of two cognitive modes: the rational and the mythical. He asserts that "culture thrives both on a desire for ultimate synthesis between [these] two conflicting elements and on being organically unable to ensure that synthesis."[33] Mythic thinking, defined by Kołakowski as the transformation of empirical, contingent experience into something meaningful and "an attempt to reveal an unconditioned reality, thanks to which the conditioned reality becomes intelligible," is "not subject to conversion into rationalized structures" and cannot be replaced by such structures.[34]

---

30. Weber, "Science as a Vocation," 155.

31. Max Horkheimer and Theodor Adorno, *Dialectic of Enlightenment*. In *Modernity and the Holocaust*, Zygmunt Baumann explores this social phenomenon in more detail. On the role of irrationality in Weber's critique of modernity, as well as a discussion of the similarities with Lukács, see Jukka Gronow, "Element of Irrationality." George Ritzer's theory is elaborated in *McDonaldization of Society*.

32. Rationalization is sometimes referred to as secularization or disenchantment. Recently, the secularization thesis has been challenged by a number of scholars. For a recent refutation of the secularization thesis, see Jason A. Josephson-Storm, *The Myth of Disenchantment: Magic, Modernity, and the Birth of the Human Sciences*.

33. Kołakowski, *Presence of Myth*, 135.

34. Kołakowski, 131–132.

The impossibility of resolving the tension between the rational and the mythic and the dangers of attempting to rid the modern world of "superstition" motivates not only Woolf's view of sociopolitical issues but also her narrative response to these issues. In her classic statement of modernist aesthetics, "Modern Fiction," Woolf links an epistemological error, mistakenly believing that one may ascertain the truth about human beings by observing their external circumstances and qualities, which is a variety of empiricism, to the "materialist" aesthetics that she finds problematic in the Edwardian writers H. G. Wells, Arnold Bennett, and John Galsworthy.[35] These authors are materialists because they "write of unimportant things. . . . They spend immense skill and immense industry making the trivial and the transitory appear the true and the enduring" ("Modern Fiction," 148). In contrast, Woolf offers a modernist vision of life as "a luminous halo, a semi-transparent envelope surrounding us from the beginning of consciousness to the end" and the individual as "this varying, this unknown and uncircumscribed spirit" that harkens back to a premodern belief in the soul (150). Degrading nonrational ways of seeing—the ambiguity and paradox inherent in intuition, imagination, and mythic and symbolic thought—within a simplistic rational materialist system restricts the imagination both in art, where it leads to a sterile and shallow realism that cannot convey "life or spirit, truth or reality," and in the social and political imagination (149).

Not surprisingly, a vehement rejection of the rational materialist worldview accompanied confidence in Western models of progress. An emerging anxiety that something had been lost in a disenchanted modern Western world gave rise to a variety of antirational views within artistic and academic circles in the nineteenth and twentieth centuries, which often imagined premodern culture as an alternative to rationalist modernity. Chief among these was primitivism, an aesthetic that shaped modernist literature and visual art, especially Fauvism, Cubism, and Expressionism. Philosophically, Giambattista Vico articulated the precursors of primitivism in his rejection of Enlightenment rationalism in his 1725 *The New Science*. Primitivism in the visual arts grew out of a response to the Classicism that dominated eighteenth- and nineteenth-century European art academies. Within this classical framework was a "presumption of reason as the governing artistic faculty. Rationality formed the core of academic precepts. . . . The foundation of academic pedagogy upon the rule of reason framed the key characteristic of 'uncivilized' imagery as unreason."[36] The lack of reason, deep passions, and spontaneous

---

35. Hereafter, citations to "Modern Fiction" will occur parenthetically in text.
36. Connelly, *Sleep of Reason*, 13. For more on modernist primitivism, see Jack Flam and Miriam Deutch, *Primitivism and Twentieth-Century Art*; Robert Goldwater, *Primitivism in*

expression freed of cultural tradition that Western primitivists presumed in so-called primitive art set it apart from the arts of so-called civilized people and made it an enviable alternative to the decadence and emptiness that some Europeans felt had befallen their own cultural and artistic traditions.[37]

Both Harrison and Woolf participated in antirational trends that directly criticized the tenets of rational materialism, and they linked this epistemology to social and political realities and to aesthetics, whether ancient or modern. As several scholars have shown, Harrison's antirationalist enthusiasm for a prepatriarchal chthonic maternalist religion and society influenced Woolf's intellectual development significantly. In *Themis*, Harrison links rationalism to patriarchy and war, arguing that the rise of rationalism in the classical period resulted in individualistic, patriarchal Olympian religion and its warlike society. Modern parallels are hard to miss. However, despite Woolf's respect for Harrison and their shared values, Woolf takes a more nuanced approach to modernist rejections of science and the subsequent turn to nonrational myth than do many of her contemporaries, especially Eliot and D. H. Lawrence.[38]

As Robert Ellwood demonstrates in his study of the tarnished political reputations of mythologists Mircea Eliade, Carl Jung, and Joseph Campbell, enthusiasm for myth as a nonrational alternative to modernity shares intellectual roots with certain twentieth-century political movements, notably fascism, that relied on myth and ritual for their propagation. While Woolf evinces enthusiasm for antirational myth, she avoids these unsavory political associations, instead deploying myth to actively resist fascism. Woolf's avoidance of the fascist implications of antirational readings of myth derives partly from her suspicion of finalized answers and the obsessive desire for order that motivates Eliot's interest in myth.[39] Throughout this study I try to balance an appreciation of Woolf's enthusiasm for archaic myth, particularly that variety which might be termed matriarchal or matrifocal, with a recognition of her concerns about the dangers inherent in an antirational turn to myth.

Woolf's appreciation of the dangers of, on the one hand, impotent intellectualism and, on the other hand, dogmatically committing oneself to politi-

---

Modern Art; Robin Hackett, *Sapphic Primitivism*; Arthur O. Lovejoy and George Boas, *Documentary History of Primitivism and Related Ideas*; and Marianna Torgovnick, *Gone Primitive*.

37. Connelly, *Sleep of Reason*, 14, 21–22.

38. On Lawrence's primitivism, see Jack Stewart, "Lawrence and Gauguin"; William York Tindall, "Lawrence and the Primitive"; John Vickery, "Myth and Ritual"; and Kingsley Widmer, "Primitivist Aesthetic." On Eliot's primitivism, see William Harmon, "Eliot, Anthropologist and Primitive."

39. For a discussion of Woolf's insistence on space for objective critique, see Koulouris, *Hellenism and Loss*. For a discussion of Woolf's complicated relationship to the causes she supported during her long career as an activist, see Clara Jones, *Ambivalent Activist*.

cal agendas, may have contributed to her skepticism of political movements. Thus, despite her documented engagement in selected political action, including the People's Suffrage Federation, the Women's Co-operative Guild, and the National Federation of Women's Institutes, her male peers judged her as, in Leonard Woolf's words, "the least political animal that has lived since Aristotle invented the definition."[40] However, this characteristic of Woolf's thought—its radical openness and her critique of both Western masculinized knowledge structures and the finalized political answers that rely on their certainty—has made her political insights perpetually relevant to new audiences. Woolf concerned herself not with political movements and parties but with the social system that crushes human beings.[41] For Woolf, not just action but also thought and vision must be transformed to effect deep and radical change of the status quo. Writing, especially imaginative writing, allowed her the space to comment upon the sociopolitical problems that arise from that system, to challenge its underlying ideologies, and to imagine alternative ways of living together. She interrogated knowledge structures and power dynamics, in part, through subtle yet rebellious adaptations of familiar symbolism and imagery from the classical period. Thus, I see resistance to rational materialism as underlying Woolf's targeted adaptation of Greek myth to comment on the social and political problems in her contemporary world.

The second reason Woolf turns to myth as a tool for thinking through social and political challenges has to do with the position of myth in modern thought. I agree with Mills and other scholars that Harrison's scholarship significantly influences Woolf's reading of Greek myth, but Harrison's feminist reading of myth has roots in the nineteenth century. Beginning with the Romantics' notion that myth could provide a privileged entrance into a realm of transcendent values and furthered by Friedrich Nietzsche's 1872 publication of *The Birth of Tragedy*, both proponents and critics of this view have associated myth with the opposite of a scientific, rational approach to reality: in the case of depth psychology, with the unconscious; in the case of Karl Marx, with fiction; in the case of E. B. Tylor, with so-called primitive cultures.[42] These various understandings of myth as opposing Enlightenment thought have gained so much traction that nowadays they dominate our commonsense notion of myth. While Nietzsche's vision of the Greeks became enormously influential in twentieth-century modernist and avant-garde art and literature, Victorian

---

40. Jones, *Ambivalent Activist*. Woolf, *Downhill All the Way*, 27.

41. For a discussion of Woolf as a political writer in this vein, see Berenice Carroll, "'To Crush Him in Our Own Country.'"

42. For a history of the modern construction of myth, see Andrew Von Hendy, *Modern Construction of Myth*.

classicists, who grounded their imperialist sense of superiority in a belief that they were "more truly 'Greek' than the Greeks themselves," largely ignored the implications of Nietzsche's theory.[43] In the Victorian era, Greek continued to represent "the source of truth and universal human knowledge, the origin and paradigm of Western thought and civilization," that had long dominated European attitudes toward the Greeks.[44] This attitude represents the type of Hellenism that Woolf attempts to discredit by killing the Greek Master in *Jacob's Room* to make room for a more Harrisonian and Nietzschean understanding of the Greeks.

A year before the publication of Nietzsche's *The Birth of Tragedy*, Tylor published *Primitive Culture*, a book that established cultural anthropology as a discipline and applied the theory of evolution to world cultures and religions, arguing that cultures progressed from savagery to civilization. Though he was not a classicist, Tylor circulated among classicists and his thought influenced later theories about myth and ritual. The combination of Nietzsche's reinterpretation of the Greeks with Tylor's theory that myth was a fundamental category of so-called primitive culture profoundly informed the work of Harrison, whose anthropological study of pre-Olympian, prepatriarchal Greek religion directly influenced Woolf's understanding of ancient Greek literature and religion. As Mills demonstrates, Woolf and Harrison engaged in an ongoing conversation, inflected through their shared political and ethical values, about ancient Greek culture. Mills rightly emphasizes the political kinship of Harrison and Woolf and the importance of Harrison's work in Woolf's aesthetic and political vision, writing that Harrison's work "gave Woolf the necessary tools to reject patterns and structures made by others and to seek out alternatives, different ways of knowing, of being, and different literary and political approaches."[45] The antirational variety of archaic, pre-Olympian myth that Harrison introduced through her research supports both her own and Woolf's ongoing efforts to resist totalizing knowledge structures, efforts motivated, for both women, by a keen awareness of the real-world consequences of masculinist rationalist thought.

Throughout this book I explore the ways that characters in *Mrs. Dalloway*, *To the Lighthouse*, and *Between the Acts*, including Lily Briscoe, Clarissa Dalloway, Peter Walsh, and Septimus Warren Smith, navigate the two modes

---

43. Spiropoulou, "'On Not Knowing Greek,'" 1.
44. Spiropoulou, 1.
45. Mills, *Spirit of Modernist Classicism*, 5.

of thought that Kołakowski argues propel culture, the mythic and the rational. Woolf's fiction repeatedly demonstrates the impossibility of eradicating the mythic from modern society and the dangers of that endeavor, as these characters embody the return of a mythic unconscious repressed by modern rationalism and the resulting incompatibility of the mythic with rationalist modernity. Far from Eliot's vision of myth as an ordering force, capable of containing the ruins of modern society in its sheltering arms, Woolf's vision within these novels shares more with Nietzsche's conception of the Dionysian. It demonstrates the ambiguous disruptive potential of the mythic—its wondrous ability to tear down the constrictive prison of rational materialism and open up new and startling visions of reality, its terrifying destruction of the human individual, and the risk that it may itself be subsumed into the totalizing system of modernity.

The characters I examine mythicize the world, experiencing publicly shared secular reality as infused with spiritual significance and symbolism borrowed from the archaic world. What is it that accounts for the different fates of these characters—the fact that Septimus drowns in the Dionysian sea while Lily Briscoe safely navigates the riptides of mythic perception to create her artwork, Clarissa Dalloway infuses mundane reality with a sense of meaning and connection with others, and Peter Walsh returns to the world of ordinary reality after a refreshing dip in the chthonic unconscious? Peter and Clarissa insulate themselves from the fate of Septimus because they never completely dive into the Dionysian irrational, instead keeping one foot firmly on the solid ground of the publicly shared rational worldview.[46] Clarissa's position in the British class system tethers her, as does Peter's imperialist and patriarchal status. Lily Briscoe seems closer to Septimus Warren Smith in being an outsider who is not firmly tethered by social position, but she represents a later, more optimistic vision of the possibility of transforming mythic vision into art through a disciplined artistic vision that does not aim at mastery. While Septimus cannot sustain his moment of artistic creation, making a hat with his wife, or invest it with identity and perspective, Lily's painting constitutes a central project in her life and represents an achievement gained through long struggle and self-reflection. Unlike Clarissa's and Peter's tentative and uncommitted forays into mythic consciousness and Lily's sustained and successful effort to formulate an artistic vision of the mythic, Septimus's embodiment of mythic consciousness suggests the crisis at the heart of Enlightenment thinking as Weber, Horkheimer, Adorno, and Georg Lukács have formulated it. In the final novel I discuss, *Between the Acts,* Woolf dis-

---

46. For more on this, see Dalgarno, *Virginia Woolf and the Visible World,* 73.

perses the return of mythic consciousness among several characters, at times an entire community, who wander in and out of the mythic over the course of an afternoon. *Between the Acts* extends Woolf's hopeful vision of Lily's ability to productively navigate the mythic within the modern world, suggesting the possibility of archaic thought and ritual to build ethical community within a village.

The mythic material that Woolf draws on most often in her novels, and which has been the focus of most feminist criticism of myth in Woolf, is the archaic, pre-Olympian myth that formed the basis of Harrison's research. In this study, I focus on an intersecting network of three groups of figures that can all be classified under this broad category of archaic myth: The Mother Goddess in her various manifestations; deities associated with the Thesmophoria and Eleusinian mysteries and myth; and vegetation gods, including Dionysus, often identified as a son of the Great Mother. These deities exemplify the characteristics of myth mentioned earlier; they are interrelated in slippery and prismatic ways, they have multiple, contradictory stories, and there is some evidence that several of them derive from the same ancestral figure. The Eleusinian Mother and *Kore* offer one possible way into this network that can encompass the Earth Mother goddess; *Korai*, such as Artemis and Athena; feminine figures of death including Hecate, Medusa, and the Sirens; and multiple versions of Persephone's seducer, alternately identified as Hades, Zeus, and Dionysus. Each of these smaller groups links to the others and to other outside figures, so that the network continues to expand outward like ripples on a pond. This material contains inherent paradox as each deity embodies irreconcilable qualities, and Woolf's treatment of it preserves and emphasizes these internal inconsistencies. According to even the most canonical interpretations, Persephone epitomizes both death and life, Dionysus combines liberation and bondage, and the Sirens embody both terror and desire. When referring to the Dionysian in Septimus Warren Smith, Woolf avoids idealizing the delirious pleasures of leaving behind the confines of reason and sanity, acknowledging both the terrible and benevolent sides of Dionysus, who is gentle to his worshippers yet terrible to his enemies.[47] When referring to the Eleusinian community of women, Woolf refuses to portray Clarissa's relation to women as wholly free of the taint of patriarchy. Likewise, she treats the Great Goddess in both *To the Lighthouse* and *Between the Acts* complexly, provoking conflicted critical responses to her mythic allusions in both novels. Each chapter of this book explores both the lines of relation between figures

---

47. See Daniélou, *Shiva and Dionysus*, 51; Versnel, *Inconsistencies*, 139; and Otto, *Dionysus: Myth and Cult*.

and the coincidence of opposites within figures and groups of figures, features through which Woolf resists narrative closure.

Woolf's mythic allusions in *Jacob's Room* anticipate the central themes of her developing mythic method. Nearly every major mythic theme that I explore in this book has precursors in *Jacob's Room*. As she will in *To the Lighthouse*, Woolf critiques the heroic individualism of Olympian religion through her satirical presentation of Jacob as an ordinary young man with philhellenic delusions of grandeur. Like *Between the Acts*, the novel shares features of Greek drama, as Mary Koutsoudaki notes.[48] As in *Mrs. Dalloway*, in *Jacob's Room* Woolf emphasizes the Nietzschean view of Dionysus, which brings to light the role of sacrifice and death, challenging the classical image of Dionysus as god of wine-fueled revelry. While Jacob's view of the Greeks once he visits Greece becomes Nietzschean, Woolf weaves this perspective on the Greeks throughout the novel. To cite just one example, the dying and reborn vegetal Rose Shaw, who is "re-born every evening precisely as the clock struck eight" (*JR*, 100), repeatedly intones variations on a Silenian theme that features prominently in *The Birth of Tragedy*: "Life is wicked—life is detestable," "Oh, life is damnable, life is wicked" (90, 99, 100).

Anticipating *Mrs. Dalloway*, *To the Lighthouse*, and *Between the Acts*, the Goddess appears in many forms throughout *Jacob's Room*, and many of Woolf's allusions reflect Harrison's understanding of these figures. The key bonds between the Mother-Maiden dyad of Demeter and Persephone and the Maiden goddesses (Aphrodite, Hera, Athena, and Artemis) reflect Harrison's presentation of the forms of the Goddess in *Prolegomena to the Study of Greek Religion*. These figures feature prominently in the novels examined throughout this study. Vara Neverow meticulously traces the numerous allusions to archaic matrifocal Greek myth in the novel, including major characters like Florinda, Clara Durrant, and Sandra Wentworth Williams, who reference Aphrodite, Artemis, Persephone, and Hera, along with minor characters like Julia Eliot whose tripod links her to Athena.[49]

The first three chapters of this study focus on *Mrs. Dalloway*, the novel Woolf composed after *Jacob's Room*, in which Woolf develops her paratactic mythic method in earnest. In the first chapter, "Clarissa's Eleusinian Desires," I examine two revisions of the Eleusinian Mysteries, the Thesmophoria and the Homeric *Hymn to Demeter* that Woolf embeds in the novel. By revising this material, Woolf offers a multifaceted critique of the power structures and modes of thought that led to World War I along with a feminist vision of

---

48. Koutsoudaki, "The 'Greek' Jacob," 73–74.
49. Neverow, "Return of Great Goddess," 205–7.

hope and renewal for England in the postwar period. First, she changes the *Hymn*'s portrayal of female community to encompass spirituality and lesbian relationships by focusing on Artemis, a minor character in the *Hymn*. This allows Woolf to replace biological fertility with a vision of spiritual and cultural renewal not grounded in heterosexuality. Second, while the *Hymn* portrays female community as cooperative and ethical in comparison to a violent and dominating patriarchal presence, Woolf's allusions to Eleusinian floral symbolism call into question the economic positioning of Clarissa's desire for women. If women's bodies are flowers, as the *Hymn* presents them, then what does it mean that Clarissa opens the novel by purchasing them while other women must sell them? Woolf destabilizes her mythic references by alluding to both Persephone and Artemis, goddesses who combine death with fertility in very different ways. By revising the Eleusinian figures to emphasize paradox and inconsistency in matrifocal material, Woolf offers a critique of imperialist, capitalist, patriarchal modes of relation that is both more sophisticated and more powerful than if she had simply portrayed women as occupying a privileged ethical position.

The second chapter, "Septimus's Dionysian Sacrifice," challenges the usual reading of Septimus as a figure of insanity, arguing that his symptoms, described in concrete symbols associated with Dionysus and other vegetation gods, suggest mythic vision, which rationalist modernity attempts to confine and eradicate. At the same time, these symptoms result from the logic of imperialist militarism, which teaches him not to feel. Septimus's impossible position, displaying an irrationality both produced and punished by imperialist rationality, suggests the persistence of the nonrational in modern Western society. As she does with the Homeric *Hymn to Demeter*, Woolf revises the motif of the dying and reborn vegetation god by emphasizing a Nietzschean vision of unity with nature, sacrifice, and cultural renewal that specifically targets modern rationalism. As she does throughout her work, Woolf balances a respect for the potential of mythic cognition with a critical perspective on naïve celebrations of the archaic irrational as a utopian site of irrationality outside modernity.

In the third chapter of this section, "Peter's Primitivist Odyssey," I examine Peter Walsh's turn to the mythic realm in his primitivist fantasies of goddesses. Woolf links Peter, just returned from administrative work in India, with Odysseus to highlight the mutual dependence of imperialism and primitivism. As he traverses London, Peter transforms women he sees into sites of supernatural fullness and exotic relief from a rationalist imperialism. Woolf bookmarks these primitivist fantasies with passages in which Peter explicitly comments on British imperialism, criticizing militarism and praising English domestic life. Woolf satirizes Peter's unwillingness to recognize that the feminine domesticity and primitivism he celebrates support the masculine imperialism he criticizes, offering a critical perspective on the dangers of utopian fantasies of non-Western cultures to escape from modernity.

Woolf continues to develop her mythic method in *To the Lighthouse*, in which she offers endlessly shifting and competing visions of the Great Goddess. In "The Goddess in the Lighthouse," I examine Woolf's adaptation of Harrison's distinction between patriarchal Olympus and societies organized around the worship of the Mother. By translating these cultural systems into a nineteenth-century context via Mr. Ramsay, who suggests a Victorian intellectual version of an Olympian hero, and Mrs. Ramsay, who suggests a patriarchal version of the Mother Goddess, Woolf exposes the domestic politics of Victorian rationalist materialism. Woolf's critical application of Harrison's categories highlights the problematic historical links between nineteenth-century theories of matriarchy, a Victorian rational materialist worldview, and feminism. By emphasizing the intellectual causes of the Victorian idealization of femininity, Woolf calls into question the wisdom of adopting Victorian notions of divine femininity as a source of feminist liberation. This mythic irruption in the projection of goddess imagery both supports and challenges rationalist modernity, an inconsistency that becomes clear in Lily's critical perspective on the Ramsay's marriage and in the artistic inspiration she draws from a mythic vision of Mrs. Ramsay.

In "Harmonious Discord in *Between the Acts*," I conclude the argument of the book with a discussion of Woolf's mythic resistance to fascist structures of thought in her final novel, *Between the Acts*. I argue that in this novel Woolf most fully implements her paratactic mythic method and most explicitly links it to her epistemologically informed political project. In the 1930s, the rising threat of fascism became a central focus for her thought. The imposition of artificial unities and clean distinctions in thought, which Woolf challenges through her political critiques, aesthetic project, and mythic allusions manifest most clearly in the phallogocentrism and hegemony characteristic of fascism. I examine Woolf's paratactic adaptation of the choral passage from Greek tragedy and her extremely indirect, piecemeal, and contradictory allusions to archaic myth in *Between the Acts*. I argue that these two adaptations represent some of Woolf's strongest tools for destabilizing meaning within a text. Building on the work of Melba Cuddy-Keane and Mahaffey, I argue that Woolf's refusal to resolve the tension between unity and dispersal constitutes her most powerful critique of exclusionary and oppressive social identities by tentatively offering a vision of community as a harmonious integration of multiplicity.

When we read Woolf's novels according to her advice in "On Not Knowing Greek," with attention to some of the seemingly irrelevant and wild passages, as many of her best critics do, we see clearly that an intricate structure of allusion and political critique is at play and that myth lies at the heart of this structure. In her nonfiction works, Woolf makes clear her political positions on specific social and political issues as well as her overall vision of their interconnectedness. Many contemporary critics agree that Woolf embodies what Jane Marcus termed a "very wide feminism" with commitments to opposing war, fascism, imperialism, the mistreatment of mental illness, and capitalism, but what has been largely ignored for years is the serious work done by mythic allusion in Woolf's novels and its significance for understanding Woolf's integrated political vision. Understanding the paratactic structure of her political vision, her mythic method, and the archaic material on which she draws sheds light on the consistency of her political vision and stylistic innovations, while also respecting her logic in giving such attention to archaic religion.

CHAPTER 1

Clarissa's Eleusinian Desires

Written a few years after the end of World War I, *Mrs. Dalloway* reveals the complexities of a future for Britain in the aftermath of soul-numbing destruction. As Woolf makes clear in *A Room of One's Own* and *Three Guineas,* she understood war as intimately connected to patriarchal domination and envisioned a renewal of life for Britain in feminist terms. Like Eliot, Woolf considers myth, and the development of a method for shaping literature around myth, to be a tool for imagining our future in literature. But her aims, her diagnosis of the underlying problem, and her mythic method differ greatly. Woolf's method does not seek the restoration of a comforting masculinist order, one truth in which we can all trust. Instead, her study of Greek literature combined with Harrison's theory of communal renewal in archaic pre-patriarchal societies motivate Woolf's development of a literary method that imagines new ways of life that might benefit the entire community and promote life. This method, modeled on the paratactic structure of archaic oral literature, exposes and destabilizes the rigid hierarchical order that necessitates and justifies nationalist war.

Woolf's changing portrayal of Clarissa Dalloway mirrors the development of Woolf's mythic method. Clarissa appears in Woolf's first novel, *The Voyage Out,* as little more than a two-dimensional society woman, but after developing her in short fiction, including "Mrs. Dalloway in Bond Street" and "The Prime Minister," and following the death of Woolf's friend Kitty Maxse, in

Mrs. Dalloway Clarissa receives a much more complex characterization.¹ Clarissa's paradoxical characterization and the paratactic allusions and revisions of myth attached to her form the core of the novel's vision of postwar renewal. To imagine new structures of community and rebirth on feminist grounds, Woolf turns in *Mrs. Dalloway* to one of the most iconic matrifocal myth-ritual clusters in archaic myth, the Homeric *Hymn to Demeter* and rituals associated with the Eleusinian figures. Woolf's allusions to the myth-ritual cluster of the Thesmophoria, Eleusinian Mysteries, and the *Hymn* illustrate Harrison's influence on her mythic method both in Woolf's attention to the ritual in concert with the literary material and because Harrison devotes lengthy attention to the Eleusinian cluster in *Prolegomena to the Study of Greek Religion*.² Clarissa, and to a lesser extent Sally Seton, becomes a locus for paratactic allusions and revisions to the Homeric *Hymn to Demeter* and the goddesses surrounding the Eleusinian Mysteries and Thesmophoria, particularly the *Korai* Persephone and Artemis.

Because of Woolf's keen awareness of the difficulties of transplanting archaic values and social structures into the modern world, she revises rather than adopts the plot, language, and values of the Homeric *Hymn* in two key ways. First, she changes the *Hymn*'s portrayal of female community and emotionally intimate relationships between women into a spiritual women's community organized around lesbian relationships rather than familial ones. Woolf draws on the *Hymn*'s floral images of fertility and rebirth to envision social renewal, but she decouples this symbolism from biological fertility and heterosexuality by emphasizing the eternal virgin Artemis, a minor figure in the *Hymn*, in Clarissa and Sally's relationship. Woolf also depicts the bond between women as both religious and sexual, characteristics that are not present in the *Hymn*'s portrayal of female community.

In her transformation of the *Hymn* to portray a revivification of Britain on spiritual and lesbian grounds, Woolf's skepticism about utopian promises prompts a second revision. While the *Hymn* portrays female community as cooperative and ethical in comparison to a violent and dominating patriarchal presence, Woolf includes women, primarily the mature Mrs. Dalloway, in her critique of patriarchy, Empire, and the class structure that led to the war. Woolf adapts the *Hymn*'s flower imagery to construct a hierarchical economy of female sexuality that shapes Clarissa's relationships with other women. In several of the novel's iconic floral passages, including the famous "match burn-

---

1. For more on the importance of Kitty Maxse as a model for Clarissa, see Fernald, *Mrs. Dalloway*, 178, and Froula, *Virginia Woolf and the Bloomsbury Avant-Garde*, 93–95.

2. Hereafter, citations to *Prolegomena to the Study of Greek Religion* will occur parenthetically in text.

ing in a crocus" scene, Clarissa and Sally's youthful kiss, and Mulberry's flower shop, Woolf uses the *Hymn*'s flower imagery to differentiate between Artemisian female communion and relations between women that resemble the *Hymn*'s portrayal of hierarchical heterosexuality. These two revisions allow Woolf to balance optimism about the political potential of a spiritual woman-centered community to counter masculinist war culture with clear-eyed attention to the ways women live within and live out structures of inequality.

Harrison's work on matrifocal ritual and female community informs these revisions of the *Hymn*. Mills lays out the influence of Harrison's thought on Woolf's "consistent striving for female-centered companionship, cooperation, and community," and "networks of feminine support."[3] Patricia Morgne Cramer reads *Mrs. Dalloway* as a narrative form of matrifocal fertility rites described by Harrison. These fertility rites consist of the ritual "exorcism of evil and the induction of good," the latter of which Woolf grounds in the lesbian body.[4] Woolf's shift away from biological fertility and familial community to spiritual rebirth and lesbian companionship reflects both the feminist communitarian values that Mills identifies in Harrison and the importance of ritual that Cramer detects in *Mrs. Dalloway*. As a leader of the Cambridge Ritualists, Harrison's approach to ancient Greek religion prioritized ritual. In her major book, *Prolegomena to the Study of Greek Religion*, she begins with analysis of ritual and proceeds to analysis of the related myths. One of the religious festivals connected to Demeter is the Thesmophoria, a pre-Olympian festival in honor of Demeter in which women participated in a sympathetic magical ritual intended to ensure a good crop and human offspring (*Prolegomena*, 120–24). Harrison argues that the myth of Persephone's abduction told in the Homeric *Hymn to Demeter* arose from the Thesmophoria and interprets the myth as representing details of the ritual. If we follow Harrison's line of thought, by starting with the religious ritual of the Thesmophoria, the female community of the *Hymn* is *implicitly* the kind of spiritual woman-centered community that Woolf emphasizes in her revisions of the myth. While Harrison's work clearly influenced Woolf's thinking, I believe that because Woolf cares about envisioning cooperative communities that offer alternatives to patriarchal competition, as she does in *A Room of One's Own*, she interrogates even women's community for traces of patriarchal modes of relation. While Woolf celebrates the ethical and political potential of lesbian relations and female companionship in the novel, primarily through Clarissa and Sally's youthful romantic friendship, she makes careful distinctions within her rep-

---

3. Mills, *Spirit of Modernist Classicism*, 60.
4. Cramer, "Notes from Underground," 182.

resentations of lesbian sexuality based on women's participation in capitalist and patriarchal power structures.

Woolf's revisions of the Homeric *Hymn to Demeter* allow for a multifaceted critique of the power structures and modes of thought that led to World War I and thus for a truly revolutionary vision of renewal and hope. By balancing her enthusiasm for the possibilities of female intimacy with an awareness of the ubiquity of human egoism, Woolf constructs a critique of patriarchal modes of relation that is both more sophisticated and more powerful than if she had portrayed women as simply occupying a position outside of patriarchy. Her unwillingness to simplify the realities of female relationships parallels her treatment of myth in the modern world as neither wholly outside rational materialism nor hopelessly enmeshed within its logic. By preserving indeterminacy through her treatment of archaic, matrifocal myth Woolf tentatively imagines a true postwar renewal that might resist recreating the same problems, protecting her critiques of patriarchy, rational materialism, and imperialism from the dangers of being swept up in the utopian primitivism that dominated modern art and myth studies. In this chapter, I begin a discussion that ranges across three chapters about three different characters' engagement with myth in *Mrs. Dalloway*: Woolf's revisions of the Homeric *Hymn to Demeter* in the characterization of Clarissa, her portrayal of Septimus as a mystical vegetation deity related to Dionysos, and her framing of Peter Walsh's romantic dreams of chthonic goddesses. In all three cases, Woolf portrays these characters as enmeshed in the logic of empire, patriarchy, and modernity, creating narrative distance from their perspectives. To varying extents, their mythic visions also provide some measure of freedom from rationalist modernity.

The Homeric *Hymn to Demeter* features a network of goddesses with interlocking symbolism and relations—Demeter, the mother goddess celebrated in the Eleusinian Mysteries and Thesmophoria; her daughter Persephone, whose abduction by Hades and seasonal return the *Hymn* recounts; Hecate, the only deity willing to help Demeter in her search for Persephone; and Artemis, a minor figure in the *Hymn* who becomes important in the thought of Harrison and Woolf. These deities overlap in various mythic narratives, a feature that makes them particularly useful for Woolf's paratactic method, and Woolf alludes to several of them in the novel.[5] Harrison argues that these goddesses and several others derive from an earlier figure, called the Cretan

---

5. For discussions of the identity of Demeter and Persephone, sometimes expanding to Artemis and Hecate, see Harrison, *Prolegomena to the Study of Greek Religion* and *Mythology*; Kerényi, *Eleusis* and *Gods of the Greeks*; Jung and Kerényi, *Essays on a Science of Mythology*; and Suter, *Narcissus and the Pomegranate*.

Earth Mother, the Mistress of Wild Beasts or the *Potnia therōn*. This ancestor, associated with the cycle of life, death, and regeneration, has both life-giving aspects and terrifying, deathly aspects, which are seen in the Eleusinian figures. When living things die, they return to the Earth Mother, and she is thus the guardian, or, in the case of Persephone, the queen of the dead.

Woolf develops her paratactic mythic method in *Mrs. Dalloway* through allusions to several of the Eleusinian deities. Beverly Schlack and Lisa Tyler have both identified references to the Homeric *Hymn* in the novel.[6] While Schlack and Tyler seek to identify specific correspondences, Woolf's paratactic method here makes such parallels impossible to isolate. Woolf alludes to features of the *Hymn*, such as torches and flowers, that suggest not just Demeter, but also Persephone, Artemis, and Hecate, and Woolf disperses these references among characters. Both Clarissa and Rezia suggest Demeter, but also Persephone; Peter and Miss Kilman recall Hades; the minor characters Maisie Johnson and Mrs. Dempster echo Persephone and Demeter, respectively. Woolf creates a kaleidoscopic allusion to the *Hymn* and its accompanying rituals, not a one-to-one correspondence between Woolf's characters and the Eleusinian figures. Woolf aims to break up the stability of mythic referents as a symbolic system, and that refusal to stabilize meaning leads her to value archaic material like the Homeric *Hymns*, not just for its matrifocal content but also for its aesthetic and epistemological indeterminacy.

In this chapter I focus on Woolf's allusions to Artemis and Persephone, two deities linked through their synthesis of fertility and death, because this troubling combination provides Woolf with a means of thinking postwar renewal. As Persephone combines death and fertility through her own descent to and return from the underworld, Artemis combines them by being both the goddess of sudden death for women and the goddess of childbirth and nurturer of young children. As Harrison writes, while Artemis "may have her aspect as death-dealer to women merely as a correlative of Apollo; on the other hand it is perhaps more likely that she here reflects the darker underworld side of the Earth-Mother."[7] In this way, they are two sides of the same coin: Persephone, the maiden taken to the underworld, embodies the passive aspect of death while Artemis, as murderer, represents the active side.

Clarissa Dalloway is famously complex. Judging from her revisions to both Clarissa and Richard Dalloway, this characterization seems to have been important to Woolf. While both characters appear as satiric caricatures of the gentry in *The Voyage Out*, in *Mrs. Dalloway* Clarissa especially has blos-

---

6. Schlack, *Continuing Presences*, 52–53; Tyler, "Loss of Roses," 64.
7. Harrison, *Mythology*, 119.

somed into a round character. Woolf's attention to this process reveals itself most tellingly in her revisions of Richard Dalloway, whose association with Clarissa might influence readers' perceptions of her. In her draft of the novel, "The Hours," Woolf presents Clarissa's suitor Richard through Peter Walsh's eyes.[8] Richard appears as an obedient conservative snob with a "tenth rate" mind who cannot appreciate books or music, requires compliance with "any law however bad," including the absurd Deceased Wife's Sister Bill, and refuses to read Shakespeare's sonnets because "he thought it indecent to talk about one's feelings" ("Hours," 72–74). Woolf removes this extended and extremely unflattering description of Richard's flaws in the published novel, and instead paints Richard as an unobtrusive partner who does not detract from Clarissa.

Woolf achieves Clarissa's complex characterization partly through shifting allusions to Persephone and Artemis, two goddesses who manifest the indeterminate nature of archaic myth. Like Persephone, Clarissa crosses the threshold from maidenhood to the status of wife, mother, and symbolic queen. Like Artemis, she remains an eternal virgin, characterized by solitude and psychological independence, never completely giving herself to another person. Both Artemis and Persephone express within themselves the same opposition as Clarissa. All three combine eternal virginity with marriage and childbirth: Persephone in her synchronistic combination of wife and maiden; Artemis in eternally retaining her virginity while shepherding women across the threshold into marriage; and Clarissa in retaining her virginity through marriage and childbirth. Fertility and youthful joy also combine with death and isolation in all three figures. Persephone, often read as an allegory of seasonal death and renewal, alternates between the chthonic realm and the Olympian realm of light; she transitions from stasis to dynamism, and the abduction that seems to bring death allows her to bring forth life by giving birth. Likewise, the maiden Artemis kills animals and women as huntress yet brings forth life as midwife. Clarissa embodies both a cold spirit and a joyous life-giving function. She combines these two facets of her personality in a way that parallels Persephone's and Artemis's synchronistic combinations. Her ebullient states of connection and intimacy are tinged with hints of darkness and exploitation.

Like Persephone, Clarissa experiences a transformation from youthful beauty and female community to coldness and isolation. Clarissa's shift from joyful integration with the world to seclusion and spiritual emptiness, when she returns home from buying flowers and discovers that Richard alone has been invited to Lady Bruton's luncheon, correlates to Persephone's separation

---

8. Hereafter, citations to Woolf's draft of *Mrs. Dalloway*, "The Hours," will occur parenthetically in text.

from her family and friends when she enters marriage. In this moment Clarissa reenters her role as wife, leaving behind the freedom of being simply Clarissa, and she experiences that transition into married identity as isolating. Clarissa's earlier reverie in the flower shop, when she participates in the archetypally feminine task of selecting flowers with the friendly Miss Pym, echoes Persephone, who gathers flowers with friends before her abduction. Just as in the *Hymn* prior to Persephone's abduction, in *Mrs. Dalloway,* women celebrate and select flowers without the presence of men. And just as Persephone is interrupted by the arrival of a chariot carrying the King of the Underworld, Clarissa's communion with Miss Pym is interrupted by a backfiring motor car that transports a mysterious personage "of the greatest importance" but only reveals "a male hand" (*MD*, 13–14).[9] The structure of this scene—intimacy with another woman mediated by flowers, which is disrupted by a masculine, vehicular intrusion—parallels not only Persephone's abduction, but also Clarissa's memory of the kiss she shared with Sally Seton in her youth. Woolf emphasizes these parallels in her draft of the novel. There Clarissa's peaceful reverie with Miss Pym is broken in upon by "a violent interruption!" ("Hours," 275), language that echoes Peter's violent interruption of Clarissa and Sally's shared flower and kiss, when Clarissa feels, "It was shocking; it was horrible! . . . . how Sally was being mauled already . . . ; she felt his hostility; his jealousy" (35).

Clarissa sometimes feels ravaged by outside forces, mirroring the *Hymn*'s representation of Persephone's movement into death as an abduction. When she learns she has been excluded from Lady Bruton's luncheon, Clarissa imagines her existence being cut into and her bed growing narrower, separating her from both other people and existence itself. Locating the cause of her separation from others outside herself, she "feared time itself . . . how year by year her share was sliced" (*MD*, 29). Clarissa's perception of herself as a victim echoes the *Hymn*'s portrayal of Persephone as a victim abducted by Hades. Woolf links Clarissa to Persephone in the latter's form as Queen of the Underworld, as well, by drawing parallels between Clarissa and the Queen of England. Both Clarissa and the Queen of England give parties on the same night, and Clarissa feels it her duty to organize and manage the experience of her guests, in a sense ruling over them. When the motorcar appears on Bond Street, the narrator is clear that "nobody knew whose face had been seen," and others guess the "Proime Minister's kyar," yet Clarissa is certain the Queen is inside (*MD*, 14). In her inner dialogue, Clarissa exclaims that "the Queen herself [was] held up; the Queen herself unable to pass" due to the crowds gath-

---

9. Page references are to the 2005 edition.

ering on the street and the traffic (17). In the next sentence, Clarissa mirrors the Queen when she too is held up, unable to cross the street. Later, when she feels reduced by Peter, Clarissa likens herself to "a Queen whose guards have fallen asleep and left her unprotected" (44).

While Clarissa often locates the causes of her loneliness outside her own agency, suggesting Persephone's passive relation to death, Woolf also links her to Artemis and the active form of death she represents. Her bed may be narrowing and her share of life being sliced, but Clarissa attributes her lack of intimacy with others, both her husband and other women, to her own "cold spirit": "through some contraction of this cold spirit, she had failed him. . . . She could see what she lacked. It was not beauty; it was not mind. It was something central which permeated; something warm which broke up the surfaces and rippled the cold contact of men and women, or of women together" (*MD*, 31). Clarissa's conviction that her spirit is cold connects her to Artemis who, as the goddess bringing sudden death to both animals and women, carries death within herself. While Richard Dalloway does appear in speech in the moment of Clarissa's transformation from relational to isolated, Woolf also describes that transition in images characteristic of virgin goddesses like Artemis. When Clarissa feels isolated from the world, a single figure against the June day, she identifies herself as "suddenly shrivelled, aged, breastless" and "a nun withdrawing, or a child exploring a tower," both images of asexuality and virginity (31). In one of the novel's many enigmatic lines, she describes herself as unable to dispel a "virginity preserved through childbirth, which clung to her like a sheet" (31). Clarissa attributes this existential virginity to an indescribable lack that prevents her from experiencing intimacy with others, most notably her husband. As Eileen Barrett notes, Clarissa's unbreakable virginity, as well as her choice of Richard over Peter, suggests her resistance to heterosexual relations.[10] Clarissa's essential solitude mirrors the virginity of Artemis, and she believes "there is a dignity in people; a solitude; even between husband and wife a gulf; and that one must respect" (120). This necessary gulf between people suggests the independence of virgin goddesses, and it leads Clarissa to reject Peter Walsh's marriage proposal because she feels that he demands too much intimacy from her, wanting to know all her thoughts.

Most notably, Persephone and Artemis are both *Korai*, youthful maidens who address the transition from child to woman. Persephone is the maiden whose virginity remains whole and untouched until the entrance of the masculine. Her transition from maiden to wife, queen, and mother reflects Artemis because it resembles that of young girls whom Artemis initiates into fully

---

10. Barrett, "Unmasking Lesbian Passion," 158.

socialized female adulthood, according to ancient Greek standards. In his study of Artemis, Jean-Pierre Vernant interprets Artemis as the goddess of boundaries who articulates and allows one to cross them. One of the functions of Artemis in ancient Greek ritual was to guide boys and girls across the threshold into adulthood and citizenship while maintaining the sanctity of the distinctions between identity categories. For girls, sexuality within marriage marks them as citizens; Artemis prepares the young girl to be a wife and mother, a transition that integrates femininity into culture.[11] Despite her role in preparing girls for marriage and heterosexuality, Artemis refuses this transition herself. She maintains a unique tension regarding marriage. She enforces it upon women whose time it is to submit, punishing those, like Atalanta, who wish to remain eternal virgins. At the same time, she remains outside this system of meaning, which defines the identity of ancient Greek women, and creates a homosocial community of maidens, hunting and running through the woods. Echoing the events of the *Hymn*, a maiden's marriage marks the end of her time with Artemis and, in the words of Vernant, signifies a type of death, since "every virgin, attaining the state of matrimony, must die first for Artemis."[12] The Artemisian framework applies to Persephone especially well, as a figure of liminality who joins two identities (virginal daughterhood with motherhood) while representing each discrete side. Both Artemis and Persephone maintain the boundary between childhood and womanhood while allowing its permeability.

Outside the *Hymn*, we know Artemis for her preference for female companions and refusal of heterosexual relations. In this, she stands in contrast to Persephone, who, according to some feminist classicists, chooses marriage and motherhood. The *Hymn*'s main version of Persephone's abduction states that she was with the daughters of Okeanos when Hades took her, but when Persephone returns from Hades and tells her mother what happened, she changes the story, saying that Athena and Artemis were present. Helene Foley interprets this discrepancy, the absence of the virgin goddesses Artemis and Athena, in the *Hymn*'s original version of the abduction as a sign that Persephone is ready for marriage. Several other aspects of the abduction support Foley's interpretation. In the *Hymn*'s version of the abduction, the girls are picking flowers in what is described as a soft meadow, a liminal site associated with both the underworld and the transition into female sexuality. Foley concludes that "the motif of abduction from a meadow and a group of maidens suggests the girl's readiness for marriage."[13] Further, in line 79, Helios describes

---

11. Vernant, *Mortals and Immortals*, 199–201.
12. Vernant, 215.
13. Foley, *Homeric* Hymn to Demeter, 34.

Persephone, Demeter's *thalos* (shoot), as *thaleron*, fertile or blooming, and the maidens with whom Persephone plays during her abduction are mature enough to be described as "deep-breasted." The fact that Persephone picks the narcissus that has been planted to lure her—the picking of which opens the earth beneath her—on her own impulse indicates to Ann Suter that the *Hymn* should be read as primarily concerning the maturation of a daughter and her mother's reaction, since Persephone "herself is thereby the active agent who, by this readiness, precipitates the action of the core story."[14]

If the *Hymn*'s main version of Persephone's abduction suggests her readiness for marriage, as these details and readings suggest, the alternative tale that Persephone tells Demeter does not. Woolf emphasizes this secondary version in her allusions to the *Hymn*. Woolf incorporates the *Hymn* into her novel through Clarissa's relationship with Sally Seton, who resonates with Artemis in several ways. By focusing on the minor character of Artemis, who appears only in Persephone's alternative tale of her abduction, Woolf decenters the *Hymn*'s main tale and its implications of predestined heterosexual fertility. In its place she prioritizes the *Hymn*'s subtext of female-centered community suggested by Persephone's noncanonical story of her abduction. By focusing on Artemis in the description of Clarissa and Sally's youthful romantic relationship, Woolf sets up her revision of the *Hymn*'s community of women from the familial to the lesbian.

Woolf references Artemis through Clarissa's attraction to Sally Seton, who is herself an Artemisian figure.[15] Clarissa thinks of Sally as "all light, glowing" (*MD*, 35), an image that suggests the bright full moon that Harrison associates with Artemis (*Mythology*, 121). In "The Hours," Woolf emphasizes Sally's link to the moon more extensively. Peter remembers "going boating in the pond by *moonlight*, one of Sally's mad ideas. . . . He could hear her talking, emphatically, about the *moon*" ("Hours," 36, emphasis mine). While in *Mrs. Dalloway*, Sally kisses Clarissa after Sally suggests that they walk on the terrace after dinner, the draft introduces this intimate moment by linking Sally to moonlight: "Sally said, 'What a shame to [stay] indoors talking—& moved to the window, & there she stood in the *moonlight* . . . they all [went] out of doors to look at the *moonlight*. They were alone together. Sally took her arm.) Then the most exquisite moment of her life" ("Hours," 49, emphasis mine).

The Artemisian quality of Clarissa and Sally's relationship stands out. Barrett argues that the relationship between Clarissa and Sally exemplifies the romantic friendships between women that were thriving at the turn of the cen-

---

14. Suter, *Narcissus and the Pomegranate*, 11.

15. For a discussion of Sally as voicing Harrison's views, see Mills, *Spirit of Modernist Classicism*, 106.

tury.[16] Barrett's illuminating contextualization of Clarissa and Sally's romantic friendship can help us see the traces of the archaic relationship between Artemis and her young companions. Clarissa describes her relationship with Sally in terms that recall the virgin goddesses, maintaining that her feeling for Sally was "not like one's feeling for a man. It was completely disinterested" (*MD*, 34). Clarissa does not depend on Sally economically or socially, and she can gain no status from her feelings for Sally; this independence and purity of emotion suggest the virgin goddesses, especially Artemis, with their emphasis on chastity, independent identity, and separateness from gods and men. Woolf also marks Clarissa's love for Sally as Artemisian through Clarissa's attention to the significance of their age. Clarissa describes their relationship as having "a quality that could only exist between women, between women just grown up" (34). The qualification of the women as "just grown up" rather than as fully mature women highlights the aspect of their romantic friendship that resembles the virgin goddesses; it is a companionship between women who are not yet embedded in the economic system of compulsory heterosexuality. Location in this liminal zone between child and adult, maiden and wife, characterizes Artemis's maidens, the girls she shepherds to the threshold of womanhood; Woolf's emphasis on the status of "just grown up" as a necessary condition thus marks Clarissa and Sally's love as Artemisian.

Throughout the novel, Woolf echoes the Homeric *Hymn to Demeter* by depicting marriage as a deadly threat, a life that makes Lady Bradshaw and Mrs. Whitbread ill.[17] Clarissa in particular thinks of this death as a threat to Sally, suggesting that Woolf alludes to Persephone in Sally as she does in Clarissa. Like maidens fearful of the transition awaiting them, Clarissa thinks of her feeling for Sally as "protective, on her side; [they] sprang from a sense of being in league together, a presentiment of something that was bound to part them (they spoke of marriage always as a catastrophe)" (*MD*, 34). In "The Hours," this fear of marriage is Sally's more than Clarissa's: "There was always this obscure dread, [(Sally felt it more strongly than she did) of marriage as a sort of doom]. . . . She certainly never felt it for herself, but Sally used to talk as though . . ." (46). In "The Hours," Woolf emphasizes the threat of Sally's death when Clarissa explicitly fears that "Sally was bound to be injured. She had an absurd, a schoolgirlish vision, of Sally . . . going out to be slaughtered" ("Hours," 45). At the end of *Mrs. Dalloway*, Clarissa links Sally's marriage to death just as Persephone's marriage equates to death. When Sally appears unexpectedly at Clarissa's party, Clarissa remembers how she used to

16. Barrett, "Unmasking Lesbian Passion," 150–51.
17. For a discussion of the novel as a critique of marriage, see Barrett, 154. For a discussion of the deadly threat of marriage as Eleusinian, see Tyler, "Loss of Roses," 64.

worry that Sally's youthful ways were bound "to end in some awful tragedy; her death; her martyrdom; instead of which she married, quite unexpectedly" (*MD*, 182). While this sentence may seem to deflate the link between marriage and death, the juxtaposition of an expected tragic martyrdom with an unexpected marriage also reinforces the link.

The friendship of Clarissa and Sally does ultimately end because they marry, move away, have children, and leave behind that magical moment of women "just grown up" and the pure feelings it made possible. But Peter intrudes upon their intimacy much earlier in a scene that resembles the abduction of Persephone:

> Then came the most exquisite moment of her life passing a stone urn with flowers in it. Sally stopped; picked a flower; kissed her on the lips. The whole world might have turned upside down! The others disappeared; there she was alone with Sally . . . the revelation, the religious feeling!—when old Joseph and Peter faced them: 'Star-gazing?' said Peter. It was like running one's face against a granite wall in the darkness! It was shocking; it was horrible! Not for herself. She felt only how Sally was being mauled already, maltreated; she felt his hostility; his jealousy; his determination to break into their companionship. (*MD*, 35–36)

Female communion that is interrupted by men; the woman's experience of this intrusion as violent, shocking, and horrible; the interpretation of this intrusion as motivated by jealousy, hostility, and a determination to rupture the bond of women; the setting of this scene among flowers and the fact that one of the girls picks a flower—all of these elements parallel the events and tone of the Homeric *Hymn to Demeter*.[18]

Here we have Woolf's first revisions of the *Hymn*, introduced through her portrayal of Clarissa and Sally's companionship as Artemisian: Woolf adapts the story of Persephone's abduction to express spiritual romantic friendship between women. By shifting her focus from the main tale to the minor, alternative version of the abduction that features Artemis, Woolf revises the *Hymn* from what Foley and Suter consider a story about a girl's readiness for marriage to a story about male sexual violence against female intimacy. This latter significance, male sexual violence against spiritual female love, lies implicitly within the *Hymn*, but the main tale does not explicitly convey it. In this passage, Woolf combines a representation of love between women as religious

---

18. Molly Hoff describes Peter as interrupting sacred women's mysteries and suffering impotence for his sin. Hoff, "Peter Walsh and Women's Mysteries."

("the revelation, the religious feeling!") with a representation of male aggression and sexual possessiveness as a threat to women's spirituality, to create a meaning that is similar to, but not identical with, the meaning of the Homeric *Hymn*. Although the *Hymn* represents masculinity as a violent intrusion upon the peace and happiness of female companionship, it does not characterize the community of the flower-picking maidens as essentially spiritual or as romantic.

It may be that these elements of Woolf's revision of the myth lie in the background of the *Hymn* and its related rituals. In her commentary on the *Hymn*, Foley notes that a Greek word connoting sexual desire expresses Persephone's longing for her mother.[19] Writing about this dynamic in *To the Lighthouse*, Tyler characterizes Demeter and Persephone's "intense desire for each other's presence and physical closeness" as what we might today term homoerotic. While "a young girl's love for her mother is, of course, not specifically lesbian . . . like the young boy's oedipal love, it encompasses the desire for physical and sexual intimacy as well as the more socially acceptable need for attention, affection, and care."[20] This analogy between daughters' and sons' love for their mother suggests that the "romantic friendship" of Clarissa and Sally may bring to the surface the homoerotic subtext of the *Hymn*'s familial relation. In transforming the nonreligious female community of the *Hymn* into a spiritual community by describing Clarissa and Sally's kiss as religious, Woolf may be drawing on the related Thesmophorian rituals that Harrison believed were the source of the myth. Thus, Harrison's ritualist interpretation of the *Hymn* along with Woolf's knowledge of Greek, and perhaps of the etymological implications of sexual desire in Persephone's longing for her mother, inform Woolf's revision of Persephone's abduction.

For Woolf, all people, especially those raised in and benefiting from imperialism, patriarchy, and the British class system, may fall into enacting the logic of exploitation and domination. Clarissa and Sally, especially once they have become Mrs. Dalloway and Lady Rosseter, are no exception. Given the different roles of Clarissa and Sally in the novel, most of my argument here focuses on Clarissa. As I have shown in my analysis of Woolf's allusions to Persephone and Artemis, Clarissa belies simple categorization. Part of this character's ambiguity derives from the multitemporal nature of the narrative, since Woolf

---

19. Foley, *Homeric* Hymn to Demeter, 130.
20. Tyler, "Mother-Daughter Passion and Rapture," 75.

positions the lesbian desires of the young idealistic Clarissa and the established Mrs. Dalloway differently within the Eleusinian value system. Unlike her relatively egalitarian relationship with Sally, Mrs. Dalloway's pleasure in women confessing their foolishness and her economic capacity to purchase flowers embody the hierarchy by which Woolf characterizes patriarchal relationships elsewhere. Woolf's sensitivity to the presence of these dangers even between women prompts her second revision to the *Hymn*, which she effects primarily by adopting the *Hymn*'s language of flowers to emphasize Mrs. Dalloway's susceptibility to embodying hierarchical power structures, complicating the feminist potential of women's community. While Clarissa may recall the *Korai* Persephone and Artemis, Woolf sometimes identifies both female community and Mrs. Dalloway's lesbian desire with the modes of relation characteristic of patriarchy, empire, and capitalism. The *Hymn* depicts relationships between women as ethical and cooperative, whereas heterosexual relationships are marked by the ownership and transfer of women as property (as when Zeus grants Persephone to his brother as a gift) and by the coercion of women (as when Hades abducts Persephone). But Clarissa's mature relation to women resembles the hierarchical nature of patriarchal Olympus more closely than it resembles the Artemisian community of maidens that precedes Persephone's abduction.

Mrs. Dalloway abounds with actual flowers and floral metaphors that establish an economy of female sexuality within the novel, in which Clarissa and other women participate in varying ways.[21] Flowers figure in the first sentence of *Mrs. Dalloway*, when Clarissa declares she will buy the flowers herself, and this moment establishes both the central role that flowers play in the novel and Clarissa's position in this symbolic economy. Woolf's second revision of the Homeric *Hymn to Demeter* takes two interrelated forms. First, in the famous "match burning in a crocus" passage, Clarissa's most explicit account of her mature desire for women, Woolf's floral imagery echoes the *Hymn*'s depiction of hierarchical heterosexuality more closely than the *Hymn*'s depiction of Artemisian female community. By contrasting Clarissa's, or rather, Mrs. Dalloway's mature lesbian desire with her youthful love of Sally, Woolf emphasizes the importance of considering social realities when envisioning the kind of feminist lesbian community she offers in her first revision of the *Hymn*. For Woolf, being a woman, even being a woman-desiring woman, may not be enough to avoid the tentacles of imperialist patriarchy. Second, Woolf revises the *Hymn*'s floral imagery to distinguish between Artemisian and patriarchal elements of female community by repeatedly remind-

---

21. On flowers in the novel, see Sparks, "Literary and Quotidian Flowers."

ing the reader that, in Mrs. Dalloway's world, flowers—and therefore women's lives and bodies—function as a commodity to be bought and sold. Woolf positions Clarissa from the novel's opening as consumer of these goods, one who, while mourning the fading of her own bloom, buys other women's blooms and relishes her temporary domination within that economy. Thus, while *Mrs. Dalloway* shows us a world in which women like the young Clarissa and Sally freely exchange flowers, working-class women like Miss Pym, Maisie Johnson, and Carrie Dempster must sell flowers to make a living, while wealthy women like Mrs. Dalloway enjoy the privilege of buying these flowers.

In both the *Hymn* and throughout literary history, flowers serve as metaphors for female sexuality, as Paula Bennett demonstrates in her groundbreaking analysis of Emily Dickinson's use of clitoral floral symbolism. Buds, berries, and seeds, the "language of flowers" has long been "the language through which women's bodies, and more particularly . . . women's genitals have been represented and inscribed."[22] In the Homeric *Hymn to Demeter*, their meaning extends to suggest the life cycle of a woman, figured as stages of a plant's life. While the *Hymn* portrays Demeter and Persephone as mother and daughter, elsewhere they function as two intertwined aspects of the same figure, one that reflects a woman's life cycle and her changing identities. Carl Kerényi notes that an inscription on Delos identifies the unity of the two goddesses, leaving "no doubt: maiden and woman (or wife) are two simultaneous aspects of the Eleusinian goddess."[23]

Arcadian myths, in which Demeter is raped by Poseidon, also suggest the identity of Demeter and Persephone.[24] A vegetation goddess like her mother, Persephone's story mirrors the life cycle of the flower, which starts as a tightly closed bud that blossoms, is fertilized, and bears fruit. Blossoming suggests both the fulfillment and the death of the bud's self-contained form of life. Marriage, symbolized in the *Hymn* as death, transforms Persephone from maiden under her mother's domain to powerful Queen of the Underworld. The Homeric *Hymn to Demeter* portrays this transformation in violent terms by which a maiden does not choose marriage and sexuality but rather assumes those roles under force. From the perspective of the maiden-bud, one mourns the actualization and realization of the maiden's potential as loss of the idyllic wholeness that constitutes her mode of existence. Once the bud blossoms into the flower and bears fruit, the flower shrivels and dies. However, while Persephone's abduction ruptures the unity of mother and daughter, it also initiates a necessary and fruitful moment in her development into adulthood. For the

---

22. Bennett, "Critical Clitorodectomy," 242.
23. Kerényi, *Eleusis*, 33.
24. Kerényi, 31.

lifecycle to continue, some force must disrupt the unity of mother and daughter and open the untouched wholeness of virginity to its own power. Though the introduction of the masculine element breaks the static circle of mother and daughter, this same event establishes the dynamic aspect of the circle in which daughter becomes mother and queen.

Woolf engages this kind of floral imagery to explore relationships between women in three key scenes of the novel: Clarissa and Sally's youthful kiss, the flowers in Mulberry's florist shop, and her description of an illuminated crocus. Within the value system of the *Hymn*, both Clarissa and Sally's kiss and the flowers on display in Mulberry's resemble the Artemisian community of maidens that Persephone enjoys prior to her abduction in the *Hymn*. These passages echo the *Hymn*'s emphasis on female collectivity prior to the intrusion of the male. Woolf's description of flowers on display in Mulberry's flower shop has received little critical attention, and certainly has not appeared significant to most readers as a figure of female community. In contrast, much critical attention has centered on Woolf's description of Clarissa's mature desire for women, featuring the now famous image of a "match burning in a crocus." (*MD*, 31) While that passage beautifully portrays Clarissa's sexual desire for other women through floral imagery, reading these three scenes in conjunction and through the lens of the Homeric *Hymn to Demeter* yields additional insights into Woolf's views on lesbian desire, female community, and resistance to patriarchy and phallic modes of loving. Woolf certainly represents lesbian sexuality in her fiction, as critics have rightly celebrated, but her interests in doing so extend beyond increasing visibility or even legitimating that sexuality. While Clarissa's mature desire for women, pictured as a flower lit by a match, suggests lesbian desire, Woolf's adaptation of the *Hymn*'s floral imagery in this scene does not align with the *Hymn*'s depiction of Artemisian community. Perversely, the isolation and heterosexual imagery of this passage echoes the *Hymn*'s portrayal of Persephone's life after Hades abducts her.

In this passage, Clarissa betrays what Shirley Panken calls "her considerable interest in the pyrotechnics of masculine power and domination" and identifies with "a dominant or masculine role in relation to" other women.[25] After describing her lack of "something central which permeated; something warm," Clarissa admits an exception to her "cold spirit" (*MD*, 31). With "a woman confessing, as to her they often did, some scrape, some folly . . . she did undoubtedly then feel what men felt" (32). While critics have tended to focus on the ways in which Clarissa's declaration that she feels "what men

---

25. Panken, *Lust of Creation*, 122.

felt" indicates sexual desire for women, the context of this declaration creates a more sinister undertone. The fact that Clarissa responds only to a woman confessing a foolish error, a woman momentarily beneath Clarissa, suggests that men's relation to women appeals to Clarissa, at least in part, because of their dominant status in a hierarchical arrangement. Clarissa identifies with patriarchal power in this passage, taking up what she understands to be the position of a man in relation to a woman, especially as exemplified by Hugh Whitbread, who sexualizes male superiority over foolish women when he forcefully kisses Sally for saying that women should have the vote. Earlier, on the receiving end of Hugh's condescension, he makes Clarissa feel "a girl of eighteen . . . a little skimpy besides Hugh; schoolgirlish" (6). Like Hugh, who responds sexually to women's folly, Clarissa finds "a woman confessing . . . some scrape, some folly" irresistible; in those moments "she did undoubtedly then feel what men felt" (32). Most significantly, Clarissa's statement at the end of this passage, "but it was enough" (32), may indicate that her temporary access to this male position offers some compensation for her lifelong subordinate status within the patriarchy.

In this position of patriarchal superiority, Clarissa experiences her most intense sensual feeling:

> It was *a sudden revelation,* a tinge like a blush which one tried to check and then, as it spread, one yielded to its expansion, and rushed to the farthest verge and then quivered and felt the world come closer, swollen with some astonishing significance, some pressure of *rapture,* which split its thin skin and gushed and poured with an extraordinary alleviation over the cracks and sores! Then, for that moment, she had an *illumination;* a match burning in a crocus; an inner meaning almost expressed. But the close withdrew; the hard softened. It was over—the moment. (*MD,* 32, emphasis mine)

Critics have generally celebrated this passage as a feminist portrayal of lesbian sexuality, given the literary history of clitoral flower symbolism, established by Bennett, and the broader literary association of flowers with female sexuality dating back to the Greeks.[26] Cramer summarizes a widespread interpretation of the image as a "symbolic equivalence for female genitalia—the match

---

26. See Patricia Morgne Cramer, "Virginia Woolf and Sexuality"; Judith Roof, "The Match in the Crocus"; Pamela Olano, "'Women alone'"; Theresa de Lauretis, *Practice of Love*; and Tuzyline Allan, "Death of Sex." Woolf employs flowers to represent lesbian sexuality in other works; for more analysis of this motif, see Jane Goldman, *The Feminist Aesthetics of Virginia Woolf,* and Erin Douglas, "'That was a terrible thing to do to a flower'" and "Queering Flowers, Queering Pleasures.'" On flower symbolism and female sexuality more broadly within literature, see King's *Bloom.*

and the crocus for clitoris and labia."[27] Many such readings situate the passage within the larger context of Western literary representations of lesbian sexuality, but situating it in conversation with Woolf's other floral metaphors for female communion in *Mrs. Dalloway* yields a different set of insights.

At first glance, this passage seems to parallel Clarissa's youthful sexual awakening when, "passing a stone urn with flowers in it Sally stopped; picked a flower; kissed her on the lips" (*MD*, 35). In both moments, sexualized flower imagery combines with religious language, the "revelation" and "illumination" of this mature arousal mirroring Clarissa's description of "the revelation, the religious feeling!" of Sally's kiss (32, 35). Yet, aside from these apparent similarities, Clarissa's mature description of desiring women differs quite a bit from her youthful description of Sally's kiss. When Sally kisses Clarissa, Peter intrudes upon their privacy to interrupt their spiritual, sexual experience. As we have seen, this structure echoes the Eleusinian narrative in which Hades abducts Persephone while she picks flowers with a group of female friends. Clarissa's mature spiritual and sexual experience with women confessing a folly also fails to reach full expression, since the inner meaning is "almost expressed" and the moment over too soon. However, in this case, the disruption comes not from an external representative of patriarchy. Woolf's description of Clarissa's mature sexual feelings (and notably, not her description of Clarissa's feelings when Sally kisses her) employs the word "rapture," a word whose origins echo Hades's seizure and abduction of Persephone, and which in the seventeenth century was sometimes used to mean rape. Linguistically, the patriarchal heterosexual treatment of women introduced by the *Hymn* lies at the heart of Clarissa's mature desire for women.[28]

In contrast to her youthful relationship with Sally, which she describes as pure and "completely disinterested . . . it had a quality that could only exist between women, between women just grown up" (*MD*, 33), Clarissa's mature attraction to women sits within an economic, imperialist, and patriarchal power structure due to her changed status from being "simply Clarissa" to the

---

27. Cramer, "Virginia Woolf and Sexuality," 187.

28. Compare Woolf's third sensual memory in "A Sketch of the Past," a synesthetic blend of sight, smell, and sound in which she looks down at the gardens of St. Ives: "The buzz, the croon, the smell, all seemed to press voluptuously against some membrane; not to burst it; but to hum round one such a complete rapture of pleasure that I stopped, smelt; looked. . . . It was rapture rather than ecstasy" (*MoB*, 66). While this passage does not help us understand Woolf's use of rapture in its distinction from ecstasy, we may note the significance of the word in Woolf's lexicon of religious experiences, as Teresa Prudente has discussed. More helpful for our purposes here, in this early memory, sensual experiences "press voluptuously against some membrane" but do not burst it, whereas the bursting of a membrane's "thin skin," gushing and pouring, is exactly what produces the famous image of the illuminated crocus. See Prudente, *A Specially Tender Piece of Eternity*.

established Mrs. Dalloway. As Tuzyline Allan writes, the "ambivalent expression of lesbian desire" in this passage manifests the "soul death that Clarissa as Mrs. Dalloway personifies," which is caused by Clarissa's "unflagging fidelity to convention" and "the menace of the bourgeois lifestyle."[29] By this point in Clarissa's life, when she has grown used to the privilege of conforming to the heterosexual and class system, she carries the logic of patriarchy within herself. She has, in moments like this, when she "undoubtedly felt what men felt," become like Hugh Whitbread who kisses Sally for her foolish ideas as a way of demonstrating his superiority and reinforcing patriarchy. As we saw in Woolf's first revision to the *Hymn,* in which she references Persephone and Artemis in her characterization of Clarissa and Sally, Clarissa represents not simply the innocent Persephone upon whom death is forced by the masculine intruder but also the more active Artemis who harms other women.

In contrast, Woolf's floral imagery in Mulberry's florist aligns with both the Homeric *Hymn to Demeter* and Clarissa and Sally's kiss. At the florist's, Clarissa anthropomorphizes the flowers she sees and associates them with feminine bodies. The roses look "fresh like frilled linen clean from a laundry laid in wicker trays," the red carnations "dark and prim, holding their heads up" (*MD,* 13). When Clarissa looks at the flowers, she imagines that girls are picking them, and it is "the moment between six and seven when every flower—roses, carnations, irises, lilac—*glows;* white, violet, red, deep orange; *every flower seems to burn by itself, softly, purely in the misty beds*" (13, emphasis mine). Here we have an Eleusinian moment that parallels Clarissa's description of Sally's kiss more closely than does Clarissa's mature description of desiring women. Like Clarissa and Sally's kiss, this description of flowers parallels the Homeric *Hymn to Demeter* in that all three passages feature a group of girls picking flowers who are interrupted by an outside force.[30]

Woolf emphasizes the parallels between the flower shop scene and Sally's kiss more explicitly in her draft of the novel. Unlike the internal disruption of Clarissa's mature sexual feeling, Clarissa's florally infused communion with Miss Pym is intruded upon in "The Hours" by "a violent interruption!" ("Hours," 275) that resembles her language in *Mrs. Dalloway* when Peter's breaks in upon the kiss: "shocking . . . horrible . . . she felt his hostility" (*MD,* 35). In the draft, when Sally kisses her, Clarissa feels that "the radiance that was inside it began to glow [burn] through; [as if she herself glowed out,] fill-

---

29. Allan, "Death of Sex," 109–10.
30. Molly Hoff discusses the echoes of the Homeric *Hymn* in this passage at length, noting the structural parallels between the two, a catalogue of flowers "neatly divided in half as the hymn is divided," and the repetition in both texts of the floral formula. Hoff, *Virginia Woolf's Mrs. Dalloway: Invisible Presences,* 38–40.

ing her with an extraordinary satisfaction" ("Hours," 51). This emphasis on a self-generated fire that glows or burns from within, the way every flower in Mulberry's "seems to burn by itself, softly, *purely*," parallels the "the *purity, the integrity* of [Clarissa's] feeling for Sally" (*MD*, 13, 34, emphasis mine). The language of both passages contrasts with the hard illumination of the crocus and Woolf's description of the accompanying revelation as sudden and swollen with a pressure of rapture that gushed and poured out. These divergent descriptions of the flower's illumination, burning by itself or illuminated by an external and potentially phallic element, suggests that "a match burning in a crocus" can also be read as an image of phallic desire or heterosexual relation between women. Here, as we shall see repeatedly in her mythic allusions, Woolf's language prioritizes indeterminacy. A match in a crocus suggests female genitalia, as Judith Roof and other scholars argue, but it can also connote an external phallic object. At the very least, we may say that this passage depicts genital sexuality, whether clitoral or phallic. In contrast, the internally illuminated flowers in the florists evoke polymorphous sensuality, sensuality that is not obsessively oriented toward an end goal of orgasm, that exists prior to the introduction of the masculine order. This polymorphic sensuality matches both Woolf's earliest memories, as she recounts them in "A Sketch of the Past," and the *Hymn*'s portrayal of female union—a spiritual and, at best, implicitly sexual intimacy among maidens and between mother and daughter.[31]

If we take the language of illumination and revelation—language I have analyzed through a religious lens, in keeping with Harrison's influence—as expressions of *jouissance*, as Roof does, then I agree that a Cixousian *jouissance* features prominently in these passages.[32] However, this passage does not straightforwardly represent Clarissa's *jouissance* in the presence of other women because, when contrasted with the illumination of Miss Pym's flowers, Clarissa's *jouissance* with women confessing a folly more closely resembles Lacan's conception of it as phallic. Allan would seem to concur when she writes that "the repressive instinct, embodied in the sentence 'she did undoubtedly then feel what men felt,' threatens to neutralize the imagined

---

31. Woolf's first memory is of gazing at flowers on her mother's dress while sitting on her mother's lap; her third memory in "Sketch" is "highly sensual" and her description of it vague: while walking to the beach she stopped to look at the gardens in which "the buzz, the croon, the smell, all seemed to press voluptuously against some membrane; not to burst it; but to hum round one such a complete rapture of pleasure" ("Sketch," 64–66). Molly Hoff links the crocus in this passage of *Mrs. Dalloway* to the floral incense burners found at sites devoted to the cult of Hera, the goddess of marriage who thus stands in contrast to the Eleusinian value system. Hoff, *Invisible Presences*, 68.

32. Roof, "Match in the Crocus," 112.

moment of lesbian *jouissance* by evoking male-centered heterosexual desire."[33] Given that illumination and burning are key images suggesting *jouissance* in this passage, the source of this illumination—from a foreign match inserted into the flower as opposed to a self-generated flame within the flowers in Miss Pym's flower shop—ought to be considered.

Despite the richness of Woolf's floral imagery in the flower shop scene, and the ways it parallels her imagery when Sally kisses Clarissa, this scene has not been widely celebrated by readers as an Artemisian image of lesbian sensuality. Pamela Olano observes that lesbian narratives can be hard to detect because "the gender specificity of representations of desire (male and heterosexual) has all but silenced lesbian representations in canonical literature."[34] This may explain why Woolf's description of the community of flowers and girls in Mulberry's flower shop has been largely ignored by critics. Unlike the patently sexual match in the crocus, the flower shop scene contains no phallic, clitoral, or orgasmic imagery that would mark this scene as obviously sexual in nature. However, the anthropomorphizing of flowers as female bodies and the parallel language of burning, which clearly functions as a metaphor for sexuality in the later passage, as well as the resemblances between the scene at the florist's and the draft version of Sally's kiss, merit reconsideration.

Moreover, the relationship between these passages and the Eleusinian context reveals itself in the distinction between a group of feminized flowers, the central image of the flower shop scene, and a solitary crocus, the central image of the later scene. This difference corresponds to that in the Homeric *Hymn to Demeter* between the all-female collective of the matriarchate, the state of affairs prior to Persephone's abduction, and the isolation, due to marriage, of a single woman from women's community. Foley, Kerényi, and Suter have linked the *Hymn*'s perspective on marriage with matriarchal cultures. Harrison goes further, arguing that pre-Olympian matrifocal cultures feature an emphasis on the group rather than the individual, and this emphasis on collectivity finds expression in the Eleusinian materials. We should not overlook the fact that Clarissa claims that with women, she is singularly able to have a passionately sexual (as opposed to sensual), hierarchical, exclusive relationship. The *Hymn* portrays relationships between women as the "soft and pure" nonsexual type;

---

33. Allan, "Death of Sex," 109.

34. Regarding the match burning in a crocus passage, Roof argues that "an inner meaning almost expressed" reflects the "representational impossibility" of lesbian sexuality: "It can be there, but it cannot be seen in its own terms since such terms to do not exist." In contrast, Teresa de Lauretis attributes the unsatisfying end of this passage instead to Clarissa's lack of desire. Olano, "'Women alone,'" 161; Roof, "Match in the Crocus," 103; de Lauretis, *Practice of Love*.

not so with Woolf. Her depiction of Clarissa's mature desire for other women conforms to the terms that the *Hymn* associates with heterosexuality.

Woolf further complicates things by framing this second revision of the *Hymn* in economic terms. While the flower shop passage presents an Artemisian image of female relationships and sexuality, especially when compared to the later description of a match in a crocus, Woolf undercuts any optimism we may feel about the Mulberry scene through this economic frame. Clarissa views the anthropomorphized, feminized flowers in order to purchase them from a subordinate Miss Pym. When Clarissa buys the flowers for her party from Miss Pym, a woman "who owed her help, and thought her kind," a wave lifts her above her monstrous hatred of Miss Kilman, a character coded as threatening lesbian in the novel (*MD*, 12). The wave that flows over her, lifting her above her hatred and pettiness, combines "this beauty, this scent, this colour, and Miss Pym liking her, trusting her" (13). Her transcendence comes from the combination of the flowers and the economically dependent and socially inferior Miss Pym. Clarissa owes her "moment of perfection" in the flower shop partly to her position as a customer with the means to purchase flowers in relation to Miss Pym, whose body is both associated with the flowers she sells and damaged by them, her hands "always bright red, as if they had been stood in cold water with the flowers" (12).

Clarissa's "exquisite moment" continues when she returns home, where she feels uplifted by her servants, whose labor and economic dependence, as well as their supposed appreciation of her generosity, buoy her against the brute inside: "Thank you, thank you, she went on saying in gratitude to her servants generally for helping her be like this, to be what she wanted, gentle, generous-hearted. Her servants liked her" (*MD*, 38). Clarissa describes the gifts of her cook and maid as "buds on the tree of life, flowers of darkness... as if some lovely rose had blossomed for her eyes only" (29). As with Sally's kiss, the match burning in a crocus passage, and the flower shop scene, Clarissa's return home combines religious imagery with floral imagery: here Clarissa "felt like a nun who has left the world and feels fold round her the familiar veils and the response to old devotions... felt blessed and purified" (28). She follows this description by saying, "not for a moment did she believe in God; but all the more... one must repay in daily life to servants... one must pay back from this secret deposit of *exquisite moments*" (28–29, emphasis mine), language that anticipates her recollection of the "most *exquisite moment* of her whole life" when Sally kisses her (35, emphasis mine).

Clarissa's quasi-religious retreat from the world into the sacred realm of her household staff mirrors the complexity of both Clarissa's mature desire for women and her moment of perfection with Miss Pym. These "buds on the tree of life" suggest the clitoral symbolism that Bennett identifies, echoing the gendered floral language we have seen in other passages. But, as with the match burning in a crocus passage, the image of a lovely rose blossoming *for her eyes only* recalls the isolation and exclusivity that the *Hymn* associates with heterosexual marriage, not the collective life of matrifocal societies. The scene in the flower shop and Clarissa's exquisite moment at home with her servants purify Clarissa of her egotism, transcending her monstrous jealousies and hatred of the lesbian Miss Kilman. While Clarissa momentarily transcends her anxieties about Miss Kilman in the presence of these socially inferior women, her adoption of the heterosexist value system that gives rise to these anxieties remains unchallenged.

Just as Peter Walsh interrupts Clarissa and Sally's kiss, the joy and peace of this moment shatters when Clarissa reads the telephone message inviting her husband Richard, but not her, to lunch at Lady Bruton's. Woolf describes Clarissa's crisis through flower imagery also, and here it further indicates her alienation. This scene, the first time in the novel that Richard enters Clarissa's thoughts, severs her connection to the fullness of life by excluding her from the social event and confirming what she perceives as her husband's abandonment of her. Now, instead of being transported and blessed by the fullness and flowering of the day around her, Clarissa feels herself "a single figure against . . . the stare of this matter-of-fact June morning; soft with the glow of rose petals for some, she knew" (*MD*, 30). While the "flowering of the day" continues, it does so outside of her body and brain, which have now failed, since she has not been asked to Lady Bruton's lunch party (31).

In the passages we have compared, Woolf presents her second revision of the *Hymn* as well as the revision of traditional heterosexual romance plots that critics have noted.[35] This collection of passages featuring anthropomorphized floral imagery, lesbian sensuality or sexuality, and religious language reveals stark and meaningful differences. In some moments, Woolf combines these qualities to suggest an Artemisian mode of relation between women that might inspire optimism about the feminist potential of women's community to counter patriarchy. In other contexts, she portrays relationships between women as having characteristics that the *Hymn* associates with heterosexual marriage, such as exclusivity, passionate sexuality, isolation from one's community, and hierarchy. While Woolf's first revision of the *Hymn* allows her to portray lesbian sexuality, her characterization of these relationships as shaped by hierarchical structures in her second revision allows her to explore other questions—notably, women's complicity in the exploitation and domination of other women. In contrast to her portrayal of the relationship between Clarissa

---

35. On the revision of the heterosexual romance plot into the mother-daughter romance, see Hirsch, *The Mother / Daughter Plot*, and Lisa Tyler, "Mother-Daughter Passion and Rapture."

and Sally, here Woolf does not characterize women's relationships as occupying a privileged ethical space. This second revision of the Eleusinian material emphasizes Persephone's paradoxical intertwining of fertility and deathliness through politically charged flower imagery, gesturing toward Clarissa's preoccupation with power and position. The novel presents female sexuality, figured as flowers, as embedded in a capitalist network of commodification, objectification, and exploitation. As men trade women and their sexuality in the *Hymn*, women sell their lives and sexuality in Woolf's novel. As we shall see in later chapters, in the modern world, the goddess, embodied here as the Eleusinian goddesses, exists within capitalist, imperialist, patriarchal, and heteronormative modes of relation, rather than wholly outside of them.

Woolf depicts the commodification of female sexuality and women's lives most clearly through the minor Eleusinian characters of Mrs. Dempster and young Maisie Johnson, who watch the advertising airplane early in the novel. Carrie Dempster and Maisie Johnson represent two negative ends of the Persephone story. Woolf introduces Maisie when she asks Septimus and Rezia for directions to Regent's Park Tube station and becomes horrified by how strange they and the whole of London feel. Maisie, whose name recalls the corn goddess, suggests the isolated Persephone who regrets having "left her people" for the terrifying metropolis (*MD*, 26). Mrs. Dempster, whose name refers to the doomsman, the official responsible in old Scotch law for announcing the court's sentence, or "doom of the court," on the accused, evokes the Hecatean crone who grieves over the disappointments of married life. Both women combine vegetation with death in their brief appearances in the novel. Maisie appears on only one page, as a passerby who is troubled by the "queer" Septimus and Rezia (26). As she ends her interior monologue, Maisie echoes Persephone's abduction to the underworld by combining death, in the form of a premonition of Septimus's death upon an iron railing, with leaving home: "Why hadn't she stayed home? she cried, twisting the knob of the iron railing" (26). Woolf follows this statement by introducing Carrie Dempster, who comments on Maisie's naïveté since Maisie has not yet suffered the degradations of marriage that occupy Mrs. Dempster's mind. Echoing Eleusinian themes, Carrie Dempster attributes her suffering to an unhappy marriage that has caused her to sacrifice "roses; figure; her feet" (27). Woolf's reference to the literary tradition of equating flowers with a woman's body continues throughout Mrs. Dempster's monologue. Carrie Dempster derides the ideological constructions of both roses and romantic love, thinking of roses as "all trash, m'dear. For really, what with eating, drinking, and mating, the bad days and good, life had been no mere matter of roses," and imploring Maisie for "pity for the loss of roses" (27).

In contrast to Clarissa's relatively happy version of the Persephone story, these women suggest a less hopeful version of female sexuality and a woman's life cycle, a life in which a woman may leave home for a terrifying city filled with omens of death or marry a man who drinks too much and betrays her, working every day of her life and sacrificing her body, seeking only sympathy and recognition of that sacrifice from other women. By contrasting Clarissa's Persephone story with those of Maisie Johnson and Carrie Dempster, Woolf demonstrates that while the life cycle of a woman—the transition from youthful maiden to crone, and the conflicts over sexuality, intimacy, and independence—may be universal, varying social positions and varying levels of agency within patriarchal, capitalist, and imperial power refract these realities. Whereas women like Mrs. Dempster can only resort to pleas for pity for the loss of their roses, Mrs. Dalloway finds herself in a position to temporarily recast herself in the patriarchal drama, purchasing her exquisite moments of perfection from other women and finding moments of intimacy that echo the *Hymn*'s depiction of heterosexuality.

Woolf's revisions of the Homeric *Hymn to Demeter* find their motivation in the problem of recovering from the war and her sophisticated feminist, socialist, and anti-imperial analysis of the factors that led to the war. She envisions a renewal for Britain through the traditional, matrifocal fertility symbolism of the Homeric *Hymn to Demeter*, but she shifts the focus away from heterosexual fertility and toward the possibility of woman-centered community. At the same time, her interest in the radical potential of woman-centered community does not blind her to the ways in which women live within patriarchal, capitalist, and imperialist power structures and the ethical implications of this situation. While the space of woman-centered community that these revisions open up may be fragile in the novel and might seem to be subsumed into heterosexuality, class domination, and conservative politics, Sally returns at the end of the novel to counter this trajectory by unsettling the closure of the heterosexual marriage plot. By bringing Sally back as a kind of deus ex machina, that lost moment of her youthful kiss with Clarissa remains a sliver of hope, and by effecting a spiritual rebirth for Clarissa through the queer and mystical Septimus, Woolf emphasizes the decoupling of fertility and heterosexuality that Artemis evokes. Clarissa's receipt of a kiss and a flower from Sally is unique within the passages I analyze here; it is the only one in which a woman freely gives her flower to Clarissa, and it takes place before Clarissa has made her devil's bargain with the British class system.

Yet, even Sally's return mirrors Woolf's second revision of the *Hymn* because, like Clarissa, Sally has also secured financial stability for herself through marriage—now as Lady Rosseter she has "five sons" who attend Eton, "myriads of servants, miles of conservatories," and "ten thousand a year . . . for her husband . . . did all that for her" (*MD*, 182–83). While the young Sally evokes Artemis, Lady Rosseter takes a distinctly masculine relation to young Elizabeth when she echoes a male onlooker's reduction of Elizabeth to nature imagery: "She was like a poplar, she was like a river, she was like a hyacinth, Willie Titcomb was thinking. . . . She was like a lily, Sally said, like a lily by the side of a pool" (184, 188). Earlier in the novel, Elizabeth has made her position on these exact natural metaphors very clear, thinking that people's insistence on comparing her to "poplar trees, early dawn, hyacinths, fawns, running water, and garden lilies . . . made her life a burden to her, for she so much preferred being left alone to do what she liked in the country, but they would compare her to lilies" (131).[36] Like Mrs. Dalloway, Lady Rosseter may have once embodied the Artemisian values of the *Hymn*, but from her financially secure perch, she embodies the male perspective more than the egalitarian community of maidens in the *Hymn*. Thus, in the case of both Clarissa and Sally, Woolf adapts the Homeric *Hymn to Demeter* to offer an indeterminate and paratactic characterization, juxtaposing Artemisian and patriarchal elements of each woman to distinguish between the different lives of women.

By creatively revising the Eleusinian material in her novel, Woolf forms a paratactic presentation of archaic myth that aims at a truly revolutionary renewal that does not simply reproduce the power structure that led to the war. Woolf develops a complex understanding of the relationship between feminism and archaic myth that celebrates the renewing qualities of matrifocal myth and feminine sensuality and spirituality while remaining sober about the effects of women's locations in hierarchical structures.

---

36. On Elizabeth's relation to other's natural metaphors for her, see Melissa Bagley, "Nature and Nation."

CHAPTER 2

Septimus's Dionysian Sacrifice

In her diary entry of October 14, 1922, Woolf wrote that in *Mrs. Dalloway* she intended to suggest "the world seen by the sane & the insane side by side" (*Diary 2*, 207). This inherently paratactic commitment to balancing opposing perspectives pervades the novel. While readers and scholars alike usually regard Septimus Warren Smith as a madman, I argue in this chapter that he embodies irrationality in a broader sense that poses deeper challenges to modernity. Through allusions to the dying and reborn vegetation god in Septimus, Woolf dramatizes the conflicted interdependence of the rational and nonrational in modernity and the dangers of attempting to eradicate the irrational. By focusing on Nietzsche's version of the Dionysian and on the experience of the sacrificial victim in Septimus, Woolf illustrates the dangers that the Romantic antirational turn to archaic myth pose for the modern agent. Through these paratactic allusions, Woolf effects a rigorous critique of rationalism and imperialism.

The epistemological legitimacy of Septimus's perspective plays a significant role in Woolf's critique of rational materialism.[1] His madness fits with Richard Seaford's description of "the initial, painful crisis of madness [as] (unritualized) possession by the spirit or god, as it is sometimes in Dionysiac

---

1. On Woolf's portrayal of Septimus's perspective as having cognitive authority, see Dalgarno, *Virginia Woolf and the Visible World*, 72. For a reading of the sexological implications of Septimus's apparent insanity, see Eileen Barrett, "Unmasking Lesbian Passion," 148.

• 51 •

myth."[2] Careful analysis of Woolf's allusions in Septimus to the dying and reborn god of archaic religion, and specifically to the Nietzschean version of Dionysus, reveals a broader critique of modernity.

Septimus manifests religion in several important ways. He embodies irrationality, both premodern religion and insanity, that an overly rational world marginalizes and seeks to contain, or worse, as Clarissa thinks of the Armenians, "hunt . . . out of existence" (*MD*, 117). While *Mrs. Dalloway* includes numerous allusions to archaic myth in Septimus's experiences, Woolf creates more explicit links to religion in "The Hours," her draft of the novel. Woolf drafts, then cuts and rewrites Septimus's religious conversion. There, reading Shakespeare leads Septimus to "a religious awakening" or, more pointedly, to "the gods" ("Hours," 107). Woolf seems to have experimented with a Catholic conversion, with Septimus making "visits to shrines, incense, services, self examinations [*sic*], & prostrations, exaltations" and attending "Holy Communion" (108). In *Mrs. Dalloway*, Woolf incorporates fewer Christian and more archaic allusions to religion. However, while Septimus reflects religious belief, which some nineteenth-century thinkers deemed superstition, because his irrationality comes from his trauma in World War I—the epitome of excessive and instrumental rationality—he also illustrates the unreason at the heart of rational modernity that many sociologists and critical theorists describe.[3] Thus, I argue that Septimus's marginalization reflects the status of all that does not fit in the discourse of reason that came to dominate British and Western European culture in the mid-nineteenth century.

Instrumental reason—the use of reason as a means of defining and dominating human life—causes Septimus's irrationality, and his resistance to this force, as it manifests in imperialist medicine, ultimately ends in his death rather than the defeat of his oppressors. Because of this, his irrational response to modernity never wholly exists outside the order of reason but is always simultaneously embedded within and struggling against it. This *both/and* presentation of irrationality parallels the ambivalence of Dionysus, the god who plunges victims into madness, in his terrible aspect, and liberates them through mystic initiation from all suffering, including human madness, in his benevolent aspect. Accordingly, during the festival of Dionysus at Sicyon "two images of Dionysos Bacchios and Dionysos Lusios were carried to the temple

---

2. Seaford, *Dionysus*, 106.

3. By instrumental reason, I have in mind the concept as defined by both Emmanuel Levinas and Theodor Adorno. See Horkheimer and Adorno, *Dialectic of Enlightenment*; Dodds, *Greeks and the Irrational*; Ritzer, *McDonaldization of Society*; Levinas, *Totality and Infinity*. On the role of irrationality in Weber's critique of modernity, as well as a discussion of the similarities with Lukács, see Gronow, "Element of Irrationality."

by torch-light."[4] In her portrayal of Septimus, Woolf alludes to Dionysus both through this structural thematic and through specific imagery and symbols associated with the god.

A paratactic treatment of irrationality through allusions to Dionysus creates an ideological flexibility for Woolf, allowing her to avoid naïve praise of antirational responses to modernity. Such responses often imagine mythic thinking as a utopian space outside modernity, a site of escape and salvation for the individual. Countering the widespread reading of Septimus as a figure of irrationality, Sabine Sautter-Léger argues that "Septimus represents an exaggerated attempt to apply the rationality on which the rules of western post-Enlightenment societies are generally based."[5] Indeed, Septimus often inappropriately applies the scientific approach to mystical perceptions, thinking that "one must be scientific, above all scientific" (*MD*, 21, 66). Likewise, Septimus's inability to escape rationalist modernity, embodied in the sacrificial overtones of his death, prompts Dalgarno to see Septimus as "a voice that although wearing the mask of the other does not represent an alternative view of the world."[6] While I too believe that Septimus's resistance to rationalist modernity is incomplete, I would not go so far as Sautter-Léger and Dalgarno.

Rather than marking him as an agent of rationalism or a pretender, Septimus's entanglement with rationalist modernity exemplifies Woolf's paratactic mythic method, through which she expresses skepticism about utopian antirational responses to modernity. As we will see in the next chapter, Woolf satirizes exploitation of the mythic for personal salvation in the character of Peter Walsh, whose fantastical mythic experiences reinforce rather than challenge imperialism. But the optimistic tone of the close of the novel, focused on the inspirational power of Septimus's suicide for Clarissa's sense of community, suggests that Woolf does not intend to cynically present hegemony as something that cannot be thought otherwise. Septimus's mythic vision parallels Clarissa's attempts to dream a new future for England through revisions to the Homeric *Hymn to Demeter*. Septimus represents the alternative nonrational or mythic mode of cognition that many thinkers argue constitutes an inevitable part of modernity.[7] This mode does not sit "outside" modernity as some may fear or hope but instead situates itself inside the very structure that it attempts—genuinely, if not wholly successfully—to resist.

As Eliot's famous articulation of the "mythical method" indicates, premodern myth and ritual, accessed through nineteenth- and twentieth-century

---

4. Versnel, *Inconsistencies*, 139.
5. Sautter-Léger, "Railed in by a Maddening Reason," 6.
6. Dalgarno, *Virginia Woolf and the Visible World*, 84.
7. See Max Weber, Georg Lukács, E. R. Dodds, Max Horkheimer, Theodor Adorno.

anthropology, shaped modernist responses to the contemporary world. The archaic figure of the vegetation god, ritually killed and reborn to stimulate fertility, exercised enormous influence on the imagination of Eliot, Joyce, and Lawrence. Frazer's multivolume study *The Golden Bough* examines the ritual killing of the King of the Wood at Nemi who, according to Frazer, represented the spirit of the tree and that of vegetation generally. Frazer argues that archaic peoples interpreted the weakness of the god-king as a sign of his impending death, which was analogous to the death of the trees. Thus, "the killing of the representative of the tree-spirit in spring is regarded as a means to promote and quicken the growth of vegetation" since the spirit of vegetation resurrects in a stronger, younger representative.[8] In some villages, villagers "carried out" Death in the form of an effigy or tree, and brought in a figure representing Spring, Summer, or Life during the same ritual. Sometimes the clothing worn by Death was transferred to the representative of Summer, a practice that Frazer claims "clearly indicates that the tree is a kind of revivification, in a new form, of the destroyed effigy." Based on this evidence, Frazer concludes that the figure of Death must be endowed with a fertilizing power over vegetation.[9] In developing his mythic method, Eliot borrowed Frazer's concept of the ritual sacrifice for his own aims, stemming the chaos of the modern world and returning to an imagined order.

Countering the ubiquity of Frazer's theory, Martha C. Carpentier demonstrates that Harrison's theory of archaic religion exercised a stronger influence on modernist writers. In fact, Septimus's death and its role in Clarissa's party suggest both Harrison's and Frazer's versions of the vegetation deity. Clarissa's party combines life and death, indicating a parallel with ritual practices Frazer describes, in which Spring and Death combine such that death belongs precisely in the midst of the May dances. Effectively a religious ritual intended to renew life, "an offering; to combine, to create" (*MD*, 119), Clarissa's party takes place on a beautiful June day full of human and vegetal fertility imagery. But, as Alex Zwerdling notes, Woolf's description of the party is full of imagery suggesting "rigidity, calcification, the exhumation of relics," which prompts him to describe the party as "a kind of wake."[10] Thus, while Clarissa fears that news of Septimus's death will ruin her festivities, it has the opposite effect: Like the fructifying death of Frazer's King of the Wood, the death of Septimus renews life. Just as, in Frazer's theory, killing the representative of the spirit of vegetation prevents that life spirit from decaying and growing feeble, Clarissa

---

8. Frazer, *Golden Bough Part III*, 212. Page references are to the 3rd edition.
9. Frazer, 233–40, 249–51.
10. Zwerdling, *Virginia Woolf and the Real World*, 134.

thinks that Septimus's death "ha[s] preserved" the spirit of life that is "defaced, obscured in her own life, let drop every day in corruption, lies, chatter" (180).

While resonating with Frazer's version of the vegetation god, the effect of Septimus's death on Clarissa's communion-making party also reveals the influence of Harrison's theory. Harrison emphasizes the social function of the vegetation god whose death grounds the community by facilitating union with the collective. For Harrison, a renewal of life comes not from the transfer of the spirit of vegetation from one exceptional individual to the next, but because the worshippers of the dying and reborn god take his life spirit into themselves (*Prolegomena,* 481, 486). As Woolf makes clear, Septimus is not an exceptionally strong or gifted young man nor a leader of his people, despite what he may think of himself, but those are qualities one might expect from a typical Frazerian figure. Septimus's ordinariness and the role of his death in unifying the guests at Clarissa's party, itself a ritual intended to regenerate life and community, more strongly suggest Harrison's communal focus (*MD,* 182).

Perhaps Harrison's thought is most relevant for this conversation because of the ways that her feminist Nietzschean theory of the Greeks countered Victorian views of Greek religion that glorified rationality and masculinist values. Frazer's theory emphasized the rational manipulation of nature and the sacrifice of the exceptional individual, reinforcing the values of imperialism and rationalism. In contrast, Harrison argued that collective emotion was the authentic core of religion and that rationalist theology contaminates and degrades this emotional core. Harrison's feminist interpretation of the Greeks grows out of and diverges from the theories of Tylor, the so-called father of British anthropology. Tylor's anthropological analysis of myth emphasized the irrational aspects of archaic religion and contributed to a growing recognition that the Greeks were not exceptional. Tylor, however, also adhered to a hierarchical, evolutionary model, which reflected the Victorian terror of the irrational, and he explained those elements of Greek myth he found distasteful as survivals from an earlier period. Harrison, by contrast, did not feel the need to purify the Greeks of their irrational, violent, chthonic, feminine traits; rather, she placed these squarely at the heart of her understanding of Greek religion and described the later Olympian, patriarchal culture as a foreign importation.

Harrison's emphasis on the emotional core of religion reflects the influence of Nietzsche's revolutionary understanding of the Dionysian aspect of Greek culture, published in his 1872 *The Birth of Tragedy*. In his classic antirational celebration of the power of myth to challenge modernity, Nietzsche defined the Dionysian as a force in opposition to the rationalist "Alexandrian" culture of post-Enlightenment Europe. Whereas philologists of his time imagined Greece as a culture of reason and measure—as what Nietzsche termed the

Apollonian—Nietzsche proposed a new model of Greek culture and art based on an interdependency between the Apollonian forces of reason and individuality and the Dionysian forces of irrationality and excess. Nietzsche criticized the progressive outlook of science and logic, which naïvely believed in the intelligibility and solvability of all the riddles of the universe, an outlook he believed dominated modern Western culture. In a move that inspired Horkheimer and Adorno, he predicted that a society that forsook faith and mythology would destroy itself and reveal the limits of logic. For Nietzsche, it is in this Dionysian tragic perception, which counters the optimism of scientific or theoretical man, that the redemption of Alexandrian or Apollonian culture lies: "How suddenly this gloomily depicted wilderness of our exhausted culture changes when it is touched by the Dionysian magic! A hurricane seizes everything decrepit, decaying, broken, and stunted."[11]

As she does with the Homeric *Hymn to Demeter*, Woolf revises the motif of the dying and reborn vegetation god theorized by Harrison and Frazer to allow for more pointed critique of contemporary social problems and structures. Through Septimus, she emphasizes a Nietzschean vision of unity with nature, sacrifice, and cultural renewal that specifically targets modern rationalism. Michael Horacki astutely notes that *Mrs. Dalloway* is organized around a juxtaposition of Dionysian truth and Apollonian elements through which Woolf communicates the necessity that the "society depicted in *Mrs. Dalloway* . . . find a way to incorporate Dionysian truths into the Apollonian structures that create the illusions of meaning that make life seem to be worth living."[12] The tension between the Dionysian and the Apollonian as Nietzsche conceives them does shape the novel, and the importance of Nietzsche's thought in the novel has implications beyond those Horacki draws. Woolf's Nietzschean tone rejects the implications of naturalness and inevitability inherent in Frazer's theory, and by extension Eliot's mythic method that it inspired. Frazer's fertility ritual revives a life spirit in danger of corruption and decay from natural forces, the normal course of life in which the human carrier of this spirit grows old and weakens. In contrast, Septimus's suicide, insofar as it functions as a fertility ritual at the novel's close, preserves "his treasure" from being defaced by the repressive Apollonian order of modern society that manifests in the medical establishment, Empire, and rationalism.

While rational materialism had gained dominance in Germany earlier, in England the war between science and religion reached a high point in the 1860s and 1870s, after the publication of T. H. Huxley's *Man's Place in Nature*

---

11. Nietzsche, *Birth of Tragedy*, chapter 20, 308.
12. Horacki, "Apollonian Illusion," 138.

in 1863 and Darwin's *Origin of Species* in 1871.[13] The propagandists of Victorian science, including Huxley, John Tyndall, and Herbert Spencer, applied the methods and physicalist assumptions of the sciences to all fields of human knowledge, seeking to replace clerical authority with scientific authority. Virginia Woolf's father, Leslie Stephen, participated in this movement, publishing a book appropriately entitled *The Science of Ethics* in 1882, the year of Virginia's birth. The works of writers like Stephen, Spencer, and W. K. Clifford extended the practice and principles of science beyond the bounds of scientific practice and elevated them to the level of an ethic, "a religious vocation," with Stephen coming close to "making unfounded belief a kind of sin" in his famous essay, "An Agnostic's Apology."[14] In this intellectual atmosphere, the mad and the mystical came to have a similar status—irrational and unfounded perceptions of reality that objective observation and consensus cannot verify, Stephen's "sin." We commonly think of *To the Lighthouse* as the book in which Woolf is conversing with her parents, and Septimus as her way of working through her own medical incarceration, interpretations that Woolf's diary entries on the novel both textually support and encourage. But Leslie Stephen's participation in Victorian rationalism and the mythic allusions in Woolf's portrayal of Septimus suggest that in *Mrs. Dalloway*, Woolf is already critically examining her father's philosophical commitments and articulating her own.

While Septimus clearly embodies the kind of irrationality that Stephen and his generation wished to eradicate, he also displays a commitment to the scientific approach and to the kind of impersonalism and mechanistic character that typify rational materialism. Septimus is not an archaic figure, alien to his culture and historical period. Rather, like other members of his civilization and time, he has internalized the detached scientific objectivity of the Victorian era and he reveals his highly rational side at seemingly inappropriate times, such as during religious visions.

Three times in the novel, Septimus insists on being scientific in the observation of phenomena. In the first instance of inappropriate scientific discourse, Septimus experiences someone saying "K . . . R . . ." as a religious revelation, yet he describes it as a "marvelous discovery indeed—that the human voice in certain atmospheric conditions (for one must be scientific, above all scientific) can quicken trees into life!" (*MD*, 21). Later, Septimus experiences a brief respite from his torments shortly before his death as a "warm place, this pocket of still air," but attempts to explain its existence through scientific reason (140). Thirdly, in a "horrible, terrible" metamorphosis reminiscent of

---

13. Burrow, *Crisis of Reason*, 39.
14. Burrow, 53.

the shaman's and archaic gods' transformations into animals, he sees a dog turning into a man. He responds to this vision by looking for "the scientific explanation (for one must be scientific above all things)" (66). He attributes what is clearly a mystical vision, his ability to see "through bodies, into the future, when dogs will become men" to "the heat wave presumably, operating on a brain made sensitive by eons of evolution. Scientifically speaking, the flesh was melted off the world" (66).

Some critics assert that Septimus's scientifically framed visions suggest new, less materialistic scientific discoveries.[15] Michael Whitworth argues that Septimus's attribution of his visions to his ability to look through bodies reflects the new technology of the X-ray, with which Woolf was familiar.[16] Likewise, Sarah Dunlap reads Septimus's injunction to be scientific in these passages not as an intrusive indicator of the influence of imperialist Victorian science on his consciousness, but rather as a sign of Septimus's perception of a new, ecological science that takes seriously invisible energies and connections between humans and the natural world.[17] I am convinced that Woolf was curious about the science of her day because of its antimaterialist potential, a topic I explore in a later chapter about *Between the Acts*. However, in these moments of *Mrs. Dalloway*, Septimus's appropriation of scientific discourse feels more satirical than celebratory. Septimus clearly possesses mystical vision in this passage; though he characterizes his statement that the flesh is melting off the world as a scientific observation, it conforms more to the realm of the supernatural than to science. In all these cases, Septimus inappropriately applies scientific discourse to explain phenomena that are essentially numinous; that is, phenomena that evade classification in rational epistemology. These passages are bizarre moments in the novel that expose the rational materialist approach to spiritual phenomena as ludicrous.

Septimus's attempts to embody perfect rationality and scientific objectivity exemplify on the personal level the impossibility of modern rationalism that critics of modernity have long discussed. The first worrisome symptom Septimus notices after the death of his friend Evans in combat is an inability to feel. When Evans dies, Septimus, "far from showing any emotion, or recognising that here was the end of a friendship, congratulated himself upon feeling

---

15. Several scholars have examined Woolf's interest in contemporary physics and ecology. Gillian Beer's work on Woolf and science is the best starting point, especially *Virginia Woolf: The Common Ground* and *Wave, Atom, Dinosaur*. For a discussion of the influence of astronomy on Woolf's thinking, see Emily Dalgarno, *Virginia Woolf and the Visible World*. Bonnie Kime Scott discusses Woolf's childhood interests in botany, a family hobby, and her renewed interest in science in the last two decades of her life in *In the Hollow of the Wave*.

16. Whitworth, "Porous Objects," 7.

17. Dunlap, "One Must Be Scientific," 130.

very little and very *reasonably*. The War had taught him. It was sublime" (*MD*, 84, emphasis mine). While Septimus succeeds in internalizing and reproducing the impersonal objective ethic of modernity, this repression of emotion has detrimental consequences for the human spirit, collectively and individually. In his reason-induced illness, Septimus embodies modern rationalism, devoid of sensual, emotional, or aesthetic experience. While he "could reason; he could read . . . he could add up his bill; his brain was perfect . . . beauty was behind a pane of glass. Even taste . . . had no relish for him" (85–86). In distancing himself from death and pain so that he may survive, he finds himself alienated from beauty and life in the process. Similarly, in removing the spiritual content of the natural world so that it could be objectively studied and mastered, positivist science alienated humans from the natural world. Septimus's situation, in which his attempts to protect himself from overwhelming pain and death ironically end up causing him unbearable pain that leads to suicide, has the same structure of reversal as Horkheimer and Adorno's description of enlightenment thinking, which, in trying to protect against superstition and irrationality, creates "political error and madness."[18]

In a literal sense, Septimus gives in to madness because he has adopted objective, rational observation and become unable to feel. When the lonely and unhappy Rezia cries, Septimus can observe her pain only in a detached manner:

> Far away he heard her sobbing; he heard it *accurately*, he noticed it distinctly; *he compared it to a piston thumping*. But he felt nothing. His wife was crying, and he felt nothing; only each time she sobbed in this profound, this silent, this hopeless way, he descended another step into the pit. At last, with a melodramatic gesture which he assumed *mechanically* and with complete consciousness of its insincerity, he dropped his head on his hands. Now he had surrendered; now other people must help him. People must be sent for. He gave in. (*MD*, 88, emphasis mine)

By scientifically observing and reducing Rezia to a machine and in eventually transforming into a machine himself, Septimus embodies the impersonal, rationalistic framework of his culture. He has been "taught by the war" how to submit human relations to mechanistic laws. Submitting to rationalist discourse leads to a complete breakdown of sanity and the inevitable loss of functionality, human relationships, and eventually, life. In this sense, Septimus's madness logically flows from the lessons he learned in the war, just as, accord-

---

18. Horkheimer and Adorno, *Dialectic of Enlightenment*, xii.

ing to Horkheimer and Adorno, the cultural illness of fascism logically follows from enlightenment thinking.

Septimus's status as a trace of modernity's disorder, and specifically as a constant reminder of modernity's war, marks him as one who must be confined or killed in order to minimize the threat he poses to civilization's order. The task of protecting the nation from Septimus's dis-order, the constant reminder of imperialist war, falls to Sir William Bradshaw and Dr. Holmes, who emerge as agents of the Empire and nation. Sir William Bradshaw worships "proportion," which allows him not only to prosper, but to make "England prosper, [he] secluded her lunatics . . . made it impossible for the unfit to propagate their views until they, too, shared his sense of proportion" (*MD*, 97). The discourse of the lunatics, who lack what Sir Bradshaw euphemistically refers to as a sense of proportion, threatens to undermine the strength of the British Empire, already unstable at the historical moment of the novel, its sovereignty severely damaged after fighting the most destructive war in modern history and stretched thin in the colonies. Woolf depicts Sir Bradshaw's confinement of the insane as a service to the state since they threaten to contaminate, through the propagation of their unrestrained energies, the "sane," who uphold and submit to the order of the Empire.

One of the most interesting elements of Woolf's treatment of Bradshaw's imperial force lies in her use of religious imagery. Woolf explicitly links the threat the insane pose to the Empire with religion in conflicting ways in this section of the novel, continuing her paratactic presentation of religion. On one hand, she presents religion as a danger to the state that must be neutralized: "These prophetic Christs and Christesses, who prophesied the end of the world, or the advent of God, should drink milk in bed, as Sir Bradshaw ordered" (*MD*, 97). On the other hand, she invokes religion in defense of the nation, since Proportion and her sister Conversion, the two forces that spread and enforce the Empire's power at home and abroad, are goddesses (97–98). The goddess Conversion explicitly evokes imperialism in "the heat and sands of India, the mud and swamps of Africa" and domestic hegemony in London, preaching at Hyde Park Corner (97–98). She "feasts on the will of the weakly, loving to impress, to impose, adoring her own features stamped on the face of the populace" (98), imposing the sameness that the sociologist George Ritzer understands as characteristic of instrumental reason.[19]

While Woolf introduces elements from matrifocal religions as alternatives to the patriarchal ills of modernity, she engages with archaic matrifocal myth and religion in more complicated ways than has sometimes been appreciated.

---

19. Ritzer, *McDonaldization of Society*.

This Conversion-Proportion passage of *Mrs. Dalloway* poses a challenge to the task of interpreting Woolf's relation to archaic religion and goddess worship. We can detect the difficulties of interpreting this passage in Kathy Mezei's characterization of it as "jarring" and her statement that it creates "an ironic space for the reader" who "balk[s] at its incongruity."[20] While Bradshaw is not a conventionally religious character, he evokes institutional religion through the converting pressures he puts upon Septimus.[21] This element of patriarchal religion manifests more clearly in "The Hours," where Woolf linked Sir William Bradshaw to the Christian God, describing him as speaking "with divine and paternal gentleness" and as "Sir William, the judge, the saviour, the super man, in whose hands powers of life & death were lodged" ("Hours," 138, 142). In the draft, Rezia sees him as "like a father, wise. She felt filial, protected, cherished . . . exposed no more" (128). Woolf removes these references to patriarchal religion in *Mrs. Dalloway,* streamlining the religious conflict in this section to emphasize Bradshaw as a priest of terrifying goddesses. By doing so she shifts away from a critique of patriarchal Christianity that we might expect from her, focusing our attention on a troubling portrayal of female divinity that contrasts with her suggestions elsewhere that matrifocal religion offer alternatives to modern patriarchy. In other words, through these revisions, Woolf crafts a more paratactic treatment of goddesses as they relate to patriarchy, working to make reading religion in the novel more complicated.

Anticipating the patriarchy-capitalism-imperialism trifecta that will be at the heart of *Three Guineas,* Conversion brings together the suppression of dangerous working-class energies and sexual nonconformity, religious and cultural indoctrination, and the repression of women under patriarchal domination. Woolf connects the goddess Conversion to social reforms, fundraising, and the founding of institutions. Conversion conceals herself under the disguise of brotherly love, duty, or self-sacrifice, as she appears in the heart of Sir Bradshaw, but she "loves blood better than brick, and feasts subtly on the human will" (*MD,* 98). Woolf links Conversion and Proportion to the patriarchal domination of women like Lady Bradshaw, who, fifteen years ago, "had gone under" (98). And, as Barrett notes, Sir Bradshaw's belief in the curative powers of conversion and proportion echoes recommendations for "curing" sexual "inversion" by the Victorian sexologist Havelock Ellis, who "advocates a kind of proportion . . . suggests methods to spiritualize the inverted impulse, to redirect the interests in a kind of conversion."[22] Woolf's description of Con-

20. Mezei, "Free Indirect Discourse," 84.
21. For a discussion of Bradshaw as a religious figure, see Groover, "Woolfian Theology and *Mrs. Dalloway,*" 44.
22. Barrett, "Unmasking Lesbian Passion," 157.

version suggests that the kind of social reform that Lady Bruton, Richard Dalloway, and Hugh Whitbread plan at their luncheon—a "project for emigrating young people of both sexes born of respectable parents and setting them up with a fair prospect of doing well in Canada"—conceals and promotes patriarchy, heteronormativity, economic domination, and imperialism (106). The fact that Sir Bradshaw, follower of the religion of Proportion and Conversion, serves as a Knight of the Empire offers a clue to the connection between the Empire and these two goddesses, and to the concealment of the bloody side of Apollonian order.

Sir Bradshaw's dismissal of "Christs and Christesses," those, like Septimus, who threaten the health of the nation and must be confined to drinking milk in bed, feels particularly appropriate given the links between Septimus and Christ in earlier drafts and stories. In the original holograph manuscript of "The Prime Minister," an unpublished short story in which Woolf drafted the first part of *Mrs. Dalloway*, Septimus "plans to sacrifice himself for the redemption of starving masses by literally offering his body as a eucharistic communion for hungry European refugees. Envisaging himself as a man-god slain to expiate the sins of a guilty community."[23] In the published version of "The Prime Minister," Woolf explicitly identifies Septimus with Christ, stating, "[He] was Christ then" ("Prime Minister," 73). In "The Hours," during his appointment with Sir William Bradshaw, Septimus thinks, "So they brought Christ before [his] judges . . . for he had taken the burden upon himself. He [could] confess his sin; & then would be crucified; & would pass through death & rise" ("Hours," 131).

In the published novel, Woolf chooses to broaden her allusions to the archaic dying and reborn vegetation god of which Christ is a symbolic descendent. In *Mrs. Dalloway*, she replaces the paragraph in "The Hours" in which Septimus identifies as the crucified Christ with a list of suffering archetypes: "the most exalted of mankind; the criminal who faces his judges; the victim exposed on the heights; the fugitive; the drowned sailor; the poet of the immortal ode; the Lord who had gone from life to death" (*MD*, 94–95). In this version, Septimus identifies himself as "the greatest of mankind, Septimus, lately taken from *life to death, the Lord who had come to renew society*, who lay like a coverlet, a snow blanket smitten only by the sun, for ever unwasted, suffering for ever, *the scapegoat, the eternal sufferer*" (25, emphasis mine). These passages hint at Christ, but Woolf's shift from overt references to Christ in the draft to diffuse mythic allusions to suffering vegetation gods and other scape-

---

23. Henke, *Virginia Woolf and Madness*, 22. For a full treatment of the holograph, see Henke, "Modernism, Trauma, and Narrative Reformulation."

goat figures in the published novel allows for the interpretive openness we often see her prioritize. Even Septimus's thought that "I have been dead, and yet am now alive" (67) applies both to Christ and Dionysus, who, as the mystical infant Zagreus in Orphic myth, is torn apart by the Titans and restored to life by Athena.

In particular, Woolf alludes to Dionysus, the most famous Greek vegetation god and the one most associated with philosophical critiques of modern society. Septimus's continuity with vegetal life suggests both vegetation deities generally and Dionysus specifically, whom Harrison describes as "tree-god" (*Prolegomena*, 426). Woolf connects Septimus with trees several times in the novel. When we first meet Septimus, he is paying attention to the tree pattern on the blinds of the mysterious motor car; later he feels compelled to tell the Prime Minister his revelation that trees are alive (*MD*, 14, 66). Early in the novel, he relates his discovery that in certain atmospheric conditions the human voice "can quicken trees into life," recalling the premodern belief in the magical relationship between the human soul and trees (22). His interest in the relationship between trees and the human soul goes beyond intellectual curiosity when he experiences his body as continuous with trees, "connected by millions of fibres with his own body, there on the seat, fanned it up and down; when the branch stretched, he, too, made that statement," a link that threatens his sanity (22). This magical connection between tree and body expands into a blurring of the boundaries and interconnections between sparrows, fountain, branches, sounds, spaces, a child, and a horn. When Septimus lies "spread like a veil upon a rock," his body "macerated," vegetation grows "through his flesh," establishing the ontological fusion of his body with the earth (66–67).

Septimus's union with nature echoes not just the archaic Dionysus, but specifically Nietzsche's understanding of Dionysian union, in which individual identity disintegrates as one merges with nature. For Nietzsche, "Under the charm of the Dionysian not only is the union between man and man reaffirmed, but Nature which has become estranged, hostile, or subjugated, celebrates once more her reconciliation with her prodigal son, man."[24] While it is tempting to romanticize the dissolution of the ego through union with the collective or with nature, Nietzsche makes plain the horrors of this disintegration. Septimus illustrates the terror of the individual faced with the overwhelming Dionysian force.[25] When he mirrors the rhythmic rising and falling of the elm trees, Septimus tries to shut his eyes, knowing the ecstasy of

---

24. Nietzsche, *Birth of Tragedy*, chapter 1, 172–73.
25. See Horacki, "Apollonian Illusion," 140.

it will drive him mad: "They beckoned . . . when the branch stretched he, too, made that statement" (*MD*, 22). While Septimus sometimes experiences his visions and union with nature as ecstatic, he also often finds them terrifying and needs Rezia to tether him to ordinary reality.

Woolf's characterization of Septimus mirrors several specific elements of Nietzsche's version of the Dionysian. In chapter one of *The Birth of Tragedy*, Nietzsche borrows from Schopenhauer to describe the Apollonian individual as a sailor who, "just as in a stormy sea, unbounded in every direction, rising and falling with howling mountainous waves . . . sits in a boat and trusts in his frail barque: so in the midst of a world of sorrows the individual sits quietly, supported by and trusting in his *principium individuationis*."[26] Later, Nietzsche describes the Dionysian tendency within culture as "the suddenly swelling Dionysian tide" that destroys "all those little circles in which the one-sided Apollonian 'will' sought to confine the Hellenic world."[27] In these passages, Nietzsche figures the Dionysian and Apollonian as ocean and boat, respectively. In parallel language, Septimus repeatedly imagines himself as a drowned sailor who returns to life after death, such as when he thinks, "I leant over the edge of the boat and fell down, he thought. I went under the sea. I have been dead, and yet am now alive" (*MD*, 67). Following Nietzsche's language, we might say that Septimus has leant over the edge of his Apollonian boat and fallen into the Dionysian ocean.

Septimus also resembles Nietzsche's Dionysian principle when he claims secret and absolute knowledge, which prompts thoughts of suicide: "He knew everything. He knew the meaning of the world" (*MD*, 65). Septimus's knowledge isolates him from humanity, especially from his wife, and he imagines this separation both positively and negatively. His status as the elect, "called forth in advance of the mass of men to hear the truth, to learn the meaning," (66) makes him feel free, but it also marks his alienation from human society. About the dangers of the Dionysian level of experience Nietzsche writes, "In the consciousness of the truth once perceived, man sees everywhere only the terror or the absurdity of existence."[28] This knowledge strips us of our ability to participate in the world since action requires the veil of illusion. Nietzsche predicts that the person who has seen into the truth of nature will be, like Septimus, led to suicide. For Nietzsche, only beautiful forms of art can save the person who has seen the truth. Unlike Lily Briscoe, who is finally able to transform her vision of reality into art in *To the Lighthouse*, Septimus lacks access to an artistic medium capable of protecting him. Before his suicide,

26. Nietzsche, *Birth of Tragedy*, chapter 1, 171.
27. Nietzsche, chapter 9, 228.
28. Nietzsche, chapter 7, 209.

Septimus does attempt a work of art when he assists Rezia in making a hat, a creative process that is explicitly identified as artistic. But while this act reconciles Septimus and Rezia, allowing them to share a momentary release from suffering, the threats Septimus faces are too great. In the end, Septimus finds no refuge from his terrible knowledge and the isolation it creates.[29]

Woolf drafted even stronger Nietzschean links in "The Hours" that she reduced in *Mrs. Dalloway*. She explains Septimus's refusal to have children with Rezia in one paragraph in the novel: "One cannot bring children into a world like this. One cannot perpetuate suffering, or increase the breed of these lustful animals" (*MD*, 87). In "The Hours," Woolf wrote and revised an extended internal monologue on the subject that heightens the Nietzschean tone. Here Septimus thinks, "One cannot bring children into a world [like his]. To have children is to perpetuate suffering; for the sake of a few years of trivial childish joy; to ensure . . . [life] . . . for the brute to feast on. . . . And then . . . more men and women; more copulation" ("Hours," 116). The pessimistic tone of this passage combined with Septimus's thought a few pages later in the draft that "it would be better not to exist than to be like that man" (121) echoes the wisdom of Silenus, the companion of Dionysus, that "what is best of all is beyond your reach forever: not to be born, not to be, to be nothing. But the second best for you—is quickly to die."[30]

Septimus echoes the Nietzschean version of Dionysus as Prometheus. For Nietzsche, "the Aeschylean Prometheus is a Dionysian mask."[31] While Prometheus, in his yearning for justice, has an Apollonian aspect that establishes the boundaries of the individual, his Titanic impulse, by which an individual strives to exceed his limits, is unApollonian. Woolf alludes to Prometheus through Septimus's emphasis on suffering and punishment for sins. For Nietzsche, violation of the law and the inevitable suffering that follows lies at the core of Prometheus. Just as the universal law punishes Prometheus for his nature, Septimus believes that he has committed a crime that he cannot articulate and concludes that "the verdict of human nature on such a wretch was death" (*MD*, 89). Sir William Bradshaw, who in "The Hours" Woolf specifically links to the Father God, stands as his judge and executioner, paralleling the role of Zeus in Prometheus's rebellion and punishment.

Woolf links Septimus to Prometheus through repeated images that recall the specific details of Prometheus's abilities and punishment. Like Pro-

---

29. For a discussion of Septimus and Rezia's hat making as a moment of spiritual vision and freedom, see Alison Heney, "Kandinsky's 'On the Problem of Form' and the Fiction of Virginia Woolf."
30. Nietzsche, *Birth of Tragedy*, chapter 3, 180.
31. Nietzsche, chapter 9, 229.

metheus, who is condemned to exposure on a rock and seemingly eternal suffering, Septimus is "the victim exposed on the heights" who suffers eternally (*MD*, 95), "lying on a cliff with the gulls screaming over him" (137), "he himself remained high on his rock" (67), his body is "spread like a veil upon a rock" (66), and he "lay very high, on the back of the world" (67). Like Prometheus, who possesses supernatural and absolute knowledge of the future, which allows him to know that his torture will end, Septimus "[knows] everything" (65). Furthermore, Prometheus functions as a scapegoat, sacrificed to bring life to the community of fledgling humans, similar to the vegetation god generally, and to Christ and Dionysus in particular. Like Prometheus, Septimus undergoes his suffering, at least in parts of the novel, to bring his message of truth to humanity through the Prime Minister and Cabinet (66).

Septimus's resemblance to Prometheus underlines the role of sacrifice for social renewal in Nietzsche's theory of the Dionysian. This model of Dionysian sacrifice resembles Frazer's theory of the sacred king in whose body the vegetation god lives and whose sacrifice ensures the health of the community. But unlike Frazer, Nietzsche attends to the suffering of Dionysian victims, whose perspectives are movingly portrayed in classical tragedies like Euripides's *Bacchae*, which we should recall Woolf read in Greek. Woolf links Septimus to these Dionysian victims who are, like Agave, driven mad, or who are, like her son Pentheus, physically dismembered. Both Pentheus, whom Dionysus drives to dress as a woman, and Agave, who leaves feminine domesticated spaces to hunt and revel in the woods with Maenads, transgress the rigid gender roles assigned in ancient Greece. Septimus also transgresses gender norms by loving Evans and, according to Holmes and Bradshaw, by failing to fulfill his manly duties to his wife. Both Septimus and Agave ecstatically reunite with a nature from which they have been alienated in the city. Agave accomplishes this Dionysian union by leaving the city, while Woolf illustrates the intrusion of Dionysian nature into the urban space. Driven mad by the war and clinging to scientific explanations of his mystical visions, Septimus resembles Euripides's Pentheus, whom Dionysus causes his mother Agave and the maenads to dismember. In *The Bacchae*, Pentheus suffers from "the painful human kind of madness and stubbornly resists the new kind offered to him by Dionysos . . . with the result that the subsequent insertion into him of 'light frenzy' by Dionysos . . . will lead only to his destruction."[32] The torments of Agave, Pentheus, and Septimus enable renewal for their societies of the sort that Nietzsche has in mind. In Pentheus and Agave's case, the Dionysian cleansing rebalances

---

32. Seaford, *Dionysos*, 106.

Thebes by sweeping away the unnatural rationalist order of Pentheus and recognizing the neglected divine authority of Dionysus.

In contrast to Nietzsche and the tragedians, Frazer betrays the conservative values Woolf detests, presenting the sacrifice of the human representative of vegetation as an inevitable requirement for the health and prosperity of society. By linking Septimus, a veteran of imperialist war, to this archaic figure, Woolf situates the death of the sacred vegetation-man within a contemporary sociopolitical context rather than presenting the murder of this individual as natural or inevitable. In fact, far from presenting this sacrifice as necessary, Woolf attributes the desire to preserve the health of a nation by purifying its undesirable elements to Sir William Bradshaw, whom she links to patriarchal religion in "The Hours." In Septimus, Woolf emphasizes the perspective of the sacrificial victim, rather than eliding it as Frazer's theory does. By linking Septimus to a Nietzschean version of Dionysus, and to Prometheus as a sacrificial face of this Nietzschean Dionysus, Woolf underscores Septimus's embeddedness within a rationalist epistemology and social system that claims universality and demands compliance.

The imperialist rationalism that requires Septimus's death to preserve the health of the nation manifests at the heart of Frazer's theory of magic and religion. Frazer portrays archaic people as using fertility magic—the sacrifice of the god-king—to manipulate the natural world in their favor—ensuring the life of plants and a plentiful harvest. Because he assumes an essentially technological motivation in religion—the manipulation of external reality—as opposed to the spiritual-emotional core Harrison asserts, he projects his Victorian commitment to instrumental reason onto archaic peoples. At the same time, because the end of the novel casts Septimus's suicide in Harrisonian terms, Woolf demonstrates the power of individuals to imagine forms of social life that are not predicated on compliance and sacrifice. Septimus's suicide benefits his community in a distinctly Harrisonian and Nietzschean way: Nietzschean because Woolf deploys it to critique rationalist society, Harrisonian because through learning of Septimus's suicide Clarissa experiences mystical union that empowers her to assemble her community.

Woolf's treatment of modernity, rationalism, and antirationalism recalls Kołakowski's view that civilization requires the interweaving dance of rational and irrational to develop. Woolf's portrayal of Septimus as a religious figure with access to authentic spiritual experience killed by rationalist order and even by imperialist religion in the form of Conversion and Proportion reflects Harrison's model of an authentic and spiritual, irrational religious experience that rationalism spoils. On this level, Woolf uses irrational, chthonic religion to critique the deadly effects of rationalism; specifically, she shows that rationalism leaves no room for the irrational, which, whether it is madness or spiritual experience, comes to have the status of sin for modern rational materialists like her father. Nietzsche's theory, filtered through Harrison, provides a framework for Woolf to comment upon imperialist reason. But because she attentively portrays the destructive effects of a Nietzschean merging with nature, she also calls into question the Romantic, antirational response to rational materialism. Woolf places the irrational firmly within the situation of modernity, both by attributing Septimus's religiously inflected madness to modern industrial warfare and by limiting his power to resist the legal authority of Drs. Holmes and Bradshaw. Her allusions to Dionysus and Nietzsche's Dionysian principle in Septimus are paratactic, suggesting both the promise of a return to the archaic irrational and the limits of such a return.

CHAPTER 3

Peter Walsh's Primitivist Odyssey

Like Septimus Warren Smith, Peter Walsh, a man "with a disposition toward the Dionysian," enters mythic consciousness as he wanders through London.[1] But unlike Septimus, instead of challenging imperialist reason, Peter co-opts his mythic vision to support imperialist aims, projecting fetishistic primitivist images onto female figures. Peter Walsh simultaneously criticizes masculine British imperialism and idealizes the feminine domestic sphere of civilization, refusing to see these two facets of Empire as interdependent. In his inconsistent reactions to British civilization, Peter assumes a distinction between two intertwined aspects of hegemonic society—the consensual form, what Antonio Gramsci termed *civil society*, which manifests here as the domestic, private sphere; and the enforced form, *political society*, represented as the government and military, especially as they manifest in colonialism and World War I. While Peter Walsh criticizes British militarism and colonialism in India, features of *political society*, he feels nostalgic for domesticity and feminine civilization, *civil society*. At the same time, his primitivist fantasies conform to the pattern Edward Said traces through the Western construction of the Orient, a project designed to consolidate the identity and power of the West. Peter's unwillingness to confront his inconsistency renders him not only pow-

---

1. See Michael Horacki's analysis of the Dionysian and Apollonian elements woven throughout *Mrs. Dalloway*. Horacki, "Apollonian Illusion," 138.

erless to resist imperialism but doomed to reinforce that which he consciously criticizes.

Woolf develops her commentary on civilization and primitivism in *Mrs. Dalloway* through references to the *Odyssey*, a highly paratactic epic that Felson characterizes as shaped by "narrative indeterminacy."[2] As Steven Monte demonstrates, Woolf draws upon elements of the epic in the novel, including extensive Homeric similes early in the novel.[3] These explicit epic allusions cluster in the early section of the novel when Clarissa returns home to find that Richard will be lunching with Lady Bruton and continue through Peter's visit to Clarissa and Peter's walk through London. The prevalence of Homeric similes in scenes featuring Peter Walsh accords with Woolf's adaptation of Homeric imagery in Peter's characterization. Peter Walsh appears to himself and others as a returning Odysseus, and Peter's journey across London, bookended by visits to Clarissa's home, resembles Odysseus's voyage home in his primitivist fantasies of women and preoccupation with British civilization. He features as a topic of conversation at Lady Bruton's lunch, where the group think of Peter as a seafarer who, like Odysseus arriving on the shores of Phaeacia, has come back "battered, unsuccessful, to their secure shores," perpetually in trouble with "some woman" (*MD*, 105). This Homeric language echoes Peter's self-conception. Having returned home by ship from India, a land he has helped govern in an attempt to civilize natives—an endeavor that echoes Odysseus's wanderings through barbarian islands—Peter envisions himself as "an adventurer, reckless . . . a romantic buccaneer" (*MD*). The *Odyssey* is perhaps the oldest Western tale that establishes the civilized identity of Europeans by contrasting Greek cultural practices with those of imagined barbarians. In this way, the *Odyssey* anticipates the links between imperialism and primitivism that Woolf exploits in her satirical treatment of Peter Walsh.

While Peter seems to willfully deny the mutual dependence of political and civil society, Woolf reminds her readers throughout her oeuvre of their reliance on one another. In *Three Guineas*, she argues that the woman shut up within the dependency of the marriage system cannot help but support imperialism and war as her only hope of security and escape, since, as "consciously she desired 'our splendid Empire'; unconsciously she desired our splendid war" (*TG*, 49).[4] Within *Mrs. Dalloway*, Lady Bruton serves as the most explicit reminder of this intersection of imperial power and domestic confinement, and she clarifies the high stakes of Peter's mythic fantasies. By using her domestic privilege to accomplish her imperialistic aims, Lady

---

2. Felson, *Regarding Penelope*, xiii.
3. Monte, "Ancients and Moderns," 594.
4. Page references are to the 2006 edition.

Bruton embodies the interdependence of civil society and political society, a characteristic that prompts Richard Dalloway to see her as representative of British tradition and identity. Like the frustrated women Woolf describes in *Three Guineas,* Lady Bruton seeks outlets for her martial nature in imperial projects like her letter to *The Times* calling for the emigration of young people to colonize Canada.

Woolf presents Lady Bruton as a woman ensconced in a domestic privilege that the British Empire makes possible, much like the young women with their "admirable butlers, tawny chow dogs, halls laid in black and white lozenges with white blinds blowing" whom Peter spies through an open door and "approves" as "a splendid achievement" of British civilization (*MD,* 53). She stands out, though, for her unusual participation in and identification with militarism. Woolf explicitly militarizes and masculinizes Lady Bruton: She once organized an expedition to South Africa during the war, advised General Sir Talbot Moore on an important advance of British troops, according to rumors, and mirrors the painting of her ancestor, "the General." This latter visual parallel prompts Richard Dalloway to muse that "she should have been a general of dragoons herself. And Richard would have served under her, cheerfully" (102). She invites Richard and Hugh Whitbread to luncheon so that she may engage their help in writing a letter to *The Times* calling for young people born of "respectable parents" to emigrate to Canada in a plan that she believes would ease domestic economic tensions and strengthen the Commonwealth. Lady Bruton bears much in common with Sir Bradshaw in that both of them work to "make England prosper" by protecting it from "the unfit" (97). This project in which she grounds her identity—"Emigration had become, in short, largely Lady Bruton" (106)—might seem to be a matter of civil society; yet repeated references to it as a "battle" suggest that it functions as political society: "Her hand, lying on the sofa back, curled upon some imaginary baton such as her grandfathers might have held, holding which she seemed, drowsy and heavy, to be commanding battalions marching to Canada" (109).[5]

---

5. Here Woolf references an actual letter to the *Times* in 1923 that called for the emigration of "eugenically sound" youth to improve the population of Canada, replacing some of the young men killed in WWI. Bonnie Kime Scott, annotation to *Mrs. Dalloway.* Kathy Phillips connects Lady Bruton's proposed emigration policy to the nineteenth-century policies of Sir John Robert Seeley. In 1883, Seeley advocated that the "superfluous population" of England be moved to the colonies. Kathy Phillips, *Virginia Woolf against Empire,* 9. As Raymond Williams points out in *The Country and the City,* emigration to the periphery of the empire offered a solution to rural poverty and overcrowded cities, allowing an expanding middle class new economic opportunity. Barrett links this letter to the fact that emigration was proposed as a solution to the problem of "sexual inverts." Barrett, "Unmasking Lesbian Passion," 156–57.

Lady Bruton combines the masculine and the feminine sides of power and privilege, using domestic luxury—a sumptuous banquet, a beautiful home, and competent domestic servants—to ensure the success of her military maneuvers and imperial projects. At the same time, her need to "eject upon some object" the "pent egotism, which a strong martial woman . . . feels rise within her, once youth is past" (*MD*, 106) motivates her imperialist project of emigration to Canada.[6] Lady Bruton stands as the type of woman Woolf describes in *Three Guineas*: Confined within the domestic sphere, limited in the scope of her direct influence as a woman, this woman who has inherited the martial strength of her male ancestors seeks and finds an outlet for her energies in advancing the cause of Empire and war.

Woolf subtly links Peter Walsh and Lady Bruton through several recurring details that represent femininity as a seductive and deceptive threat to masculine consciousness. In both sections of the novel, red carnations that are associated with women's bodies mesmerize men; visions rise up or float before the eyes of men, obscuring their perceptions of reality; and men fall into a dreamy feeling of peace with the universe under the sway of femininity. While Peter willingly seeks out the enchantments of women and dreams, abandoning the burdens of awareness, Lady Bruton wields feminine charms like a weapon to accomplish her objectives. Further, of the characters in the novel, only Lady Bruton and Peter Walsh take naps in the middle of the day; these naps represent the retreat from consciousness that Woolf more fully develops through Peter Walsh's adventures.[7] Mentioned sparingly in the novel, as possessions of Lady Bruton and the privileged girls whom Peter admires, chow dogs serve as a clear reminder that the products of British imperialism in China were imported into domestic situations. Along with Lady Bruton's use of domestic privilege to support militarism, these parallels between Peter and Lady Bruton—their shared Homeric characterizations of Peter, the unusual presence of imperialistic and domestic chow dogs, and the presentation of feminine charms as undoing masculine consciousness—highlight both the intersections of militaristic conquest and domestic privilege that Peter refuses to acknowledge and the means by which he evades this acknowledgement.

Lady Bruton's luncheon, while revealing the marriage of empire building and culture, also exposes the role of deceptive ideological narratives in obscuring and protecting this union. Both Lady Bruton and Peter obfuscate the interconnections of domestic luxury and imperialism. Lady Bruton's household has a religious quality to it, the mystery of which perpetuates the

---

6. On Lady Bruton as one who exiles others, see Bowlby, *Feminist Destinations*, 82.

7. Clarissa Dalloway is ordered to take a nap in the afternoon but never actually does so.

illusion that the domestic and militaristic spheres are independent while echoing the archaic religious imagery of Peter's fantasies. The practice of esoteric mystery associated with Lady Bruton's maids, "*adepts* in a *mystery* or grand deception practiced by hostesses in Mayfair from one-thirty to two" (*MD*, 102, emphasis mine), suggests secretive, archaic mystery religions. In her enchanted home, domestic privilege transcends the capitalist economy and conceals the role of labor in production, since the food has not been paid for and the table "spreads itself voluntarily with glass and silver" (102). Similarly, Peter imagines that the girls he spies, privileged "girls in their security," stand outside of the "empire and army" he dislikes (54). By spinning a myth composed of religious symbols to conceal the ideological forces they support, Peter and Lady Bruton express Nietzsche's and Marx's conception of myth as an ideologically motivated lie.

Woolf's reminders about the links between civil and political society in this section of the novel create for the reader an ironic distance from Peter's perspective, particularly his naïve assumption that he could praise one aspect of British society and blame the other. Woolf establishes this distance by contrasting Peter's celebration of British civilization with the novel's general presentation of the state of England. When he observes Septimus hallucinating the dead and Rezia desperately trying to snap him back to reality, a scene that Woolf has just narrated in excruciating detail, Peter describes it all as "amusing" and glibly reads it as a lover's quarrel, one of the charms of British civilization: "Lovers squabbling under a tree; the domestic family life of the parks. Never had he seen London look so enchanting . . . the richness; the greenness; the civilisation, after India" (*MD*, 69). This scene does indeed represent civilization, but not in the idealized way Peter thinks; rather, it signifies the destruction of human relations and life caused by civilization's wars and rationalist discipline. Similarly, Peter's interpretation of the change in English society between 1918 and 1923, while he was in India, stands at odds with the novel's presentation of this change. He recognizes that "a change of some sort had undoubtedly taken place," but he focuses on the greater social freedoms that young people experience, especially on sexual freedoms—women making up their faces in public, boys and girls openly displaying affection without being engaged, and newspapers publishing articles about water closets (70). Whereas Peter sees the liberating aspects of this transition from repressive Victorian society, elsewhere in the novel Woolf paints a very different picture of postwar England. Early on, Clarissa muses that "this late age of the world's experience had bred in them all, all men and women, a well of tears. Tears and sorrows; courage and endurance" (9). When Mr. Bowley, "sealed with wax over the deepest sources of life," watches the crowd gathering at the gates of Buckingham Palace, he becomes "unsealed suddenly, inappropriately, sentimentally" (19). In Mr. Bowley's sudden excess of emotion, Clarissa's statement about this late age of the world, and Septimus's inability to hold back his overflowing well of grief and madness, we see the dark side of this cultural transformation: The war has catastrophically disrupted a relatively stable, if repressive, social order. A realistic sense of this damage tempers even Clarissa's most optimistic efforts to reassemble and revive English society. In these ways, Woolf marks Peter's glib perspective on a changed London as oblivious.

Rachel Bowlby suggests another way that Woolf distances the reader from Peter's perspective. She teases out the allusions to the classical *passante*, or passing woman, of Baudelaire and Proust in Peter's vision of the young woman he follows through the streets. Peter imagines this young woman in language that echoes Baudelaire's in "*A une passante*," as "tall, slim, in deep mourning, majestic grief . . . the softness that fascinates and the pleasure that kills."[8] Working with many of the same passages I focus on later in this chapter, Bowlby argues that Woolf parodies this literary stereotype, the *passante* pursued by the *flâneur*, which is "pure projection, pure fantasy . . . a creature of masculine imagination."[9] Woolf's version of the *flâneur-passante* encounter reproduces Proust's generic feminine fantasy of an everywoman but concludes by deflating Peter's desire for a climax to his amorous adventure. As Bowlby writes, in *Mrs. Dalloway*, "the inclusion of the *passante*'s angle of view has produced a parody of a scene whose conventions are clearly understood by both parties." When the young woman in black looks directly at Peter and produces a latchkey more powerful than his fingered pocketknife, the scene transforms into a "power game where she comes out with the victory," and the female gaze substitutes for Peter's impotent gaze.[10] Woolf does mockingly mimic this modern version of a universal feminine fantasy, which Bowlby calls a death-dealing, life-giving mother. But as we have seen repeatedly, Woolf crafts multifaceted allusions. The modern *flâneur*'s *passante* also echoes an ancient universal mother, a set of images with which Woolf was intimately familiar. Her descriptions of this woman create not just a space for female walking and writing, as Bowlby compellingly argues, but also a commentary on modernity and imperialism.

By distancing us from Peter's perspective and his tendency to fetishize women, Woolf critiques modernist primitivism, the fascination among some early twentieth-century Western artists with non-Western art forms and culture as a lost paradise in contrast to repressive European modernity. But

---

8. Baudelaire, "A Une Passante."
9. Bowlby, *Feminist Destinations*, 202–3.
10. Bowlby, 206.

Woolf's paratactic approach indicates a particularly nuanced relationship to the nostalgic, antirational tendencies that characterize much avant-garde art of her period. Like Peter, who seeks an alternative to imperialist logic in images of the spiritually integrated archaic, Woolf turns to archaic mythic models, especially chthonic matrifocal myth as described by Harrison, to forge her feminist response to imperialism and rational materialism.[11] To an extent, then, Woolf shares the modernist tendency to see archaic myth and art as alternatives to the ills of modernity, à la Fry, Lawrence, and Eliot. However, as Whitworth argues, Woolf was keen to distance herself from the mythic modernism of her contemporaries and its implicit support of dangerous political movements. In his brief discussion of this topic, Whitworth suggests that Peter Walsh's "'primitivist haze' . . . may indicate Woolf's dissatisfaction with the modernism of her contemporaries, and its dangerous potential to blur real political issues."[12] Peter's 'primitivist haze' deserves more sustained exploration. Woolf's employment of primitivist imagery in her novels suggests that while she may have sympathized with primitivists' dissatisfaction with sterile rationalist modernity, she had reservations about their proposed solution. Because Woolf read Greek literature carefully and had grown up in a family damaged by the Angel in the House mythology, she displays skepticism about utopian mobilizations of divine femininity that promise escape from the restrictions of modern life.

The nostalgic side of modernity, which looks back longingly upon a lost, and largely imaginary, premodern world, has formed a counterpoint to progressive confidence since the Romantic Movement.[13] In the early twentieth century, this tendency manifested in Orientalism and primitivism because its adherents often envisioned non-Western cultures as possessing what the alienated modern Western world was felt to lack, "believing that, largely through the power of myth and ritual, primal humanity was better integrated spiritually and cosmically than moderns."[14] If, in the modern age, one feels transcendentally homeless, alone, and unsure of one's place in a godless universe of natural processes, as theorists of the modern novel like Lukács have argued, then one may dream of a return to a simpler time when the natural world was saturated with supernatural meaning.

---

11. On Harrison's influence on Woolf's ability to seek out alternative approaches, see Mills, *Spirit of Modern Classicism*, 5.

12. Whitworth, "Virginia Woolf, Modernism, and Modernity," 116.

13. This nostalgia is often identified with the counter-Enlightenment. Despite Isaiah Berlin's attempts to situate the counter-Enlightenment in eighteenth-century thought, Robert Norton has argued that the concept was an invention of the early twentieth century in "Myth of the Counter-Enlightenment."

14. Ellwood, *Politics of Myth*, xiv.

The fantasy of a premodern paradise appears in psychological theory as well where theorists link it to the unconscious. As Gretchen Holbrook Gerzina reports, James and Alix Strachey, adherents and advocates of Freudian psychoanalysis, thought of Africa as "a more direct expression of the Freudian unconscious," a sentiment that Gerzina links to Freud's "reference to women as the 'Dark Continent,' a phrase which he himself 'borrowed from Victorian colonialist texts.'"[15] The Jungian psychologist Erich Neumann, in *The Origins and History of Consciousness*, repeatedly merges the ontogenetic and the phylogenetic, drawing parallels between infancy and prehistoric human beings. When theorizing uroboric incest, which he defines as the budding "ego's tendency to dissolve back into unconsciousness," Neumann describes infantile consciousness as "easily tired," "passive, having no real activity of its own," and "mainly receptive, though even this receptivity is exhausting and leads to loss of consciousness through fatigue."[16] Compare his description of "primitives, who, if they are not actively occupied with something, drowse off and are easily tired by conscious effort."[17] To extend his parallel between infants and his imagined version of early humans, Neumann describes the uroboros itself, the state of primal unconsciousness into which the awakening ego returns, as the symbol of "the prehistoric world. Before the beginning of history, mankind exists in a state of nameless amorphousness of which we know, and can know, very little, because at that period 'the unconscious' ruled."[18] Neumann articulates links between nostalgic fantasies of the premodern and depth psychology that permeate Woolf's portrayal of Peter's fantasies of women. As we shall see, Peter displays many of the symptoms of uroboric incest.

This gendered fantasy of uroboric dissolution manifests also in the dynamic that Robert Young terms colonial desire, the obsessive attraction and fear felt by colonizers for black sexuality that culminates in a fascination with miscegenation. The modern Western subject has traditionally imagined itself as masculine/subject and the non-Western as feminine/object.[19] The power dynamics of this gendered colonial relation may seem straightforward, but

---

15. Gerzina, "Bushmen and Blackface," 50–51.
16. Neumann, *Origins*, 277.
17. Neumann, 275.
18. Neumann, 281.
19. On the gendering of races, see Young's discussion of Gobineau, who "rationalizes the apparently irrepressible sexual relations between the Aryans and the other races of the world by characterizing the active Aryans and the 'pre-eminently male groups' and the desirable yellow and black races as the 'female or feminized races'" (*Colonial Desire*, 102). Gerzina notes the binding together of exotic and erotic in both African sculpture and photographs of Africans and their art, a discourse that shapes the reception of Fry's Post-Impressionist Exhibition of 1910 ("Bushmen and Blackface," 51–52).

as Neumann's analysis of uroboric incest reveals, "modern man" often takes a masochistic relation to the dominating uroboric Mother. Uroboric incest is "simultaneously pleasurable and painful. . . . The dissolvent sadism of the uroboros and the masochism of the dissolved ego germ coalesce in an ambivalent pleasure-pain feeling. This 'death in ecstasy' is symbolized by the pleroma, the 'fullness' known to the ego as a borderline experience."[20] The sadomasochistic relation of ego consciousness to the unconscious uroboric mother, which Neumann links to the prehistoric situation, resembles in some ways the ambivalence of colonial desire, a simultaneous obsessive attraction and repulsion, which Young identifies in racialist writings of the nineteenth century.[21] The ambivalent desire for death or unconsciousness, symbolized as the exotic or primordial feminine, came to be pictured by some as a relief from the tensions of modern life, or consciousness in Neumann's language. As Young illustrates, this became a particular fantasy of white colonial masters seeking to lose themselves in sensual pleasure with native women, who were often represented in poetry in classical terms, such as "The Sable Venus."[22] But at the same time that white men were "so enthralled by 'their infatuated attachments to black women,' that they refuse[d] to marry white women," miscegenation was believed to produce "the offspring who initiates the degeneration that eventually brings about civilization's end."[23] Not surprisingly, Young explicitly identifies this obsessional colonial desire as "no doubt complicit with colonialism itself."[24]

The picture that emerges blends anxiety about repressive and sterile Western rational materialism, imperialism envisioned as a male activity, primitivist imagery of exotic femininity, and the psychosymbolic fetishizing of an uroboric womb. Peter illustrates this constellation because he indulges in three fantasies about women he encounters during his walk across London, and because Woolf frames these fantasies with three passages in which Peter comments ambivalently on the political and civil aspects of the British Empire. In short, his primitivist fantasies evince the complicity with colonial power that Young notes, though they are framed within passages in which Peter is critical of the political side of British imperialism. In this way, Peter willfully denies the mutual dependence of the political and civil aspects of imperialist society, and in so doing avoids acknowledging the complicity of his primitivist fantasies in supporting imperialism.

20. Neumann, *Origins*, 277.
21. Young, *Colonial Desire*, 142.
22. Young, 143–48.
23. Young, 141, 102.
24. Young, 2.

Having recently returned from his colonial administrative position in India, Peter Walsh wanders through the streets of London on a fanciful adventure and experiences three mystical visions of the divine feminine that lift him out of profane modern life. In evoking the archaic goddess, Peter's mythic visions of women he encounters in London—a young woman dressed in black, a nurse on a park bench, and an old beggar woman—mirror the discursive construction of some contemporary cultures as primitive. Woolf communicates this primarily through allusions to chthonic feminine figures from archaic Greek religion, not directly through images of contemporary non-Western women. Woolf could conjure primitivism for her reading public by alluding to Greek religion because nineteenth-century British anthropology, led by E. B. Tylor and sometimes called "Mr. Tylor's science," repeatedly associated the cultures and beliefs of contemporary indigenous peoples with the pre-Olympian religion of the Greeks since both were imagined to represent earlier stages in human development. Due to these links, references to archaic Greek religion could have gestured toward cultural constructions of contemporary non-Western societies for Woolf's reading public.

Peter's fantasies suggest modernist primitivism not only because Woolf describes them in language that evokes archaic Greek religions but also because they share the abstraction typical of Western primitivist art. Both archaic religious figures and the women Peter envisions occupy a liminal position, neither disembodied concepts nor fully developed characters. This shift away from anthropomorphic and realistic representation of the human form typified art of the period. Primitivist visual art often blended tribal motifs with sexualized imagery of the female body and the tantalizing threat of death. In this sense, they present a fitting example of uroboric incest when viewed through a Jungian lens. This combination can be seen in two masterpieces by Paul Gauguin and Pablo Picasso. Gauguin's 1894 *Oviri* [Savage], a clay sculpture named after the Tahitian goddess of death and mourning, *Oviri-moe-aihere* [The Savage Who Sleeps in the Forest], features a naked, bloody woman holding two dead wolves. Gauguin's presentation of an abstracted non-Western nude feminine figure with dead bodies in this sculpture, which was displayed at the 1906 artist's retrospective that Picasso attended, may have inspired Picasso's 1907 painting *Les Desmoiselles d'Avignon* [The Young Ladies of Avignon]. Picasso's *Desmoiselles* exemplifies the primitivist aesthetic and lays the foundation for cubism with its two-dimensional female nudes broken into geometric planes. Just as Woolf alludes to archaic Greek goddesses as shorthand for primitivism, Picasso blends premodern Western imagery (archaic Iberian art) with African masks and juxtaposes these with flattened angular female nudes. Sketches for this painting included two men who were removed from the painting, one of whom was a medical student carrying a skull, a *memento mori* that references death in much the same way as the bleeding lupine bodies in Gauguin's sculpture.

Woolf presents Peter's visions of women in terms similarly abstract to Picasso's and Gauguin's portrayals of women. In each of Peter's visions an actual woman inspires Peter, but the reader never directly sees these women. Instead, they are available only through Peter's perspective, and his fantasies, which "ceaselessly float up, pace beside, put their faces in front of, the actual thing," eclipse each woman (*MD*, 56). Even this level of narrative certainty requires some interpretation. Woolf imbues these passages with ambiguity, since the reader cannot access objective occurrences outside Peter's perception, and Peter's experience of the events, even while awake, feel dreamlike. Woolf does not definitively mark the transition from external reality to Peter's dream on the park bench. In waking reality, Peter sits next to a "grey nurse" who knits as he falls asleep, at which point she becomes for Peter "one of those spectral presences which rise in twilight woods made of sky and branches" (55). Even before he transforms this woman into a nonanthropomorphic earth goddess, Peter's waking language of a "grey nurse" conflates her dress with her being, engaging in the merging of internal and external that Neumann argues characterizes regression to the uroboric state, "when we plunge into the world of dreams," and the "dawn period of mankind."[25]

Further, Peter's visions of the archaic feminine are primitivist both in the qualities with which he endows these goddesses and in his emotional relation to them. When Peter gazes at the young woman in black, the nurse on the park bench, and the old beggar woman, their discrete particularity dissolves into the world around them and into universal concepts, impersonal forces, and states of mind. Peter's fantasies suggest the universal, infinite, and generative characteristics of the uroboric Great Goddess: She contains all potential forms of Being, merges all disparate elements and particularities, and makes no distinction between inside and outside, subject and object, self and other. He identifies the female vagrant who meanders through the background of the novel and the grey nurse on the park bench with the earth and with eternity, suggesting an eschatological function. Peter identifies the old woman with the infinity of the universe itself, thinking that when she dies "the pageant of the universe would be over" (*MD*, 79). He envisions her as an eternal entity who sings "through all ages" of "love which has lasted a million years . . . love which prevails" (79). Several characters in the novel experience the female vagrant as a kaleidoscope of many things—a rusty pump pouring song from

---

25. Neumann, *Origins*, 276.

the earth, a tree, a hole in the earth from which issues a bubbling song that fertilizes the earth, a "battered old woman with her hand exposed for coppers" (80). She is in fact the most paratactic figure in *Mrs. Dalloway*, since everyone who looks at her sees something different. Peter participates in this symbolic vision of the beggar woman and extends it to other women. The figure in his dream is likewise part woman, part force of nature in which "myriads of things merged in one thing" (56). She too suggests the infinite and eschatological in Peter's mind, becoming "the giant figure at the end of the ride," a being that Peter believes exists because "he can conceive of her" (56). This earth goddess appears to him as a spectral presence made of "sky and branches he rapidly endows . . . with womanhood," and his vision blends the feminine and divine when he thinks of her as rising "from the troubled sea to shower down from her magnificent hands compassion, comprehension, absolution" (56). This transcendence of human categories highlights the primitivist aspects of Peter's fantasies because it echoes archaic religion, especially as Harrison describes it. Peter imagines nonanthropomorphic figures that recall Harrison's archaic Mountain Mother as well as the Sirens and the Erinyes, which Harrison categorizes as early manifestations of this central female divinity. At an early stage of culture, before humans make a clearly drawn boundary between themselves and other animals in anthropomorphic religions, humanity "makes his [sic] divinities sometimes wholly animal, sometimes of mixed monstrous shapes" (*Prolegomena*, 257–58, emphasis in original).

These feminine figures provide Peter with access to a transmundane realm that exceeds the limits of human personality since Peter's visions blend women with external objects. Peter's mythicized fantasy of the young woman in black whom he follows similarly echoes a feature of the archaic Goddess that Harrison emphasizes, the embodiment of an impersonal, abstract concept. Harrison notes that the goddess Dike embodied Justice and that Themis embodied divine law (*Prolemogena*, 506, 261). Echoing this archaic practice, Peter calls the young woman he follows through the streets "this excitement" and refers to her using the pronouns "it" and "which" instead of "she" and "who" (*MD*, 51–52). For Peter, she seems to "shed veil after veil" until she transforms from an attractive young woman into "the very woman he had always had in mind" (51), transcending her particularity to enter the category of the universal and the abstract ideal. Peter's relationship to all three women is not to ordinary human beings. Rather, another being or force hidden within each has been unveiled, and this other being or force draws Peter to it. For

Peter, the woman—no longer anthropomorphic and discrete—embodies an impersonal force, abstract concept, or state of mind, much like the goddesses Harrison studied.

While the grey nurse/nature goddess and the female vagrant suggest the archaic earth goddess in general terms, the young woman in black whom Peter follows specifically evokes the chthonic feminine figures of death: the Erinyes, Keres, Sirens, and Persephone. These chthonic deities are among the most visible examples of the nonanthropomorphic forms of the Great Goddess that Harrison theorizes. Woolf uses them to suggest primitivism, uroboric incest, and colonial desire. Peter describes the young woman he follows in unusual language that reflects a common theological construction. "Young, but stately; merry, but discreet; black, but enchanting" (*MD*, 51), she suggests the *coincidencia oppositorum* that characterizes the divine in many cultures. The specific dichotomies contained within this woman recall Persephone who, in the timeless world of myth, is equally young, enchanting, and merry (as the maiden picking flowers with her companions) and black, discreet, and stately (as the terrifying and cold queen of the underworld).

Within the list of paradoxes embodied in the young woman, "black, but enchanting" stands out. Modern readers might not at first associate blackness, and its suggestions of destruction and death, with the description of a woman as enchanting, since to modern readers that adjective commonly connotes delight and pleasure in relation to women. However, these two characteristics, black and enchanting, intersect in the psychosymbolic realm of mythology and literature, in which figures like the femme fatale combine deathly terror with seductive charms, employing feminine charms to bring about the death of the male hero. The description of the woman as black references archaic descriptions of the black Keres and the black Erinyes. As predators and seductresses, the Keres are both black and enchanting, combining terrifying death with feminine sexuality. Greek art depicts them as both "pursuing a man out of erotic desire or sitting aside him to have intercourse with him" and "attacking him to tear him to shreds and devour him."[26] The word enchantment and its Greek correlatives are paratactic, implying the casting of a spell and the overpowering of another by dangerous magic and delightful charm. This ambivalence repeats throughout ancient literature. Consider Kirke, who combines both sides of the enchanting woman in her threatening and comforting qualities. She literally enchants Odysseus's shipmates in book ten of the *Odyssey*, casting a witch's spell on them, and they originally enter her house trustingly because her delightful song and youthful beauty enchant them. The

---

26. Vernant, *Mortals and Immortals*, 103.

double meanings of enchantment, then, reveal that the seeming opposition of "black, but enchanting" is, in fact, not an opposition at all, as the deathly terror implied in "black" is also implied in "enchanting." As we shall see later, this ambivalence echoes the attraction and fear that Robert Young identifies in colonial representations of black sexuality and interracial unions.

Woolf suggests the "primitive" in Peter's visions of the young woman he trails and of the female vagrant through what he imagines to be their nonverbal communication. The nonsensical or nonhuman language Peter perceives coming from these women aligns them with the "primitive," whose languages the primitivist artist strips of their meaning and imagines as signs of their exoticism rather than as modes of communication. Hugo Ball's dada poem, "Gadgi Beri Bimba," for example, a classic example of primitivist art, features an almost incoherent collective chant in imagined tribal style that consists of African-sounding nonsense words such as "rhinozerossola," "elifantolim," and "negramai." The made-up language that Woolf's brother Adrian Stephen crafted during the Dreadnought Hoax to simulate the Abyssinian language and gain entry for the "blacked-up" hoaxers similarly consisted of "a mixture of Latin, Swahili and nonsense words."[27] Following this tradition, the beggar woman seems to produce a sound "with an absence of all human meaning" that emanates from what the narrator alternately describes as a hole in the ground, a tree, a pipe, and an old woman (*MD*, 79).

Similarly, Peter thinks that the young woman in black calls nonverbally to him. This call, which Peter feels emanate from her body and clothing, echoes the Sirens' call to Odysseus:

> This woman, this excitement, which seemed even with its back turned to shed on him a light which connected them, which singled him out, as if the random uproar of the traffic had whispered through hollowed hands his name, not Peter, but his private name which he called himself in his own thoughts. "You," she said, only "you," saying it with her white gloves and her shoulders. (*MD*, 51–52)

This call, described as a light emanating from "it" and as the sound of the traffic, occurs outside phallogocentric language and expresses a force that exceeds the human. The fact that the woman calls Peter by a supposedly private name instead of his public name, singling him out from all other men, evokes the song that the terrifying and irresistible chthonic Sirens sing exclusively to Odysseus, a figure with whom Peter identifies. However, the fact that,

---

27. Gerzina, "Bushmen and Blackface," 52.

as Bowlby notes, the private name this woman calls Peter turns out to be the outrageously generic *you* undermines Peter's romantic image of the "primitive" feminine and, by extension, primitivist fantasies.

Peter perceives the young woman he follows as having an ontological bond with a red carnation, an association that links her to Lady Bruton, another woman bonded with a red carnation, and connects her to two chthonic forms of the Great Goddess—the *Kore* and the Sirens. Kerényi suggests that Persephone, the most recognizable *Kore*, has an ontological bond with flowers in the Homeric *Hymn to Demeter*.[28] Vernant writes that Homer links the Sirens to flowers through the flowering meadow in which they are permanently fixed.[29] The Greeks connected female sexuality with flowers as we do in English when we speak of a woman being "deflowered." *Leimōn*, "meadow," including the flowering meadows of the Sirens, is one of the Greek words used for female genitalia.[30] Carnations, in particular, have a long literary history dating back to ancient Greece and suggest several associations with the Goddess. *Dianthus*, the species that includes the carnation, may derive from the Greek *dios* and *anthos*, meaning "divine flower" or "flower of the gods." The flower attaches to the Roman Diana, another deathly aspect of the Goddess, who plucked out the eyes of a shepherd boy, red carnations growing where the eyes fell. In Christianity, carnations are said to have grown from Mary's tears as she watched Christ carry the cross.[31] All these cases link carnations, and specifically red carnations, with the loving yet deadly Mother.

The permeable physicality of the young woman Peter pursues merges with "the red carnation he had seen her wear as she came across Trafalgar Square burning again in his eyes and making her lips red" (*MD*, 52). Woolf does not describe the carnation as making the woman's lips *appear* red. Rather, the carnation makes them red, establishing an ontological bond between the woman's body and the flower like the ontological bond Kerényi sees between Persephone and flowers. The flower appears again at Lady Bruton's luncheon, strengthening the links between Peter's adventurous walk through London and Lady Bruton's lunch party. Echoing the language of Peter's dream on the park bench, Hugh Whitbread falls under a spell at Lady Bruton's lunch table that evokes Kirke's enchanting meal in book ten of the *Odyssey*. With the appearance of wine and coffee that are explicitly "not paid for," suggesting a domestic magic that exceeds the strictures of the capitalist economy, Hugh finds himself under the spell of "jocund visions" that rise "before musing eyes;

---

28. Jung and Kerényi, *Essays on Science and Mythology*, 108.
29. Vernant, *Mortals and Immortals*, 104.
30. Vernant, 104.
31. Mercatante, *Magic Garden*, 9.

gentle speculative eyes; eyes to whom life appears musical, mysterious; eyes now kindled to observe genially the beauty of the red carnations which Lady Bruton . . . had laid beside her plate" (*MD*, 102).[32] The effect of Hugh's vision of the red carnations resembles remarkably the effect on Peter of "those spectral presences which rise" to shower down on him "compassion, comprehension, absolution" (55–56). Like Peter, under this influence, Hugh feels "at peace with the entire universe and at the same time completely sure of his standing" (102). Taken together, these red carnations and their effects suggest that, as in Peter's mythic adventure through London, the symbolism of the Goddess saturates Lady Bruton's lunch party.

As we have seen, the feminine figures that Peter envisions as he walks around London evoke primitivism because he endows them with qualities Harrison identifies in the archaic goddess. They resemble the Great Goddess in their impersonal, nonanthropomorphic nature, which manifests as merging with the external world or with abstract concepts in Peter's mind and as their nonhuman language. Woolf's repeated suggestions of death and her emphasis on chthonic imagery in these figures strengthen these links. Beyond the content of Peter's fantasies, Woolf implies modernist primitivism through Peter's relation to his fetishes, which echoes both Young's description of colonial desire and Neumann's theory of uroboric incest.

Like modernist primitivists, Peter desperately seeks relief from profane reality and the confines of the individual ego in mythicized feminine figures that he imagines embody an escape from modern reason. Peter nurses these soteriological desires despite his professed atheism. In his visions of the three women, he experiences moments of ecstasy in altered states of consciousness that free him from profane modernity. As he drowses on a park bench, watched over by a grey nurse, he thinks that the only thing outside the individual is "a state of mind . . . a desire for solace, for relief, for something outside these miserable pigmies [*sic*], these feeble, these ugly, these craven men and women" (*MD*, 56). In his wish for "something outside," he finds the solace he seeks in a nature goddess he self-consciously invents to provide him "compassion, comprehension, absolution" (56). This figure offers Peter reunion with the impersonal collective, suggesting the *ecstasis* that Harrison argues lies at the heart of religion before rational theology overshadows its importance. For Harrison, the twin phenomena of myth and ritual arise out of the overflow of ecstatic emotion that worshippers experience in union with the godhead and the collective. Peter expresses his desire to rejoin the collective

---

32. Ironically, as Woolf's readers would have known, the red carnation was the flower of socialists, "the emblems of workers' movements in most European countries." Watts, *Elsevier's Dictionary of Plant Lore*.

most profoundly when he wishes to "walk straight on to this great figure, who will, with a toss of her head, mount [him] on her streamers and let [him] blow to nothingness with the rest" (56).

Peter enters altered states of mind passively in a moment of *enthousiasmos*, in which an external force overtakes him. Instead of fearing spiritual intrusion into his rational ego, he embraces loss of identity and self-control as an escape from the burdens of consciousness, civilization, and even life itself. In this sense, Peter resembles modernist primitivists like Georges Bataille, whom Marianna Torgovnick describes as yearning "for death (even violent death) as a way out of the intolerable uncertainty and limits of being."[33] Prior to Peter's first mythic fantasy, about the young woman in black, he reports that "inside his brain by another hand strings were pulled . . . he having nothing to do with it" (*MD*, 51). This experience leaves him feeling free and younger than he has for years, having escaped "from being precisely what he was" (51). Under this external influence, his mind is like an unguarded flame that bows and bends, about to be blown from its holding. He experiences the danger of his fragile flame of consciousness being blown out as freedom and escape, as something delightful, rather than as a threat to guard against.

When Peter escapes his identity and ordinary state of mind, he feels "like a child who runs out of doors," escaping the watchful eye of his minder (*MD*, 51). Woolf repeats this association with infantile consciousness in Peter's second encounter with a supernatural feminine force, his dream on the park bench. In this moment, as Kathy Phillips argues, he "is shown up *as* the baby he is *next to*. . . . Woolf allows the baby to serve as both environment to Peter and image of Peter."[34] Once again, an external force—in this case, "a great brush" that sweeps "smooth across his mind"—transforms Peter's mind (55). Echoing his recent description of the young woman in black as "feathered, evanescent" (53), Peter now sinks "down, down . . . into the plumes and feathers of sleep, sank, and was muffled over," a series of descriptions that prepares the reader to connect feathers, unconsciousness, and mythicized women (55). This portrayal of Peter as a drowsy infant resembles Neumann's description of the awakening "feeble" ego, in the "uroboric phase, of which infancy and sleep are typical," which finds dissolution "back into unconsciousness . . . pleasurable."[35]

Peter's fantasies also suggest modernist primitivism because they marry a yearning for liberation from rational individualism with racialized imagery of the feminine, who is "black, but enchanting." While the woman Peter follows

---

33. Torgovnick, *Gone Primitive*, 190.
34. Phillips, *Virginia Woolf against Empire*, xviii. Emphasis in original.
35. Neumann, *Origins*, 277.

wears a black cloak, he identifies this blackness with her being rather than her appearance, just as he does with the "grey nurse." According to Young, colonial discourse positions the colonial subject as "black, but enchanting" in much the same way as the Keres, Sirens, and Erinyes. Sander Gilman points out that sex became linked to race in the nineteenth century through fantasies based on stereotypes of blackness as embodying an attractive yet dangerous sexuality and a limitless fertility.[36] For this and other reasons, Young argues that colonialism was a machine "of fantasy, of desire . . . a desiring machine."[37] Peter Walsh, susceptible to feminine charms, fingering his pocket knife to soothe his nerves, and trailing a young woman through the streets, embodies this tendency to sexual fantasy. His description of the young woman as black but enchanting matches the "ambivalent axis of desire and aversion" that Young argues characterizes both colonial desire and the very idea of race.[38] Beyond reinforcing Western civilization, desire for the "primitive" body forms an ambivalent dialectic of escape into the exotic and a threat to racial purity, which parallels the uroboric escape-threat dialectic that Peter manifests and that Torgovnick points out in the work of Bataille and other modernist primitivists.

As far as this goes, we may see in Peter a not very surprising example of modernist primitivism. But Woolf presents Peter's primitivist fantasies of women within framing passages in which Peter explicitly comments on British civilization and colonialism in India. Unlike Septimus, who becomes absorbed in and destroyed by mystical vision, Peter protects his ideological worldview and social standing from the potential disruption of mythic thinking through an alternating pattern of rationalist commentary on Empire, expressed in the framing passages, interspersed with mythic consciousness, expressed in Peter's mythic fantasies. Whereas theorists like Harrison envision archaic mythic thinking as a viable alternative to the strictures of masculinist rational modernity, through Peter, Woolf demonstrates the ways that patriarchy and imperialism may subvert myth's radical potential.

The passages that frame Peter's fantasies reveal a fundamental inconsistency both within Peter and between Peter's perspective and that of the novel.[39] The soul-crushing discipline of imperialism and militarism repulses him, yet its domestic charms appeal to him. Peter reveals his ambivalence about Empire most often by rejecting the militaristic masculine realm of Empire and celebrating the feminine domestic sphere of civilization. He willfully dissoci-

---

36. Gilman, *Difference and Pathology*, 76–128.
37. Young, *Colonial Desire*, 92–93.
38. Young, 18, 102.
39. On Peter's hypocrisy, see Phillips, *Virginia Woolf against Empire*, 17.

ates the two faces of hegemonic society, the civil and the political, the mutual dependence of which Woolf is intent to highlight in the novel.

A passage in which Peter expresses both nostalgia for and criticism of the masculine realm of militarism and politics introduces his first encounter with a mythicized woman, the young woman in black he follows through the streets. After dejectedly leaving Clarissa's house, he wanders the streets of London, and a column of boys passes him carrying a wreath to the Cenotaph commemorating soldiers who died in World War I. Peter criticizes the boys' support of imperial power even as their rhythmic marching draws him in and invades his mind such that he begins "to keep step with them" (*MD*, 50). He resists the regimented uniformity of the boys because it cannot allow "life, with all its varieties, its irreticences," which lay "under a pavement of monuments and wreaths and drugged [it] into a stiff yet staring corpse by discipline" (50). Yet, despite Peter's refusal of militarism and his claims that he is "not old, or set, or dried in the least" (49), he feels romantic nostalgia for a military training he calls "very fine" (50–51). This nostalgia leads him to regress to his boyhood worship of Major General Charles George Gordon. Peter identifies, though with regret, with the ethos of the marching boys and the statues of imperial heroes Gordon, Vice Admiral Horatio Nelson, and Major General Sir Henry Havelock. Like these men, Peter feels he has made "the great renunciation" that yields a "marble stare." Yet here Peter displays his ambivalence, distancing himself from the expectations of imperial masculine heroism: "But the stare Peter Walsh did not want for himself in the least; though he could respect it in others" (50). Peter, in his maturity and with "all that [he had] been through," consciously embraces the life that this stifling order suppresses, but he is unable to turn his back on it (51). As he will later under the influence of his primitivist fantasies, here Peter passively succumbs to outside forces, letting his mind shift back and forth between criticism and praise of, even participation in, the imperialist display. His susceptibility to nostalgia in this passage anticipates his wish to be swept away by overwhelming feminine fantasies, to sink into sleep, to be blown to nothingness, to be taken in by "arms that would open and take the tired" (55, 56, 52).

In the second of three framing passages, after the young woman he followed enters a door, Peter shifts direction and praises civilization:

> Admirable butlers, tawny chow dogs, halls laid in black and white lozenges with white blinds blowing, Peter saw through the open door and approved of. A splendid achievement in its own way, after all, London; the season; civilisation. Coming as he did from a respectable Anglo-Indian family which for at least three generations had administered the affairs of a continent (it's

strange, he thought, what a sentiment I have about that, disliking India, and empire, and army as he did), there were moments when civilisation, even of this sort, seemed dear to him as a personal possession; moments of pride in England; in butlers; chow dogs; girls in their security. (*MD*, 53–54)

In this passage Peter momentarily acknowledges both the inconsistency and the internal logic of his sentiments about political society, which he thinks of as "India, and empire, and army," and civil society, which appears as "London; the season; civilisation . . . butlers; chow dogs; girls in their security" (*MD*, 54). Though he acknowledges the disparity of his feelings as "strange," he limits this recognition to a parenthetical aside that never receives sustained reflection. In fact, the pride and possessiveness Peter feels about the "splendid achievement" of British civilization align perfectly with his role as a colonial administrator, despite the fact that, as a passerby looking in on a world from which he is excluded by class barriers, he might seem disconnected from it.

While she was writing *Mrs. Dalloway*, Woolf attended the 1924 British Empire Exhibition at Wembley and wrote "Thunder at Wembley." In this essay, Woolf describes the visitors at the exhibition that reproduced the British Empire in miniature for the British populace, a spectacle of enormous proportions and civic pride, and imagines the exhibition's destruction. Her description of the visitors as "creatures of leisure, civilization and dignity; a little languid perhaps, a little attenuated, but a *product to be proud of*" ("Thunder," 411, emphasis mine) illuminates Peter's language in this passage. Woolf's characterization of Peter's pride in the Empire's privileged domesticity and her description of the visitors to the British Empire Exhibition as products mirror Laura Chrisman and Patrick Williams's claim that "the colonial subject could be derivative from, as well as dominant over, the colonized."[40] In both "Thunder at Wembley" and this passage of *Mrs. Dalloway*, Woolf anticipates Chrisman and Williams's suggestion by reversing the usual imperialist notion of the Empire as a product of which the British subject may be proud, a conceptual framework that underlies the exhibition and, according to Woolf, that its visitors share. By portraying the civilized Londoner, rather than the colonized subject, as a dehumanized product forged by colonial power (despite her refrain that her contemporaries are revealed to her "simply as human beings"), Woolf suggests the extent to which the colonial encounter forms and re-forms the colonizer's subjectivity and the nature of civilization. In doing so, Woolf intrinsically links the privileged young women on whom Peter spies to his primitivized feminine fantasies: Both are feminine prod-

---

40. Williams and Chrisman, *Colonial Discourse*, 16.

ucts of British imperialism, imaginative constructions sustained by the work of men like Peter Walsh, by "India, and empire, and army" (*MD*, 54). And, equally important, in both cases, Peter Walsh imagines the feminine sphere, whether it takes the form of privileged girls protected (or confined) in the security of the upper-class home or of exotic fantasies, as fetishistic objects located *outside* British imperialism, pure sites from which he can escape the burdens of empire building.

The third framing passage, which comes after Peter awakens from his nap on the park bench with the phrase "the death of the soul" on his lips (*MD*, 57), further demonstrates Peter's ambivalence regarding hegemonic society. As his thoughts come into focus, Peter interprets his dream and "the death of the soul" as a response to a day spent at Bourton in his youth. On the day in question, Clarissa introduces her set to Richard Dalloway, the man she ultimately chooses over Peter and Sally. That day, a neighboring squire and his housemaid-turned-wife have come to visit. When Clarissa discovers that the woman has had a child out of wedlock, her disdain over their marriage turns to what Peter characterizes as prudish disgust (58). Peter considers this moment to be the death of her soul, the moment when the arrogance of the privileged domestic world triumphs over the "irreticences" of life, as represented by the coupling of squire and housemaid without regard for the civilized laws of marriage. The nineteenth-century jurist, J. J. Bachofen, who invented the modern notion of matriarchy, associates unregulated sexuality of the type illustrated by the squire and his housemaid with archaic prepatriarchal societies. From this perspective, the death of the soul would seem to suggest the deathly disciplining of hegemonic society, expressed in both its political aspects, as the militaristic marching boys Peter watches, and its civil aspects, as young Clarissa's bourgeois disgust at unregulated sexuality.

However, the dream that Peter interprets as representing the death of the soul renders that interpretation ambiguous. While Peter's explanation implies that the death of the soul signifies the smothering of life by civilization's rules, death functions quite differently within the dream itself. Instead of a death imposed by civilization, in the dream, death brings a desired escape from the anomie of modern life that resembles the "death in ecstasy" of uroboric incest.[41] The conflict between these two possible meanings of "the death of the soul" reveal Peter's ambivalence regarding civilization and empire. They suggest both the undesirable restrictions that political society and civil society place upon the individual and the primitivist desire to escape from these restrictions.

---

41. Neumann, *Origins*, 277.

In the three passages that frame Peter's encounters with the mythic feminine, Woolf demonstrates Peter's unwillingness to extend his critique of political society to civil society. Peter's equivocation about Empire and his drowsy indulgence in colonial desire and uroboric incest ultimately renders his resistance to imperialism impotent. But more damaging, as Young claims about colonial desire, Peter's indulgence makes him complicit in the forces he wishes to resist because it strengthens the bonds between the political and civil aspects of hegemony. Peter co-opts the mythic vision that could destabilize his ideological imperialist and patriarchal worldview and instead uses it to support imperialist modernity. In this way, Peter resembles Lady Bruton and the mature Clarissa Dalloway, who—unlike Septimus and the young Clarissa, whose outsider status renders them open to the disruptive power of mythic vision—are firmly entrenched in the power system. Their attachment to privileges that stem from the status quo, from Empire, patriarchy, and the British class system—features of rational modernity—prevents them from being transformed by mythic thought. For them, myth functions not as the disruptive force Harrison envisions, but as the deceptive tool of ideological power that Nietzsche and Marx fear, reinforcing the very structures of thought and social power that Woolf sought to dismantle.

Woolf draws her primary tool for resisting this taming of the power of myth from an archaic aesthetic itself, the paratactic method. By refusing to settle meaning for the reader, by making the reader responsible for constructing meanings from the fragmentary allusions and characterizations she assembles and by then destabilizing those meanings, Woolf avoids appropriating the mythic for imperialist, patriarchal, and rationalist ends. In contrast to avant-garde primitivists who appropriate "primitive" cultures to reinforce Western and modern superiority, Woolf understands myth as exceeding our attempts to read it. She finds inspiration for this in her study of Greek, shaped by Harrison's theories of the archaic, but also in her nuanced understanding of political reality as an intersecting network of power relations, and her realization that we must challenge not merely action but also structures of thought in order to make real change.

CHAPTER 4

The Goddess in the Lighthouse

In *To the Lighthouse*, Woolf uses her paratactic mythic method to explore a tension within feminism regarding matrifocal societies and the Great Goddess. By presenting competing allusions to ancient goddesses side by side, she disorders her portrayal of Mrs. Ramsay, a feature that has led to a wide variety of critical interpretations of the role of goddesses in the novel. Woolf arranges the mythic figures she references in a kaleidoscopic way so that at times Mrs. Ramsay suggests Demeter, and at others Artemis, Hera, Athena, Aphrodite, or even Persephone.[1] This overlapping structure reflects both the structure of myth generally and Harrison's theory of a common ancestress that lies behind several of the goddesses in the Greek pantheon. In keeping with the paradoxical nature of myth, each of the goddesses associated with Mrs. Ramsay is multifaceted, looking very different depending on the perspective. Woolf's mythic allusions make use of this, and of indeterminate narration, to destabilize the characterization of Mrs. Ramsay through other characters' shifting mythic visions of her, frustrating our attempts to identify one-to-one representations that might provide a stable sense of meaning. At times she appears as a unifying theophany that transforms the profane world and at others as an oppressive enforcer of marriage and motherhood, often to the same character.

---

1. Woolf references mythic feminine archetypes from the Christian tradition, too, as Beth Rigel Daugherty has shown in her analysis of the Eve and Mary myths in the novel in "There She Sat."

Lily's perspective sheds revealing light on this situation because she maintains a consistent interpretive openness regarding Mrs. Ramsay's goddess-like qualities. She vacillates between ecstatic absorption into Mrs. Ramsay's divinity and criticism of her complicity in patriarchy, her acceptance of the myth of the divine feminine, and her unwillingness to give up the privileges it affords her. Lily's shifting perspective, between emotional absorption and critical distance, proves central to Woolf's commentary on the limitations both of rational materialism and of feminist matrifocal alternatives to these rationalist excesses. Neither Lily's mythic vision of the Mother nor her commitment to modern values is sufficient on its own to lead Lily to her ultimate artistic vision at the end of the novel.[2] That vision becomes possible only because Lily balances an insistence on individual liberty and a critical perspective on Mrs. Ramsay's archetypal character with an openness to a genuine religious experience of her as theophanic that exceeds patriarchy and rational materialism. Frequently, Lily sees Mrs. Ramsay as the Great Goddess and experiences mystical union with something larger than herself, an opening of her perception that allows for new artistic vision. This ecstatic communion and absorption of the small individual into a greater whole, often perceived by Lily as the natural world, correlates to Harrison's description of the emotional core of religion, which gives rise to myth, ritual, and art. Through Lily's artistic-religious perception of Mrs. Ramsay, Woolf references Harrison's core views on mystery religions centered on a mystery god or goddess. But Lily also offers the novel's primary critical perspective on Mrs. Ramsay's archetypal role, drawing attention to the ways that patriarchy co-opts mythic images of divine femininity to restrict women's self-determination and autonomy.

In the middle of the nineteenth century, Eduard Gerhard and J. J. Bachofen both theorized a prehistoric matriarchal society and a universal mother goddess that manifested in the various goddesses of the Greek pantheon.[3] While Bachofen's study was largely unknown in Britain, Harrison knew of it, and she credits Gerhard with first observing "the fundamental unity of all the Greek goddesses" and bemoans that his "illuminating suggestion has been obscured

---

2. Kathy Phillips argues that Lily accepts from Mrs. Ramsay only that which will support her painting. Phillips, *Dying Gods*, 191. For an alternative reading, see Lilienfeld, "'Deceptiveness of Beauty,'" 349, 355.

3. Gerhard, *Greichische Mythologie*; Bachofen, *Das Mutterrecht*. Bachofen does not use the word *matriarchy* to describe the second of his four evolutionary stages of civilization, preferring instead "mother-right," but for purposes of consistency, *matriarchy* befits this discussion. Four years after Bachofen's 1861 publication of *Das Mutterrecht*, John Ferguson McLennan published *Primitive Marriage* in England, which, independently from Bachofen, promoted the view that the earliest societies featured "the absence of a paternal head, and the system of female succession" (189–90).

for half a century" (*Prolegomena*, 260n1). In the twentieth century, Harrison built upon Gerhard's and Bachofen's theories of a universal mother goddess.

Harrison gave the theory of a universal primordial goddess one of its earliest feminist interpretations, and though her influence has not been widely acknowledged, her feminist version of the goddess gained prominence during the 1970s in the form of feminist theology and the Goddess movement. Despite the popularity of this theory, it has become controversial in recent years. Arguing against the theory of matriarchy and the notion of a prehistoric Great Goddess, Lynn Roller and Cynthia Eller point out that early theories of mother goddesses and of matriarchal societies such as Bachofen's reflect a traditional Victorian value system and patriarchal expectations about women's natures.

Woolf's treatment in *To the Lighthouse* of the Great Goddess and of social structures associated with Her worship anticipates this recent controversy and responds to a similar tension within nineteenth-century feminism. Some strands of nineteenth-century feminism like the Maternalists celebrated an essential feminine self as the ground of emancipation, while others emphasized the rights of the unfettered liberal self.[4] A conflict emerges when one translates the values attributed to ancient matrifocal societies—such as communal identity and the required sublimation of the individual will to the good of the group, and an emphasis on fertility and maternity as the destiny and nature of women—into a modern context. Archaic values conflict with post-Enlightenment ideals of a liberal subject whose freedom is predicated upon self-determination, a notion of freedom that lies at the heart of many modern feminist struggles for equality and emancipation. Thus, while a certain branch of feminism envisions matrifocal societies as protofeminist, Lily Briscoe and Mrs. Ramsay's daughters, who wish for independent lives in which they are "not always taking care of some man or other," suggest that the rule of the Mother may be experienced by modern women as antifeminist, heteronormative, and oppressive in its essentialism (*TTL*, 10).[5] From this perspective, Mrs. Ramsay dominates the younger men and women around her, coercing them into marriage and prescribing dependence and conformity for women in service of the values of fertility and maternity. These values technically accord with what we know of matrifocal society and of the Great Goddess, but in the

---

4. According to Gerda Lerner, one strand of nineteenth-century feminists, termed "maternalists," accepted biological sex differences, or women's historic training as nurturers, and a sexual division of labor as the basis for political claims about women's suitability to civic leadership based on their supposed natural ethical inclinations. See Gerda Lerner, *Creation of Patriarchy*, 20, 28.

5. Page references are to the 2005 edition.

modern era the disregard for individuality implicit in them more readily suggests patriarchal domination.

To explore the dangers of returning to ancient social structures and religious symbols in the modern era, Woolf adapts a distinction that Harrison develops throughout her career between the Homeric patriarchal Olympian religion and the "worship of the Mother." Harrison linked these religions with social structures: the Olympian with a "heroic state of society" that emphasized the individual over the group, and the archaic goddess religion with societies that focused on "the group, the race and its continuance" and "the facts of fertility and the fostering of life" (*Mythology,* 63; *Prolegomena,* 276–61). Woolf transplants this key idea from Harrison into a Victorian domestic context through the characters of Mr. Ramsay, who suggests a Victorian, intellectual version of an Olympian hero, and Mrs. Ramsay, who evokes a patriarchal version of the Mother Goddess. In doing this, she echoes Harrison's own discussion in *Themis* of the parallel between the Olympian heroic society and the modern patrilineal family.

By depicting the Victorian patriarchal features of the modern Goddess, Woolf problematizes the optimistic view that nineteenth-century theories of matriarchy offer radical alternatives to patriarchy. While Mrs. Ramsay embodies some of the positive aspects of the Great Goddess and matrifocal societies, she by no means represents a feminist source of power and liberation. Mrs. Ramsay's goddess-like qualities position her as an exploited substitution for a lost Father God and an inspirited natural world—both Creator and Creation—when faith in traditional theology has been shaken by scientific discoveries. At the same time, she emerges as an ironic enforcer of patriarchal and heterosexual normativity.

Woolf's refusal to present a unilateral image of the goddess, in part through Lily's vacillating perspective, represents one manifestation of her paratactic mythic method. Unlike some twentieth-century thinkers who turn to myth, Woolf avoids naïve views about the radical outsider status of myth. Her work reveals instead the ways that archaic myth both permeates modernity and provides potential challenges to modernity. Bonnie Kime Scott describes Woolf as having serious "reservations about goddess figures as patriarchal pawns," and as being "wary and irreverent toward many of the goddesses that enter her texts . . . as inventions of patriarchal culture."[6] Woolf's critical perspective on the Great Goddess may reflect an awareness of the intellectual roots of matriarchal theories, which developed out of Victorian gender norms. Victorian theories of matriarchy were originally intended to justify patriarchal civiliza-

---

6. Scott, *In the Hollow of the Wave,* 205.

tion. Bachofen, for instance, positioned matriarchal societies as an earlier and lower stage of human development prior to our evolution into patriarchy.[7] Woolf's early exposure to these gender norms and their religious valence as the Angel in the House, coupled with direct reading of Greek literature, may have shaped her critical perspective on Victorian theories of matriarchy.

By transplanting Harrison's conception of matriarchy into a modern context and emphasizing the troubled intellectual heritage of it, Woolf complicates our understanding of the intellectual relationship between Woolf and Harrison. The influence of Harrison's research on Woolf's fiction makes itself plain to readers familiar with both women's work, and several scholars have convincingly documented this. But Woolf pursued objective critiques even of writers and ideas she admired, and her portrayal of a modern version of the Great Goddess in *To the Lighthouse* reveals that she makes no exceptions to this objectivity in her reception of Harrison's research and the theory of matriarchy within the feminist movement. Unlike some admirers of the premodern, Woolf's treatment of myth respects the tension between the mythic and the rational that Kołakowski argues propels culture. As we have seen in the preceding chapters, Woolf refuses to resolve this necessary tension, satisfied neither with rationalist attempts to rid the world of superstition nor with primitivist attempts to return to an imagined premodern utopia.

Woolf's characterization of Mr. Ramsay recalls Harrison's description of the Homeric patriarchal Olympian value system. Echoing the "warlike and migratory conditions" that Harrison theorizes led to the Olympian system, Mr. Ramsay constantly recites lines from Tennyson's "The Charge of the Light Brigade" and envisions himself as being on a voyage of exploration to remote regions. These voyages suggest Victorian patriarchal imperialism, as Phillips notes, the "great scientific expeditions which Mr. Ramsay admires are likely to precede colonialism.... Mr. Ramsay casts himself not only as the leader of a 'desolate expedition across the icy solitudes of the Polar region,' but also as the captain of a ship's company, suggesting commerce, and as a soldier, implying war."[8] Twice within two pages he refers to himself as a hero (*TTL*, 38–39). Seeking the solitude of his private thoughts where he is happily "safe ... restored to his privacy," Mr. Ramsay values individual achievement over the progress of civilization more generally (36). Mr. Ramsay's obsession with

---

7. Eller, *Gentlemen and Amazons*, 9.
8. Phillips, *Virginia Woolf against Empire*, 105.

his legacy recalls Homeric heroes such as Odysseus and Achilles, who exemplify the heroic emphasis on the memorialization and immortality of the exceptional individual. Woolf links Mr. Ramsay even more explicitly to the Olympians in the holograph draft where he thinks, "Who shall require of men that they be as gods in strength and in endurance?" (*TTL* holograph, 69).[9] In a moment of defeat when he confronts the limits of his life work, Mr. Ramsay seeks consolation for the depressing realization that "his own little light would shine, not very brightly, for a year or two, and would then be merged into some bigger light, and that in a bigger still" (*TTL*, 39). His anxiety about the insignificance of the individual's "little light," which will inevitably merge into the larger light of what Harrison terms "the group, the race," marks his Olympian character. In Harrison's view, pre-Olympian matrifocal culture more likely would celebrate this merging of the individual light with the greater light of the species, since it promotes the subordination of the individual's "prowess" to the needs of the community or the human race.

Conversely, Mrs. Ramsay shares many of the characteristics of both the Great Goddess and the society Harrison associates with Her worship. Woolf links Mrs. Ramsay to Greek goddesses and classical women throughout the novel, both through the eyes of other characters and in her own self-perception. Woolf repeatedly likens her to a queen and compares her to Helen of Troy (*TTL*, 11, 85, 30). Like Aphrodite, Demeter, and other Greek goddesses, Mrs. Ramsay possesses a beauty that cannot be hidden. About Mrs. Ramsay's obvious beauty, Woolf writes that "she bore it about with her, she could not help knowing it, the torch of her beauty; she carried it erect into any room she entered; and after all, veil it as she might . . . her beauty was apparent" (44). This image of the torch recalls the centrality of torches in the Homeric *Hymn to Demeter*, where Demeter and Hecate search for Persephone by torchlight, and in the Eleusinian Mysteries, where Dadouchos (the torch bearer), the second priest of the Eleusinian Mysteries, lit by torch the ritual procession to Eleusis.[10] Woolf describes Mrs. Ramsay's beauty as "splendour" (32) and "radiant" (103), echoing the divine revelations of Demeter and Aphrodite in their respective Homeric *Hymns*. When Demeter enters the house of Keleos in Eleusis, she "stepped on the threshold and touched the roof with her head and filled the doorway with *divine radiance.*"[11] When golden Aphrodite appears before Anchises in mortal form, her splendor, radiance, and luster reveal her divinity: "She was clothed in a robe more *brilliant* than gleaming fire and wore

---

9. Hereafter, citations to the holograph draft of *To the Lighthouse* will occur parenthetically in text.

10. Kerényi, *Eleusis*, 23, 63.

11. Foley, Homeric *Hymn to Demeter*, lines 188–89, emphasis mine.

spiral bracelets and *shining* earrings, while round her tender neck there were beautiful necklaces, lovely, golden, and of intricate design. Like the moon's was the *radiance* round her soft breasts, a wonder to the eye."[12] Mrs. Ramsay's beauty inspires worship and marks her as separate from and above other women, suggesting the role that superhuman beauty played in constituting the divide between mortal women and goddesses. In ancient literature, mortal women like Mrs. Ramsay who are exceptionally beautiful, such as Helen of Troy and Psyche, often either descend from or become goddesses.[13]

Woolf's very clear allusions to goddesses have prompted many critics to identify mythic parallels in the novel. A number of critics have noted the novel's references to Demeter, while Carpentier finds echoes of Themis in Mrs. Ramsay, Lise Weil interprets her as the triple goddess, Jean Wyatt sees her as Aphrodite, and Jane Lilienfeld reads her as the archetypal Great Mother with whom Lily must come to terms.[14] Woolf's portrayal of Mrs. Ramsay refers to several goddesses from the ancient Mediterranean world, and these goddesses vary widely in their qualities and values, making any clear message about the meaning of Woolf's mythic referents difficult to discern.

Some of Woolf's mythic allusions are momentary, as when she references Athena through Mrs. McNab's perspective in the "Time Passes" section. Four times within a single page, Mrs. McNab remembers Mrs. Ramsay as a lady in a grey cloak, suggesting grey-eyed Athena (*TTL*, 140). After her death, Lily thinks of Mrs. Ramsay as she has been described by William Bankes, as "wearing a grey hat" and "in grey" three times on a single page (180). These brief but intense allusions to the father-identified virgin goddess seem hard to reconcile with Mrs. Ramsay's ties to the goddess of love or to the maternal Demeter. Other allusions permeate Mrs. Ramsay's being more deeply, such as her kinship with Hera, which Woolf suggests through Mrs. Ramsay's obsession with marriage.

Mr. and Mrs. Ramsay, identified only by their married name, suggest the divine couple of the *hieros gamos,* the sacred marriage of god and goddess, a

---

12. Athanassakis, Homeric *Hymn to Aphrodite*, lines 86–90, emphasis mine.
13. Clader, *Helen*.
14. On Mrs. Ramsay as Demeter, see Tina Barr, "Divine Politics"; Anne G. Hoffman, "Demeter and Poseidon"; Jean O. Love, *Worlds in Consciousness*; Joseph Blotner, "Mythic Patterns"; Jane Marcus, *Art and Anger*; K. J. (Kathy) Phillips, *Dying Gods*; Lisa Tyler, "Mother-Daughter Passion and Rapture"; and Harvena Richter, *Inward Journey*. On Mrs. Ramsay as Themis, see Martha C. Carpentier, *Ritual, Myth, and the Modernist Text*. On Mrs. Ramsay as Aphrodite, see Jean Wyatt, "The Celebration of Eros." While not explicitly identifying Mrs. Ramsay as Demeter, Lise Weil reads her relationship with Lily through the lens of the Triple Goddess and the mother-daughter relationship celebrated at Eleusis. Weil, "Entering a Lesbian Field of Vision."

role filled by Zeus and Hera in Greek religion. In fact, when Lily looks upon Mr. and Mrs. Ramsay, she sees them transformed into "the symbols of marriage, husband and wife" (*TTL*, 75). The *hieros gamos* serves as a model for human matrimony, and according to Kerényi, Hera "preceded mortal women as an example."[15] Like Hera, Mrs. Ramsay is a champion of marriage, enforcing it upon those young people in her care as an imperative, regardless of their wishes. Lily experiences the force of this pressure most pervasively, perhaps because she feels the most intense resistance to it. Even years after Mrs. Ramsay's death, Lily sees her "standing at the end of a corridor of years saying, of all incongruous things, 'Marry, marry!'" (178). Beyond referencing the *hieros gamos*, Woolf introduces specific references to Hera through Paul and Minta Rayley, whose marriage, arranged by Mrs. Ramsay, alludes to the union of Zeus and Hera. Paul and Minta's marital troubles, which resemble the troubled relationship of Zeus and Hera, are resolved when Paul takes a mistress. In Lily's brief story of the Rayleys, we learn that Paul breeds hares and Minta is bored by them. *Hare*, an anagram of Hera, suggests the legend of the White Hare in English folklore, in which a betrayed woman in the form of a white hare haunts an unfaithful man. Woolf had earlier employed hares and rabbits to comment on the constrictions of marriage in "Lappin and Lapinova," a story written before 1919 but not published until 1939, in which a young bride unsuccessfully attempts to survive her new life by constructing a secret world of rabbits and hares with her husband.[16] Lily's vision of Paul also evokes Zeus's role as ruler of the gods, in that his political views become increasingly important in his life, growing "more and more pronounced" (*TTL*, 177). Woolf describes his mistress as a serious woman, "with her hair in a plait and a case in her hand . . . who went to meetings and shared Paul's views," a woman with whom Paul can build what Lily thinks of as an "alliance," at the heart of which is their shared political vision (177).

In exhorting other women to marry, Mrs. Ramsay resembles not only Hera. As Carpentier argues, "the mundane Demeter, guardian of hearth and home, who *coerces through the force of 'social imperative'*" also finds her parallel in Mrs. Ramsay.[17] It also suggests Artemisian qualities. In Greek cultic practice, Artemis helped children cross over into their adult roles of wife-mother

---

15. Kerényi, *Zeus and Hera*, 97.

16. Woolf notes the gap between writing and publication of this story in the fifth volume of her diary. See Katherine Simpson, "'Lappin and Lapinova.'"

17. Carpentier, *Ritual, Myth, and the Modernist Text*, 184, emphasis mine. Phillips reads Mrs. Ramsay as a complicit Demeter figure who leads Prue, a Persephone figure, into marriage and death. Phillips, *Dying Gods*, 182.

and soldier-citizen.[18] Like Artemis, Mrs. Ramsay attempts to shepherd young men and women into marriage and praises men for fulfilling traditional patriarchal roles. Mr. and Mrs. Ramsay view their children Prue and Andrew as the perfection of their own social roles, Andrew destined to be a better man than his father, Prue a great beauty (*TTL,* 72). Prue's and Andrew's fates are both emblematic and ironic: Prue dies in childbirth a year after marriage, and Andrew dies in battle during World War I. The Artemisian roles their parents encourage lead to their deaths, which seems a scathing comment on the dangers of transplanting archaic values into the modern era.

I have shown in the preceding paragraphs how difficult Woolf makes it to determine the proper mythic parallel for Mrs. Ramsay, since she shifts allusions from one goddess to another and highlights the areas of overlap between goddesses. This unstable, paratactic structure of allusion in the characterization of Mrs. Ramsay reflects both the structure of myth generally and Harrison's theory of a common ancestress that lies behind several of the goddesses in the Greek pantheon. Therefore, I argue that the most accurate mythic parallel to Mrs. Ramsay is not any particular goddess but rather the broader Great Goddess or "Mountain Mother" from whom Harrison derives Artemis, Hera, Athena, Aphrodite, Demeter, Persephone, Pandora, Medusa, and the Eumenides-Erinyes. As Harrison writes, "To Hera she lent her 'sacred marriage,' to Demeter her mysteries, to Athena her snakes, to Aphrodite her doves, to Artemis all her functions as 'Lady of the Wild Things'" (*Mythology,* 65). By emphasizing Harrison's broader Great Goddess rather than individual goddesses, Woolf can use her mythic allusions to address the forms of social organization that Harrison associates with the worship of the Great Goddess. This turn, from simply alluding to various Greek goddesses to following Harrison in exploring the relationship between gender, divinity, and social structure, allows Woolf to use myth for critical commentary related to social and political issues.

There is clear evidence and critical consensus that Woolf wrote *To the Lighthouse* in part to work through her parents' relationship and influence on her life. In her diary entry for May 14, 1925, as she was writing *To the Lighthouse,* Woolf wrote that she planned "to have father's character done complete in it; & mothers; & St Ives; & childhood" (*Diary* 3, 18). After completing the novel, on November 8, 1928, Virginia Woolf wrote of her parents, "I used to think

---

18. Vernant, *Mortals and Immortals,* 198–99.

of him and mother daily; but writing the Lighthouse laid them in my mind" (208). Fernald and Lilienfeld have demonstrated that Woolf fictionalizes not only her parents but also herself in the novel.[19] Other details in the novel derive from moments in Woolf's life as well. James's disappointment about not being allowed to travel to the lighthouse draws on an incident Woolf recorded in the "Hyde Park Gate News" in 1892 when she and Thoby were invited to sail to a lighthouse and their brother "Master Adrian Stephen was much disappointed at not being allowed to go."[20]

In this chapter, I do not wish to pursue a biographical interpretation of Woolf's use of archaic myth as a response to her parents' relationship. Rather, I want to suggest that Woolf's use of myth for social commentary makes sense in the context of rational materialism because she was acutely aware of the consequences of the epistemological and metaphysical views held by her parents and their friends. Mark Gaipa describes Leslie Stephen's view of the universe, common to his time, as "a world without a knowable god, in which evolution (time passing) changes the living without any certain divine guidance, and in which people are probably bodies without immortal souls."[21] While Woolf communicates this subtly in the novel, she presents this context more explicitly in the original draft where religion plays a more prominent role in the narrative. In the draft, she describes Lily as "worshipping God" and going to church on Sundays in contrast to the Ramsays and Mr. Bankes, who "in spite of his own view, & a lifetime spent in investigation that [tended] to the opposite conclusions some[how] made him think all the better of a woman" (*TTL* holograph, 34–35). When Mrs. Ramsay seeks comfort in the sound of the waves, she hears "the old cradle song, murmured by nature, who, in her cosmogony, had long supplanted for reasons she could scarcely name, the hierarchy of Heaven" (*TTL* holograph, 24). Perhaps most striking, in the draft, when Mr. Ramsay doubts his ability to reach R, Woolf quotes Matthew Arnold's "Thyrsis," an elegiac poem written in honor of Arthur Hugh Clough. Here we have an explicit allusion, removed in the published novel, to the midnineteenth-century religious crisis among the intellectual class, since Clough became a representative figure of this crisis who famously resigned his teaching post because he was unwilling to teach Anglican doctrine. While Woolf removed many of her explicit references to religion and the Victorian crisis of

---

19. Lilienfeld, "'Deceptiveness of Beauty,'" 346; Fernald, "*To the Lighthouse* in the Context," 14.
20. Woolf, Bell, Stephen, and Lowe, *Hyde Park Gate News*.
21. Gaipa, "Agnostic Daughter's Apology," 2.

faith in *To the Lighthouse*, she continues to explore these themes throughout the novel.[22]

Some proponents of the Victorian materialist worldview believed that the essence of life was purely physical and that science was on its way to eventually explaining all phenomena, including consciousness and life itself, as deriving from matter alone.[23] T. H. Huxley, a contemporary of Leslie Stephen, believed that scientific progress implied "the extension of the province of what we call matter and causation, and the concomitant gradual banishment from all regions of known thought of what we call spirit and spontaneity."[24] This quest for a totalizing, rational explanation of the world sought to replace God and traditional religion—which Enlightenment philosophers deemed superstition—with science. Auguste Comte's Positivist Religion of Humanity, to which Stephen was sympathetic, was one such self-conscious attempt.[25] During the French Revolution, founders of the Cult of Reason, the radical atheist religion intended to replace Christianity in France, envisioned Rationality as a goddess. But these religions of reason, as well as Romantic attempts to transfer some of the attributes of divinity to nature, proved unsatisfactory for many Victorian intellectuals. Walter Houghton describes the pessimistic outlook prompted by the mechanistic view of nature that, in the Victorian era, replaced both natural theology and the Romantic view of nature as imbued with the divine spirit. Once the findings of geology and evolution became known, poets like Tennyson and Matthew Arnold began to imagine nature as "a battleground in which individuals and species fought for their lives and every acre of land was the scene of untold violence and suffering."[26]

Gaipa reads the central conflict of *To the Lighthouse* through this cultural context: "For many Victorians the triumph of the new materialism, represented by worldviews like utilitarianism, positivism, and naturalism, failed to provide the emotional security that religion had offered."[27] Despite the modern conflicts between religion and science outlined above, many historians of science have recently argued that Western science and Enlightenment reason developed out of a Christian worldview and with the historical support of the

---

22. For a discussion of Woolf's engagement with Matthew Arnold's "Dover Beach" in the novel, see Smith, "Virginia Woolf Reads 'Dover Beach.'"
23. Burrow, "Crisis of Reason," 35.
24. Huxley, "Physical Basis of Life," 20.
25. See Burrow, "Crisis of Reason," 78. For a full discussion of the Religion of Humanity, see T. R. Wright, *The Religion of Humanity*.
26. Houghton, *Victorian Frame of Mind*, 68.
27. Gaipa, "Agnostic Daughter's Apology," 6.

Church.[28] In this context, Woolf's turn to archaic, irrational religion takes on a new significance. Her choice of archaic religious traditions, as opposed to Christianity, as a source of inspiration and discourse, makes sense not only as an antipatriarchal gesture but also as a challenge to the rationalistic foundations of Western Enlightenment thought, which ironically developed out of Christianity.

Mr. Ramsay displays the symptoms of this headlong dive into reason, and it is reflected in his characteristically Victorian version of heroism. Mr. Ramsay's form of heroic individualism differs significantly from the version that Harrison attributes to Olympian religion. It echoes John Stuart Mill's vision of the rational individualistic hero who exercises "independent reason" in the face of the masses. Mill, the quintessential nineteenth-century defender of both the liberal self and women's rights, feared that on both a personal and social level, individuality and autonomy were in danger of falling into weakness and entropy under the pressure to conform to modern society. In contrast to Homeric heroes' battlefield exploits, Mr. Ramsay's heroism consists of a battle of the mind akin to Mill's vision, conquering Q and R to advance the cause of human reason. Mr. Ramsay's heroic individualism also takes on a typically Victorian pessimistic tone expressed most often in quotations from poems by Tennyson, one of the first to publicly worry over the unsettling effects of replacing religion with science. In his analysis of Victorian anxiety, Houghton identifies doubt, ennui, and pessimism as characteristic emotions among intellectuals of the period, attributed by several writers of the period to the crisis of faith and the breakdown of traditional metaphysics.[29] This tone differs significantly from Homeric heroism. While Homeric heroes like Achilles and Odysseus appear confident in their fated memorialization as heroes, Mr. Ramsay, while sharing their obsession with creating a legacy, mourns his failure to do so, echoing Sophocles's tragic Ajax or Tennyson's Victorian Ulysses.

Mr. Ramsay's Victorian worldview leads him to fill the void with the Angel in the House, a woman expected to fulfill the spiritual needs of secular man, much as it did for Leslie Stephen. Stephen self-consciously filled the void of religion with his marriage to Julia Duckworth, Virginia's mother, writing to her during their courtship, "I have not got any Saints and you must not be angry if I put you in the place where my Saints ought to be."[30] Woolf thought deeply about the ramifications of a marriage shaped by the cultural forces of

---

28. On the role of Christianity in the development of Western science, see Peter Harrison, *Territories of Science and Religion,* and David C. Lindberg, *Beginnings of Western Science.*

29. Houghton, *Victorian Frame of Mind,* 64–65.

30. Stephen, *Mausoleum Book,* 53.

Victorian secular anxiety and gender politics, describing her experience of the years after her mother's death, when her father withdrew into mourning, as "tortured ... made numb with non-being" (*MoB*, 136). By alluding to multiple aspects of the Great Goddess in characters' perceptions of Mrs. Ramsay, particularly Mr. Ramsay's view of his wife as a Mother Goddess, Woolf addresses the ethical problems of an uncritical compensation in the domestic sphere, sought mostly by men, for the spiritual and emotional desolation created by the Victorian crisis of faith.

According to Harrison, the Great Goddess and the social structure associated with Her worship emphasize the collective over the individual, a value that manifests in three related features of the Great Goddess. The first is a general emphasis on fertility; the second is the nonanthropomorphic forms taken by the early versions of this Goddess, which suggest Her ties to the natural world and a lack of emphasis on the human individual; the third is a subordination of individuality under generic social roles in support of fertility. Woolf turns these characteristics on their heads through Mrs. Ramsay, whose divine feminine attributes are either deployed in support of or reabsorbed into patriarchy, drawing attention to the inappropriateness of archaic values in the modern world. Woolf translates the archaic subordination of individual variation to generic fertility-oriented social roles into Mrs. Ramsay's requirement that individuals conform to gender roles and heterosexual productivity as prescribed by Victorian patriarchy. Mrs. Ramsay views men indiscriminately, both as beloved childlike worshippers and as heroes whose virtues must be celebrated and to whom virgins like Minta and Lily must be sacrificed. In turn, she views women indiscriminately as wives and mothers, and the law of marriage coerces all people into their proper roles. Like the Great Goddess, Mrs. Ramsay boasts of possessing extraordinary, life-giving powers and practices fertility magic, but this Victorian patriarchal goddess pours her supernatural efforts into the sterile field of her husband's intellectual projects and egoistic goals, which he uses to perpetuate a fundamentally flawed vision of the world. Likewise, while Lily sees Mrs. Ramsay as part of nature, merged into a greater whole, a quality that reflects the nonanthropomorphism of archaic goddesses, her husband's parallel vision of his wife casts her as mere support for his own philosophical musings, subordinating nature and human life to the realm of ideas.

Mrs. Ramsay's interactions with her husband early in the novel introduce her maternal powers and fertility magic. While Mr. and Mrs. Ramsay might appear to balance the Olympian value of heroic individualism with the matrifocal value of community and family, Woolf demonstrates the patriarchal appropriation of the Goddess's fertility magic and maternal powers to make the demands of Victorian materialism sustainable. Whereas these two forces—patriarchal Olympus and the worship of the Mother—are opposed to one another in Harrison's ancient world, in Woolf's Victorian context, the battle has already been lost, since the fertility magic and maternal power of Mrs. Ramsay exist only within the realm of the Father.[31] In *To the Lighthouse*, Woolf illustrates this co-opting of the goddess into Zeus's domestic domain, building on the association that Harrison establishes in *Themis* between Olympian patriarchy and the modern family.

Mr. Ramsay exploits his wife's fertility to uphold an unsustainable and barren rationalism. Woolf characterizes masculine intellect as dried up several times throughout the novel in ways that suggest Harrison's characterization of Olympian gods. Harrison identifies Olympians with rationalism and individualistic thinking, describing them as "the last product of rationalism, of individualistic thinking. Cut off from the very source of life and being, the emotion of the *thiasos*, they desiccate and die."[32] This description of the Olympian god separated from his attendant group of worshippers, the *thiasos* that Harrison identifies as characteristic of the matrifocal religion, aptly describes the individualistic rationalist hero embodied in Mr. Ramsay. Echoing Harrison's language about Olympian individualism, Mrs. Ramsay describes "very clever men" as "dried up" (*TTL*, 102), and Mr. Bankes, a laboratory scientist, fears that he may have "dried up and shrunk" (25). Early in the novel, when Mrs. Ramsay comes to his wife for comfort and spiritual renewal, Woolf describes him as "arid," "barren," and having a "fatal sterility," while the language used to describe Mrs. Ramsay in the same scene suggests liquidity and fertility.

Mrs. Ramsay's fertility magic appears early in the novel through descriptions of her knitting needles. When her husband comes to her for sympathy for his intellectual despair, Mrs. Ramsay sits knitting a stocking for the boy in the lighthouse. Descriptions of Mrs. Ramsay's knitting project repeatedly interrupt Woolf's narration of their conversation. In his archetypal study of the Great Goddess, which he calls the Great Mother, Neumann specifically identifies spinning and weaving as activities of the Great Mother because of their connection to fate and to fertility. When the human being depends on the powers of nature, the feminine, associated with the natural world, holds an inescapable power of fate that controls human life and death; many have imagined this power as the Goddess weaving the web of life and spinning the

---

31. On Demeter as contained by Zeus in the modern world, see Moore, *Short Season between Two Silences*, 85.

32. Harrison, *Themis*, 48.

threads of fate. According to Neumann, the "crossing of threads" serves as a symbol of sexual union, the basic form in which the Feminine weaves life.[33]

Mrs. Ramsay's knitting needles hold magical power and repeatedly suggest reproduction and even divine creation. Woolf's most explicit depiction of the fertility magic of the needles comes when Mr. Ramsay demands that his wife fill the drawing room, kitchen, bedrooms, and nurseries with life: He "must be assured that he too lived in the heart of life; was needed; not here only, but all over the world. Flashing her needles, confident, upright, she created the drawing room and kitchen, set them all aglow; bade him take his ease there, go in and out, enjoy himself" (*TTL*, 41). Her knitting needles bear the power to create the life-filled drawing room and kitchen and to set them aglow, assuring him of his place within her Creation when he falters in his faith. Through them she takes her husband within the circle of life, restores his senses to him, and makes his barrenness fertile by creating these rooms filled with life. Mrs. Ramsay functions here as a replacement for a lost God. As the Creator, her Creation goes beyond perpetuating mere life to provide a home in the universe for her husband, assuring him that "he too lived in the heart of life; was needed." Mr. Ramsay's demands are symptoms of the transcendent homelessness that Lukács diagnosed as the condition of secular modernity, and Mrs. Ramsay provides the balm to soothe that endless pain.[34] In this passage, Mr. Ramsay demands, and presumably receives, not just creation, but Creation, a sanctified universe that is a home for Man.

Woolf's depiction of Mr. Ramsay's violent exploitation of the Goddess in this section emphasizes the extent to which, as Madelyn Moore intuits, in the Victorian era, the Goddess functions as a tool of patriarchal domination by substituting for a lost Father God. The things that Mrs. Ramsay implores her husband to look at and feel are symbols of fertility. The house symbolizes the containing womb, their offspring demonstrate their shared procreativity, and the world outside the window with its garden and wild vegetation exemplifies the earth's fruitfulness. Woolf intensifies this tone through her revisions of the novel. In the published version of this passage, but not in the holograph draft, Mrs. Ramsay takes a mothering relation to her husband, boasting of her capacity to "surround and protect" him, saying that if he has faith in her, nothing should hurt him, and he will never be alone, no matter how deeply he buried himself or how high he climbed (*TTL*, 41). Mrs. Ramsay's promise that faith in her will protect him echoes the Christian doctrine that Christ will never forsake his true believers, suggesting again her role as

---

33. Neumann, *Great Mother*, 227.
34. Lukács, *Theory of the Novel*.

divine feminine substitution for the lost God of Christianity. Mrs. Ramsay's capacity to surround and protect suggests the nurturing, containing womb of the Mother Goddess. Her womblike protection of her husband positions him as her child, an image Woolf repeats in Mr. Ramsay's irritation when his wife does not worry about him as she does the children (71), in Mrs. Ramsay's description of her husband as "a fractious child" (41), and in his response when she has provided him with spiritual nourishment: He is "filled with her words, *like a child* who drops off satisfied, he said, at last, looking at her with humble gratitude, restored, renewed, that he would take a turn" (42, emphasis mine). His position of infant in this passage recalls that of the tiny human worshipper who clings at the side of a mountainlike mother in an archaic statue. Woolf's portrayal of Mr. Ramsay as a child seeking the protection of his spiritually charged wife also continues the Lukácsian tone of a fragile human specimen seeking comfort in a meaningless, godless universe, a psychic state that is most notably associated in literary history with Tennyson, Mr. Ramsay's literary touchstone.

In this section of the novel, Woolf generally aligns Mrs. Ramsay with life. While this is not consistently the case since, as Lilienfeld notes, Lily's vision of Mrs. Ramsay emphasizes the deathly aspects of the Great Mother, in this passage her life-giving side sets her in contrast to her death-identified husband, and she conceives of herself as having the superhuman power of a goddess to defy death. Mr. Ramsay, described as "barren" and "fatal," seeks comfort from his wife. Again, Woolf intensifies this contrast through her revisions to the novel. In the published novel, but not in the holograph, Mr. Ramsay refers repeatedly to "the waste of ages and the perishing of the stars" (*TTL*, 39). And Woolf revises this section so that Mr. Ramsay, throughout the first part of the novel, repetitively paces in front of urns, which, given his fantasies of death through exposure and self-identification as "a dying hero," suggest their funerary associations (39). Because Mr. Ramsay obsesses about mortality, and because climbing repeatedly correlates with death in this section and burial in the earth suggests the grave, Mrs. Ramsay's promise to protect her husband no matter how deeply he buried himself or how high he climbed suggests that she will protect him from a death he brings upon himself. Mr. Ramsay's rationalist, overly intellectual orientation renders him sterile and underlies his connections with mortality. Thus, this passage implies that those suffering the fallout of a hubristic rationalist worldview may seek refuge and rebirth in fantasies of "primitive" cultures, especially in Goddess figures that substitute for a now inaccessible faith in the Christian God.

Woolf describes Mr. and Mrs. Ramsay's interaction as both sexual and violent, reinforcing the political critique implicit in this section. She portrays both Mrs. and Mr. Ramsay as reproductive organs; the wife as the surrounding womb, "this delicious fecundity, this fountain and spray of life," into which Mr. Ramsay, identified as the generic and fatally sterile "male," plunges his "beak of brass, the arid scimitar" (*TTL*, 41). Critics have advanced divergent interpretations of the sexual imagery of this scene, ranging from Ruth Vanita's discussion of Mr. Ramsay's phallic beak of brass to Helen Corsa's reading of Mrs. Ramsay as a phallic mother, Annis Pratt's argument that Mrs. Ramsay embodies male orgasm to Matt Franks's interpretation of the scene as "an act of male-male oral sex" in which "Mrs. Ramsay inseminates her husband in a nonprocreative, perversely queer sex act that exceeds her maternal role."[35] Despite their varied conclusions, these scholars agree that Woolf does not confine phallic imagery to Mr. Ramsay in this scene. Woolf endows Mrs. Ramsay with three phallic symbols, which she employs to meet her husband in their union/battle. The first is the energy that she "pours erect into the air" in a "column of spray" (40). The second is her knitting needles, which, like Clarissa's sewing needle in *Mrs. Dalloway,* function as a symbol of her feminine power. The third phallic symbol is James himself whom Woolf describes twice as standing stiff between Mrs. Ramsay's knees (41). James, who displays Oedipal jealousy toward his father and receives his mother's transferred affections for his father, fits the characteristics of the Mother Goddess's son-lover.[36]

I read this as a scene of sexual violence and exploitation that, in its allusions to Hera and Zeus, echoes the cultural battle between patriarchal Olympus and goddess religions that Harrison theorized. In Woolf's retelling of this conflict, Olympus, in the form of Mr. Ramsay's rationalism, already dominates the life-giving power of the divine feminine, redirecting its power to its own ends. The holograph draft makes Mr. Ramsay's association with Zeus explicit when James feels that his father "fell . . . like an eagle upon them," alluding to the Eagle of Zeus (*TTL* holograph, 71). While Mrs. Ramsay overtly seems happy at her husband's approach—she confidently laughs while she knits, she reassures her husband, she boasts—the text reveals another level of relation between husband and wife. When Mr. Ramsay approaches her, she "brace[s] herself, and half turning, seem[s] to raise herself with an effort" (40). The fact that Mrs. Ramsay assumes a stance of self-protection and preparedness belies the conflicted nature of her marriage. After she has provided the reassurance that Mr. Ramsay needs to return to life and his heroic philosophiz-

---

35. See Ruth Vanita, "Bringing Buried Things to Light"; Helen Corsa, "*To The Lighthouse*"; Annis Pratt, "Sexual Imagery in *To the Lighthouse*"; and Matt Franks, "Mrs. Ramsay's Queer Generationality."

36. Neumann argues that the son-lover functions as the Goddess's phallic consort and symbol of the fertilizing phallus. Neumann, *Origins,* 49.

ing, "there was scarcely a shell of herself left for her to know herself by; all was lavished and spent," and she "felt not only exhausted in body (afterwards, not at the time, she always felt this)" (41–42). Given Mr. Ramsay's express intention in coming to his wife—to be renewed and rescued from his spiritual barrenness—and the repeated language of consumption in the image of a child dropping off the breast and the beak of brass drinking her energy—we should not be surprised that the interaction leaves her depleted of energy and strength. However, the violence of this passage goes beyond consumption of Mrs. Ramsay's life force; Mr. Ramsay also "quenches" and "mercilessly" smites his wife's strength with a scimitar. While this scene clearly depicts a sexual relation, it also depicts the defeat of an enemy in battle, an agonistic relationship that reveals the political and mythic subtext of their marriage. In this way, Woolf here recalls the strained and combative relationship between Zeus and Hera, the *hieros gamos,* which Philip Slater and other scholars interpret as symbolizing the tensions between the old matrifocal culture and religion of the Greek islands, and the patriarchal culture and religion of the invaders from the North.[37]

For Harrison, the mystery god or goddess manifests the experience of primal unity with all life—human, animal, divine, vegetative—and through the god or goddess the worshipper experiences membership in that larger community. Harrison argues that, in contrast to later Olympian goddesses, the earliest forms of the Goddess are not yet fully anthropomorphized, but rather are closer to nature, even taking animal forms (*Prolegomena,* 258). The nonanthropomorphic forms of the Great Goddess, in which she merges with nature, the second feature listed above, provides entry into primal unity. Mrs. Ramsay takes on such nonhuman forms, exceeding the boundaries of her human body, throughout the novel. Among these are the bee and beehive, emblems of Artemis in the Ephesian cult, the Cretan name for whom is Britomartis, which translates as "bee-maiden" or "honey-maiden."[38] After experiencing an intense moment of closeness with Mrs. Ramsay, in which she seeks unity and intimacy, Lily sees Mrs. Ramsay as a beehive. Lily likens her desire for Mrs. Ramsay to a bee haunting "the dome-shaped hive . . . with [its] murmurs," and afterward Lily sees Mrs. Ramsay as having "the shape of a dome" (*TTL,* 55). Cretan tombs of the Mycenean period were made in this beehive shape, and G. W. Elderkind specifically links them to Artemis.[39]

Several characters view Mrs. Ramsay's body as saturated by and coexistent with features of the natural world that go beyond these animal forms. Early in

---

37. Slater, *Glory of Hera.*
38. G. W. Elderkin, "Bee of Artemis."
39. Elderkin, 206–7.

the novel, Charles Tansley has a mystical vision of Mrs. Ramsay "with stars in her eyes and veils in her hair, with cyclamen and wild violet" (*TTL*, 18). But Lily and Mr. Ramsay sustain the most significant perceptions of Mrs. Ramsay fused with the external world. The differences between these offer a key insight into Woolf's adaptation of Harrison's distinction between matrifocal worship of the Mother and Olympian patriarchy.

In her mystical vision of Mrs. Ramsay, Lily experiences true *ecstasis* of the kind that Harrison rapturously describes in ritual worship and dance. Both Harrison's and Woolf's portrayal of the experience emphasize the absorption of the individual ego into the larger spiritually saturated natural world and the ways that this ecstatic experience transforms the worshipper's perceptual landscape. Despite her criticisms of Mr. and Mrs. Ramsay as tyrannical and overbearing, when Lily looks upon them as a couple, she perceives them as ontologically permeated with an extrahuman meaning and continuous with the world outside their individual bodies and identities: "What she called 'being in love' flooded them. They became part of that unreal but penetrating and exciting universe which is the world seen through the eyes of love. The sky stuck to them; the birds sang through them" (*TTL*, 50). Just as her painting of Mrs. Ramsay and James shows only the impersonal in them—their universal, mythic dimension—Lily directs her feeling of "being in love" with Mr. and Mrs. Ramsay toward them not as particular, flawed human beings, but as embodiments of an impersonal power, in this case the *hieros gamos* that manifests in them. Woolf's use of the word "through" in this passage—"the birds sang through them"—indicates that, in Lily's vision, the Ramsays are a medium through which nature expresses itself, constituted by and inseparable from it. For Lily, Mrs. Ramsay lies at the center of this "unreal" universe as she experiences the same state when alone with Mrs. Ramsay. In that situation, Lily feels compelled to "fling herself (thank Heaven she had always resisted so far) at Mrs. Ramsay's knee and say to her—but what could she say to her? 'I'm in love with you?' No, that was not true. 'I'm in love with this all,' waving her hand at the hedge, at the house, at the children" (*TLL*, 23). Here again Lily identifies Mrs. Ramsay with the outside world, and particularly with aspects of the outside world associated with fertility (plants, a home, children), recognizing that she is in love with this extrahuman quality of Mrs. Ramsay, not with Mrs. Ramsay as a particular, flawed individual. In both passages, Lily identifies Mrs. Ramsay with external objects, seeing her as interchangeable with them.

Mr. Ramsay also sees the external world in place of people when he looks at Mrs. Ramsay, but with different implications. His perception of his wife and son introduces the subordinate position of her divinity in relation to masculine intellect. In contrast to Lily's reverent vision of Mrs. Ramsay as the Great Goddess, his parallel nonanthropomorphic vision of her ultimately reabsorbs her under patriarchy and rationalism. Mr. Ramsay's instrumentalizing perception of his wife reflects both the primacy of the Olympian heroic individual, expressed here through his heroic intellectual adventures, and the Victorian exploitation of women as emotional compensation for a lost Christian God necessary to sustain an inherently unsustainable rational materialist worldview. Early in the novel, Mr. Ramsay looks upon Mrs. Ramsay and James and finds his efforts to attain clarity about a philosophical problem consecrated by the sight of them. However, he fails to see their particularity as individuals, since he only looks at them "without distinguishing either his son or his wife" (*TTL*, 36). Like Lily, Mr. Ramsay assimilates them to nature, but whereas Lily sees the singular individuals saturated by the natural world, which sings through them, for Mr. Ramsay his family members are *equivalent* to "a farm, a tree, a cluster of cottages" (36). These images, which one briefly glimpses "as one raises one's eyes from a page in an express train" serve merely as "an illustration, a confirmation of something on the printed page to which one returns, fortified and satisfied" (36). Throughout the novel, Mr. Ramsay treats the natural world as secondary to his intellectual efforts; when he looks up from his book during the family's eventual voyage to the lighthouse, it "was not to see anything; it was only to pin down some thought more exactly. That done, his mind flew back again and he plunged into his reading" (193). Mrs. Ramsay, James, a farm, a tree, a cluster of cottages, the world—mere scenery—all support the realm of intellect and rationality, all serve to fortify Mr. Ramsay's intellectual efforts.

For both Lily and Mr. Ramsay, Mrs. Ramsay's essence resides not within her person; rather, like the Earth Mother, her being merges with the external world, extending to objects that symbolize fertility, such as trees, houses, cottages, farms, and children. Lily's assimilation of Mr. and Mrs. Ramsay to nature suggests a mystical transformation of the world, the main quality of which is being in love, implying religious adoration and absorption of the worshipper in the divine-beloved. Mr. Ramsay's identification of Mrs. Ramsay and James with nature distorts this religious imagery. His vision of wife and son does not imply the adoring dissolution of the human worshipper's ego in the oceanic fullness of the divine, but instead reduces these individuals to props for his rationalist, philosophical efforts. Instead of the absorption of the self into the Earth Mother, here Mr. Ramsay employs the Earth Mother to enable his own self-absorption, the very flaw for which Lily criticizes him.

The third feature of the Great Goddess reflected in Woolf's characterization of Mrs. Ramsay is the subordination of individuality into generic social roles that support fertility. This emphasis on the strength of the group, expressed in a commitment to perpetuating human life generally, characterizes the Great Goddess and the society associated with Her worship. This can sometimes take the form of compelling individuals into gendered social roles—husband and wife, soldier and mother—that promote fertility and the welfare of the group. This aspect of Mrs. Ramsay's character parallels Neumann's description of the Great Mother's indifference to the individual ego even in the most healing and positive aspects of the Great Mother: "It is not an ego, much less a self or personality, that is reborn; rebirth is a cosmic occurrence, anonymous and universal like 'life.' . . . All vegetation is the same."[40] When translated into Western post-Enlightenment societies, individuals like Lily will likely experience this element of the value system that Harrison links to the worship of the Mother as oppressive. Woolf not only reveals the inherent problems with translating an archaic matrifocal value system into a modern context, she also emphasizes the inconsistencies between this value system and the values of modern feminism. She achieves this by revising the archaic tendency to prioritize generic social roles over individuality into Mrs. Ramsay's tendency to privilege men, imperial patriarchy, and rational materialism over the well-being and liberty of human beings.

Mrs. Ramsay embodies the Great Goddess's emphasis on fertility by emphasizing collective identity and dismissing individual variation and freedom. Positively, this makes her a unifier within the community of the novel; she brings characters out of their isolation and into communion with others. Lily feels this one-making, which she likens to a work of art in which "she brought together this and that and then this" most intensely in its absence (*TTL*, 164). For instance, when Mrs. Ramsay leaves the dinner party, "directly she went a sort of disintegration set in; they wavered about, went different ways" (114). After Mrs. Ramsay's death, Lily feels "as if a link that usually bound things together had been cut" (150).

But Woolf portrays Mrs. Ramsay as promoting the group over individual freedom to an excessive degree, echoing Artemis and Hera, with tragically ironic results. Woolf emphasizes the ruin brought on by Mrs. Ramsay's coercion of young people into her generic categories. Just as Woolf critiques Mrs. Ramsay's conviction that marriage is best for all people by revealing the disastrous results of Mrs. Ramsay's matchmaking in the case of Paul and Minta, she parenthetically informs us that Prue Ramsay dies in childbirth and that Andrew Ramsay dies in the war. By enforcing gendered destinies, Mrs. Ramsay resembles Artemis, who guides children into their gender-specific adult

---

40. Neumann, *Origins*, 51–52.

roles of wife-mother and citizen-soldier, and enforces conformity to normative heterosexuality and gendered social identities. The paths into which she leads her children and other people's children (marriage, war, and childbirth) lead to failure or death, a consequence that undermines her status as life giver in the novel and that emphasizes the inappropriateness of transposing matrifocal structures into modern society. Lily highlights this repressive aspect of the Great Goddess most frequently and passionately through her resistance to it, as she imagines begging for an exemption from "the universal law" of compulsory marriage (*TTL*, 53). Paradoxically, Lily's desire to remain a virgin, her refusal to cross over into her prescribed adult role of wife and mother, marks her as Artemisian as well. Like Atalanta, who values her independence and wishes to remain a follower of Artemis beyond the time given to her, Lily justifies her desire for exemption from Mrs. Ramsay's universal law by the fact that "she liked to be alone; she liked to be herself; she was not made for that" (53). While Artemis demands that women move from female community to heterosexual marriage, in some myths Artemis punishes her followers for heterosexual activity, even a nymph like Callisto, who has been raped by Zeus while he took the form of Artemis herself. Allusions to Artemis, like all mythic allusions, are far from straightforward, and here Woolf splits up elements of Artemis among characters to great effect. In the conflict between Mrs. Ramsay's Artemisian qualities (compelling the young into gendered roles) and Lily's Artemisian qualities (refusing to enter marriage), Woolf's paratactic method reveals some of the problems with archaic models for feminist liberation in the modern era.

Mrs. Ramsay's claim that only marriage can provide the path to fulfillment for all women, as she dismisses Lily's artistic dreams and remains blind to her daughters' dreams of a different life, demonstrates that, like the conservative aspect of Artemis, she views all women generically through the categories of fertility, as wife and mother. Mrs. Ramsay views men in a similarly generic and categorical way; for her, all men, regardless of their peculiarities, are the same, members of a larger category. Extending her treatment of her husband, she holds "the whole of the other sex under her protection," assuming the role of divine mother and guardian, "for reasons she could not explain" (*TTL*, 10). Men worship her as a goddess and affirm her position as divine mother. The relationship of goddess and worshipper is bidirectional; she views individual men through the generic category of worshipper, and men likewise worship her as a goddess. In his defense of realism, while objecting to Lily's abstraction of Mrs. Ramsay and James into a triangular purple shape in her painting, William Bankes refers to them not as particular individuals but as "mother and child . . . objects of universal veneration" (55–56). Woolf emphasizes the religious elements of Bankes's relation to Mrs. Ramsay with the words "miraculously," "reverence," "rapture," "sublime," "heavenly," and "worship" (51–52). Her description also relies heavily upon gender dichotomies, reflecting Mrs. Ramsay's ideology of gender that reduces men to generic worshippers of the divine female, and women, generalized as future wives, follow her divine model of marriage. Lily notes that women categorically cannot worship Mrs. Ramsay as men do, "They could only seek shelter under the shade which Mr. Bankes extended over them both" (52). At the same time, praise of Mrs. Ramsay extends to all women and Lily feels the benefit of William Bankes's worship, taking "shelter from this reverence which covered all women; she felt herself praised" (51). Just as Mrs. Ramsay views men as a generic group of worshippers, men worship Mrs. Ramsay as *woman*, a universal category she embodies more perfectly than other women, and not as a specific individual.[41]

Woolf employs Mrs. Ramsay's generic view of men as worshippers and their impersonal worship of Mrs. Ramsay as a goddess to revise Harrison's matrifocal value system in ways that undermine its radical feminist potential. William Bankes's impersonal rapture has strong implications for advancing the cause of civilization, particularly of imperialist and rationalist society. While gazing at Mrs. Ramsay, he feels "as he felt when he had proved something absolute about the digestive system of plants, that barbarity was tamed, the reign of chaos subdued" (*TTL*, 51). Like Mr. Ramsay, who seeks to feel at home in the world through his wife's comforts, Bankes reveals the anxiety of the Victorian age and the function of the domesticated goddess in perpetuating the march of progress. Mr. Bankes's identification of Mrs. Ramsay with scientific knowledge and civilization, and the confidence and sense of peace she brings him reflects the cultural construction of the goddess as a representative for reason, the Enlightenment's Goddess of Reason. Mr. Ramsay's relation to his wife reflects the other side of the goddess's function within the process of secularization and rationalization; when rationalism and materialism fail to produce the promised security and sense of mastery, a spiritualized woman must reanimate and reinspire the world. In turn, Mrs. Ramsay's abstract and generalizing view of men, and her protection of them as a group—her goddess-like behavior—supports the advancement of masculine civilization and particularly of the British Empire. Despite her professed inability to explain her inclination to protect "the whole of the other sex," Mrs. Ramsay immediately offers two reasons for this generalizing view of men. These two reasons reveal a strange combination of two value systems, patriarchal and

---

41. On Mrs. Ramsay's embodiment of the Virgin Mary archetype, see Daugherty, "There She Sat."

matrifocal, that we usually imagine as opposites. They are one more way that Woolf demonstrates how in modernity the goddess has been subordinated to rational materialist patriarchy.

First, Mrs. Ramsay protects "the whole of the other sex" because they display "an attitude towards her . . . something trustful, childlike, reverential" (*TTL*, 10). By relating to men as members of the generic category *male*, and by imagining herself as protecting all members of this group indiscriminately because of their childlike trust and reverence of her, she reflects the value system Harrison associates with the worship of the Mother. According to Harrison, the Goddess, "being concerned with the group rather than the individual is attended not only by her subordinate son and lover but by *groups* of daemonic persons, Curetes, Telchines, Corybantes, Satyrs, and the like" (*Mythology*, 63, emphasis mine). Mrs. Ramsay's other reason for her soft spot toward men reveals a privileging of traditional patriarchal values; she loves men because they possess chivalry and valor—traditionally heroic virtues—and because they uphold the institutions of civilization by negotiating treaties, ruling India, and controlling finance. In this way, she resembles the women Woolf describes in *A Room of One's Own* who support patriarchal civilization by having "served all these centuries as looking-glasses possessing the magic and delicious power of reflecting the figure of man at twice its natural size" (35). Without recourse to this magical power of women, Woolf goes on to ask, how would man continue making wars, writing laws, and civilizing natives? This combination of value systems, with the result of privileging men as a group, reveals Mrs. Ramsay's status as a patriarchal form of the Mother Goddess.

Woolf transplants these three features of the Great Goddess into an early twentieth-century context and revises them to emphasize the extent to which the Goddess in the modern world is a tool of patriarchal domination. The awesome fertility powers of the Mother no longer serve as a life-affirming challenge to the rationalist materialist culture of death; rather, in Woolf's version, that worldview has already violently co-opted the Goddess's fertility to provide a pressure valve for its desiccated intellectual heroes. Likewise, while Lily experiences ecstatic dissolution of the ego through the Goddess's manifestation in nature, Mr. Ramsay undergoes no such transformation of the self, easily subsuming theophany to his abstract philosophical reasoning. Finally, Woolf revises the matrifocal emphasis on the group over the individual into Mrs. Ramsay's prescriptive enforcement of heteronormative and militaristic roles and her admiration of men who conform to imperial patriarchal norms. It is widely accepted that Woolf employs the Angel in the House to critique the Victorian cult of domesticity and to reflect on her parents' marriage. Her indeterminate mythic allusions in this section of the novel expand this critique to a diagnosis of its intellectual causes, demonstrating the hubris of the aim of Victorian science to not only rid the world of mystery, subordinating nature to the expansion of reason's empire, as Mr. Ramsay does when he reduces his wife and child to illustrative scenery, but also to establish reason and materialism as objects of worship.

Critics have disagreed about whether Lily ultimately rejects or incorporates the influence of Mrs. Ramsay. Lily, more than any other character, suggests a version of feminism founded on the freedom of the liberal self to self-determination rather than on a universal maternal essence. According to Moore, Lily "experiences the ecstasy which she associates with Mrs. Ramsay, and recognizes it as false (feeding as it does on the inferior position of women)."[42] In contrast, Franks argues that "Lily's feminist genealogy does not involve rejecting Mrs. Ramsay, but incorporating the mother figure into herself and her modernist vision."[43] Franks asserts that Lily appropriates Mrs. Ramsay's "queer generationality" through a practice of temporal drag, in which cultural objects are repurposed in "unpredictable and unfaithful ways" to resist hetero-reproductive narratives of progress.[44] Lily's unwillingness to comply with the demands of heterosexual procreativity has prompted critics like Olano and Weil to argue that Lily exemplifies lesbian consciousness within the novel.[45] Through her nonanthropomorphic vision of Mrs. Ramsay discussed above, with its emphasis on female background instead of patriarchal foreground, Lily enacts what Weil calls an implicitly Eleusinian shift into "lesbian vision," a "reorientation of attention" that makes possible "an alternative human economy in which women's emotional and creative resources are not funneled into men and their projects."[46] Friedman accounts for this tension within our understandings of Lily's relation to Mrs. Ramsay through the interplay between two modes of writing that Friedman terms the lyric and the narrative. On the level of the narrative, Lily rejects the maternal plot of Mrs. Ramsay, but on the level of the lyrical, Lily and Mrs. Ramsay are drawn together.[47]

---

42. Moore, *Short Season between Two Silences*, 86.
43. Franks, "Mrs. Ramsay's Queer Generationality," 17.
44. Franks, 15–17.
45. Olano, "'Women alone,'" 164. Weil, "Entering a Lesbian Field of Vision."
46. Weil, "Entering a Lesbian Field of Vision," 245–46.
47. Friedman, "Lyric Subversion of Narrative."

Yet, I believe this critical disagreement ultimately misses the point. Through Lily's shifting vision of Mrs. Ramsay, Woolf presents an indeterminate characterization of Mrs. Ramsay that reflects various forms of feminism. Lily's vision of Mrs. Ramsay embodies both a liberal feminism that values individual freedom and self-determination, and a Harrisonian feminism that values the life-affirming alternative to patriarchy exemplified in matrifocal societies. We might ask, which feminism does Woolf promote in the novel? But due to the contradictory visions of Mrs. Ramsay that her daughters and Lily sustain, it is not clear that Woolf aims to promote one vision of feminism against others at all. As Daugherty writes, by continually re-envisioning Mrs. Ramsay, Lily "attempts to do more than criticize her society's codes," aiming instead to "see from a position outside those codes and myths."[48] Lily resists Mrs. Ramsay's domineering enforcement of compulsory heterosexuality and essentialist, fertility-oriented destiny for women, but her ecstatic religious experience of Mrs. Ramsay's divine aspects provides a different way of seeing that inspires her art. Lily needs both perspectives on Mrs. Ramsay to complete her painting; she must practice both absorption in and resistance to the Great Goddess as it presents itself in the modern world, and she must refuse the persistent temptation to resolve the tension by choosing one approach exclusively. Rather than seeking one vision of feminism within Woolf's novel, we ought to take Lily's vision of Mrs. Ramsay seriously in all its puzzling inconsistency. Doing so provides insight into some of the struggles for feminist identity and vision, struggles that are at the heart of the movement to this day and which greatly concerned Woolf.

Lily's inconsistent perspective emblematizes Woolf's refusal to order competing perspectives into a single truth for readers or to give her readers a nugget of pure truth to be kept on the mantelpiece forever. She performs this narrative indeterminacy on both the level of narration and through her mythic allusions. This paratactic method, inspired both by the nature of archaic myth and by Harrison's conception of an ancestress from which several goddesses derive, drives the form of Woolf's allusions and the explicit content of these allusions in the novel. Woolf's relationship to Harrison has been of perpetual interest to Woolf scholars, and *To the Lighthouse* suggests a complicated relationship. Harrison inspired Woolf's feminist theories of archaic religion; at the same time, Woolf maintains critical distance about those theories' utopian potential in the modern era, just as for Lily to carve out the space for her own inspired art, "so much depends . . . upon distance" (*TTL*, 194). In this chapter I have emphasized the critical aspect of Woolf's treatment of Mrs. Ramsay in

---

48. Daugherty, "There She Sat," 298.

order to bring attention to a productive tension within Woolf's work, but, as many critics have shown, Woolf found inspiration in the chthonic, matrifocal myth Harrison studied, drawing on it heavily in her fiction.

As Woolf makes clear in her adaptation of Harrison's Olympian and matrifocal value systems in *To the Lighthouse,* while Woolf feared the excesses of the isolated rational will that characterizes post-Enlightenment rational society and the communal erasure of individuality that characterizes archaic matrifocal society, she recognized the value in moderate forms of both. These two perspectives combine in *To the Lighthouse* to form one of Woolf's strongest statements in favor of the androgynous mind through her emphasis on the problems created by a spiritual "division of labor" in culture that confines men to dispirited intellectual efforts and contains women as patriarchal goddesses relegated to providing spiritual wholeness. Myth, with its reputation as nonrational, and particularly Harrison's feminist interpretation of myth, provides the most appropriate vehicle for this analysis, pointing the way toward nonrational, spiritual, and antisystematizing visions of reality, but Woolf refuses to apply this cure uncritically lest it become a poison.

CHAPTER 5

Harmonious Discord in *Between the Acts*

In the introduction to this book, I argue that myth matters to Woolf studies because both its structure and Woolf's paratactic method of allusion integrate her epistemologically informed political vision. Her intersectional political vision takes on many fronts, and in the 1930s the rising threat of fascism became a central focus for her thought. The phallogocentrism and hegemony characteristic of fascism embody the structures of thought that Woolf repeatedly challenges in her political critiques, aesthetic innovations, and mythic allusions. Epistemology lies at the heart of Woolf's interrelated aesthetic and political visions; specifically, she responds to a conception of knowledge and truth that imagines the world in overly simplistic, rationalist, and materialist terms. To break up the imposition of artificial unities and clean distinctions characteristic of fascist thought, Woolf promotes a vision of reality as multifaceted, overlapping, and divergent, a fragmentary paratactic structure that parallels that of archaic myth. Woolf realizes that not simply action but also thought and vision must be transformed to effect radical change. This understanding of the depth of political and social issues—of the dangers of, on the one hand, intellectual impotence and, on the other hand, dogmatically committing oneself to a political agenda—may have led to the judgment of her male peers that, in Leonard Woolf's words, she was "the least political animal that has lived since Aristotle invented the definition."[1] However, this

---

1. Woolf, *Downhill All the Way*, 27.

characteristic of Woolf's thought—her constant questioning and destabilizing of masculinist knowledge structures—gives her political vision its radical force and lasting relevance.

In the 1930s, fascist discourse concerned both Virginia and Leonard Woolf who both wrote satirical nonfiction works, Virginia's *Three Guineas* and Leonard's *Quack, Quack!*.[2] Woolf's critique of fascism is crystal clear in *Three Guineas*. Her antifascist mythic method in fiction of the period demands more attention. Throughout this book, I have discussed instances of Woolf's paratactic adaptation of archaic mythic themes and figures for the purposes of social critique. A paratactic structure can be found in other aspects of Woolf's fiction but the status of myth in the twentieth century brings it to the fore. In this chapter, I argue that Woolf's paratactic method of alluding to myth finds its fullest expression and embodies most explicitly her commitment to resisting totalizing systems of thought in her posthumously published novel, *Between the Acts*.

The critical conversation about *Between the Acts* has tended to focus on the conflicting tendencies toward disruption and unity, a tension that one could argue forms the central theme of the novel. Critics generally acknowledge both sides of this tension as operative but have tended to prioritize one perspective over the other. Many critics argue, from readings of the pageant written and directed by Miss La Trobe, that in the novel Woolf attempts to reject fascism through a privileging of the disruption and splintering of a falsely unified image of identity. Michele Pridmore-Brown emphasizes the power of Miss La Trobe's gramophone during the village pageant to disrupt images of fascist authority and nationalist unity. The insertion of random noise, static, into the information technology often used for authoritarian ends "suggests a way out of the totalizing construct" through interpretive possibilities encouraged by noise.[3] While Pridmore-Brown acknowledges the back-and-forth movement of "unity and disparity," she ultimately argues, "This grand moment of unity orchestrated through the gramophone is not sustained."[4] Likewise, Madelyn Detloff reads the famous mirror scene of La Trobe's pageant as revealing "a contingent and disparate national populace" rather than "a unifying vision of

---

2. Rosenfeld, "Monstrous Conjugations," 123. Many critics have written about Woolf's engagement with fascism; some sources include Merry Pawlowski, *Virginia Woolf and Fascism*; Elsa Högberg, *Virginia Woolf and the Ethics of Intimacy*; Patricia Klindienst Joplin, "The Authority of Illusion"; Patricia Laurence, "A Writing Couple"; Jeanette McVicker, "Woolf in the Context of Fascism"; Marlowe A. Miller, "Unveiling 'The Dialectic of Culture and Barbarism' in British Pageantry"; and Judy Suh, "Woolf and the Gendering of Fascism."

3. Pridmore-Brown, "1939–40," 411–12.

4. Pridmore-Brown, 414.

British subjecthood."⁵ In contrast, while acknowledging Woolf's representation of collectivity in *Between the Acts* as dispersed and fragmentary, Galia Benziman finds in Woolf's consistent portrayal of the community and nation as an individual self "a contrasted yearning to see the dispersed fragments as belonging to a unified whole."⁶ Jed Esty similarly sees the pageant-play as a helpful mechanism to promote English nationalism without resolving into fascism, redefining rather than eschewing national tradition.⁷

Despite the different emphases of critics, they generally agree, going back as far as Erich Auerbach's 1946 and Warren Beck's 1948 readings of the novel, that *Between the Acts* offers a way of reimagining collectivity in inclusive, antifascist ways. The critical disagreement outlined above is particularly relevant to our analysis, however, since it points to the ambiguity and destabilizing structure of the text's message. I agree with the critical consensus that in *Between the Acts* Woolf thinks through the challenges of forming an inclusive group identity.⁸ Woolf's insistence on maintaining an irreconcilable tension between unity and dispersal, her unwillingness to coherently and finally come down on one side, constitutes Woolf's most powerful critique of exclusionary and oppressive social identities like fascism. Along these lines, in this chapter I examine two aesthetic strategies that draw on Woolf's knowledge of Greek, her fragmentary adaptation of the choral passage from Greek tragedy and her indirect, piecemeal, and contradictory allusions to myth. Her fragmentary choral passages, which share the paratactic style of her mythic allusions, function as part of what some critics have identified as a larger project to disrupt the plot.

Woolf recognizes fascism not solely as a political issue but rather as an omnipresent threat in human relations, grounded in ways of seeing and conceptually organizing, or *disciplining,* the world in all its aspects, domestic and public.⁹ In La Trobe's pageant of English history, the Constable Budge gives voice to imperial domestic power, proclaiming, "Our rule don't end there. . . . Over thought and religion; drink; manners; marriage too, I wield my truncheon" (*BTA,* 111). Woolf links empire and English history more explicitly in an earlier draft of the novel, then titled *Pointz Hall,* identifying Budge's character in the play as "the Victorian Age" who directs "the traffic of Her

---

5. Detloff, *Persistence of Modernism,* 35.
6. Benziman, "'Dispersed Are We,'" 55.
7. Esty, *Shrinking Island,* 55.
8. See also Hinnov, "Each is part of the whole," and Foster, "History, Ethics, and Community in Virginia Woolf's *Between the Acts.*" On the influence of Jane Harrison on this theme, see Cramer, "Virginia Woolf's Matriarchal Family of Origins in *Between the Acts.*"
9. For a discussion of Woolf's queering practices in the novel as a response to the surveillance of sexuality and ethnicity, see Camarasana, "Trespassing the Nation," 10.

Majesty's Empire . . . crossing the Ocean to proclaim her Empire" (*Pointz Hall* ETS, 149).[10] Fascistic power structures manifest in a network of control over elements of life as disparate as knowledge, authority, gender and sexuality, and racial classifications.[11] Though Woolf pares back this section of *Between the Acts*, in *Pointz Hall* she makes explicit the racial elements of Budge's imperial enforcement, ending Budge's extended monologue, "That's the price of Empire; that's the white man's burden . . . a whole-time white man's job" (*Pointz Hall* ETS, 149–50). In her draft version of Budge, Woolf connects global politics, imperialism, and racial domination with control of daily life and thought. Woolf's artistic representatives, aspiring poet Isa Oliver and playwright Miss La Trobe, reject these fascist tendencies as they appear in the very structures of thought and art, echoing Woolf's diary entry of May 15, 1940, as she was finishing *Between the Acts*, in which she writes, "Thinking is my fighting" (*Diary* 5, 281).

Critics like Fernald and Detloff have widely recognized the political import of Woolf's aesthetic emphasis on fragmentation and narrative disruption.[12] What Fernald and Detloff characterize as a fragmentary aesthetic I take to be part of a broader paratactic strategy to withhold fixed meanings and counteract readers' conventional expectations of authorial power and the masterability of narrative. *Between the Acts* may be more paratactic and fragmentary than her other novels because Leonard published it posthumously, and Virginia did not complete final edits to the manuscript. However, considering whether Woolf would have created greater unity in her allusions had she been able to complete final revisions of the novel, Mitchell Leaska concludes that her revisions would likely have "heightened its ambiguity, and made the mysterious whole an even more defiant riddle than it already seems."[13] Indeed, Woolf's revisions throughout the two published typescripts and *Between the Acts* tend toward condensing and removing explanations and background, a practice that dates back to her description of her newly discovered method in *Jacob's Room*, which amplifies the novel's parataxis.[14] Leaska attributes the

---

10. Hereafter, citations to Woolf's drafts of *Between the Act*, originally called "Pointz Hall," will occur parenthetically in text. I have abbreviated the early typescript of the draft as ETS and the later typescript as LTS in parenthetical citations.

11. For a discussion of this network, which he calls "the Western code," see Mignolo, *Darker Side of Western Modernity*, xii, xv.

12. Fernald, *Feminism and the Reader*, 38, 40; Detloff, *Persistence of Modernism*, 39. See also Nora Eisenberg, "Virginia Woolf's Last Words on Words."

13. Leaska, Preface to *Pointz Hall*, xiv.

14. As Woolf wrote in her diary of January 26, 1920, her "new form for a new novel" was characterized by "no scaffolding; scarcely a brick to be seen; all crepuscular" (26 January 1920: *Diary* 2, 13–14).

opacity of the novel to Woolf's mature style of allusion in which "a private system of symbols over the years grew into and merged with a public system of symbolic representations." This results in passages that "are not open to analysis or description. And the harder we try to tap them into speech, the more reticent they become."[15]

Woolf's mythic allusions in *Between the Acts* represent one of the most significant and undertheorized forms of Woolf's paratactic aesthetic. The mythic allusions in this novel are so much more disjointed and fragmentary than in her earlier novels that they can be difficult to detect and even harder to interpret. Barrett's award-winning study of Woolf's feminist allusions to myth in the novel, Patricia Maika's and Cramer's analyses of the influence of Harrison's research and theories on the novel, and Evelyn Haller's detailed work on the Isis myth in *Between the Acts* have gone a long way toward illuminating this level of discourse.[16] However, while Woolf's allusions clearly convey a feminist and matrifocal tone, because the referents are not stable and singular, their greatest significance lies in their intentional refusal to signify. By undermining an artificially unified conception of the Great Goddess, which Woolf problematizes in *Mrs. Dalloway* and *To the Lighthouse,* these paratactic references destabilize concepts like community and identity that have been ideologically constructed as unified and homogeneous.

Myth does not necessarily lead one away from fascism, as Ellwood illustrates in his study of accusations of fascism and anti-Semitism against Jung, Eliade, and Campbell, because romantic images of the premodern can be used to justify attempts to Make the West Great Again. Woolf repeatedly confronts the dangers of idealizing the premodern and mythic while still respecting the radical potential of myth to counter modernity. She wields the labrys of mythic images so effectively, when Jung, Eliade, and Campbell may fumble with it, precisely because she is not a system builder; that is, precisely because she refuses the simplicity of unilateral answers, preferring instead the intellectual freedom allowed by parataxis, her mythic allusions challenge rather than reinforce fascistic thought structures.

Woolf scatters mythic allusions throughout the novel, often in animal imagery, but she clusters inconsistent mythic allusions primarily around the four main female characters in the novel: Lucinda (Lucy) Swithin, Isa Oliver,

---

15. Leaska, Introduction to *Pointz Hall,* 14.
16. Barrett, "Matriarchal Myth"; Maika, *Virginia Woolf's* Between the Acts *and Jane Harrison's Con/spiracy*; Haller, "Isis Unveiled"; Cramer, "Matriarchal Family of Origins." See also Marcus, "Some Sources for *Between the Acts*"; Little, "Festive Comedy in Woolf's *Between the Acts*"; Callan, "Exploring the Confluence of Primitive Ritual and Modern Longing in *Between the Acts.*"

Miss La Trobe, and Mrs. Manresa. These allusions extend beyond Greek myth to include the Egyptian Isis and Hathor, the Mesopotamian Ishtar, Roman Venus and Juno, and the Greek Persephone and Nemesis.[17] Woolf often brings archaic myth into this novel through nonanthropomorphic forms of the Great Goddess—notably, birds, trees, fish, cows, a donkey, a toad, and a snake. She links Isa with a donkey, and La Trobe with a cow through her village nickname, "Bossy" (*BTA*, 44). Woolf suggests the mythic valence of her animals most famously in swallows. As Marcus and Barrett note, the novel's repeated references to swallows combined with Isa's reading of a newspaper story about the gang rape of a young woman in an army barracks points to the myth of Procne, Philomela, and the rapist Tereus. Woolf's paratactic approach to the Goddess, her pattern of alluding to several goddesses within one character and one goddess among several characters, creates an unstable network of mythic signification that disrupts readers' attempts to pin down the text's meaning. For instance, while Woolf links Manresa to a patriarchal vision of Aphrodite, she also suggests Athena in being "solemn as an owl" (31). Woolf links Isa, Lucy, and La Trobe to fish, which Barrett identifies with the Goddess.[18] But later Woolf undermines this association by likening Lucy's brother Bart, a character aligned with patriarchy and scientific reason in contrast to Lucy's faith, to the fish Lucy tries to feed, when "like a fish rising to a crumb of biscuit, Bartholomew snapped at the paper" (146).

Besides these animal forms of the Goddess, Woolf emphasizes various versions of the triple goddess—the maiden, mother, and crone. She signals the importance of the triple goddess early in the novel when Isa sees "three separate versions of her rather heavy, yet handsome, face" in a trifold mirror (*BTA*, 10). But notably, Woolf provides no stable system of allusions that might suggest an equivalency or easily lend itself to interpretation. Rather, a shifting, kaleidoscopic pattern emerges in which Isa is alternately Artemisian maiden, Demetrian mother, and chthonic crone; Lucy is crone, Demetrian mother, and maiden; La Trobe is crone; and Manresa, besides her more obvious Aphroditean aspects, suggests the maidens Athena and Artemis and, according to Maika, the earth mother Demeter.[19] By referring to ancient myth and ritual in this dispersed, inconsistent manner, Woolf strips the twentieth-century conception of "the Goddess" of its monolithic veneer, exposing and developing the tensions within the Great Goddess. The Lady of the Beasts, the Vegetation Goddess, Mother, Maid, Crone—these feminine images of the divine do not align coherently into a single meaning. In emphasizing the paradoxical nature

---

17. Maika, "Alpha Not Omega."
18. Barrett, "Matriarchal Myth," 31.
19. Maika, "Alpha Not Omega," 64.

of ancient images of goddesses, Woolf continues her broader project of rejecting falsely unifying readings, splitting open the apparently uniform to reveal the spectrum within.

Woolf often links Lucy Swithin to Artemis and her Roman counterpart Diana. The variations on Lucinda's name evoke the moon goddess and maiden Artemis via Diana in multiple ways; Lucinda suggests Artemis through its combination of the Latin *Lucida*, meaning shining, bright, and clear, with *Lucina*, an older title for Juno, the feminine principle of light (*BTA*, 158n5).[20] Further, Lucy identifies with the unnamed Artemisian woman in the portrait as she and William Dodge climb the stairs. The woman in the painting is a spiritual ancestor for Lucy, described "in her yellow robe, leaning, with a pillar to support her, a silver arrow in her hand, and a feather in her hair" (26), and Lucy likes "her best in the moonlight" (47). The arrow, feather, and yellow robe of the woman in the painting, as well as her links to moonlight, suggest Artemis. The novel merges this Artemisian woman of the painting with the real world of Lucy when the satin dress in the painting appears to spread outside the bounds of the canvas. As Barrett notes, "Though it is clearly Lucy who 'shook her head,' the ambiguous 'She' of the last line fuses Lucy and her ancestress, life and art."[21] In fact, when Woolf revised this moment in the novel she emphasized the fusion of Lucy and the woman in the painting.

Lucy's mythic associations extend beyond Artemis to Demeter when, alone with William Dodge, the curtains are blown by the breeze as if "some *majestic* goddess, rising from her throne among her peers, had tossed her *amber*-coloured raiment, and the other gods, seeing her rise and go, laughed, and their laughter floated her on" (*BTA*, 50, emphasis mine). This breeze opens an alternate space, in which Lucy is physically transformed into this "amber" goddess when, in response to William, she "smiled a ravishing girl's smile, as if the wind had warmed the wintry blue in her eyes to *amber*" (50, emphasis mine). This passage, too, received attention from Woolf in the revision process; through several drafts the hypothetical goddess who moves the muslin curtain is "good-natured," but in her final revisions Woolf makes her "majestic," a description much more in line with Demeter (*Pointz Hall* ETS, 90; LTS, 306). With others Lucy appears as an old woman, "old Mother Swithin" (*BTA*, 24), but now she has the ravishing smile of a girl. Like the doubled Demeter-Persephone, she is simultaneously young girl and old woman, an association that links her to the *Kore* Artemis. Like Demeter in the Homeric *Hymn to Demeter* and the Eleusinian Mysteries, her ravishing, divine nature

---

20. See Barrett, "Matriarchal Myth," and Cuddy-Keane, "Introduction to *Between the Acts*."
21. Barrett, 26.

only appears to worshippers in private. Demeaned by others as "Batty" (104) and "old Flimsy" (19), humored and mocked, now this simultaneously old and young woman is worshipped and loved by William, who "wished to kneel before her, to kiss her hand, and to say, '... I'm a half-man, Mrs. Swithin; a flickering, mind-divided little snake in the grass, as Giles saw; but you've healed me'" (51). This worship by the goddess's traditional chthonic and phallic snake-consort remains unspoken, and the moment of theophany ends when another appearance of the breeze "went lolloping around the corridors, blowing the blinds out" (51).

Building Isa's association with the triple goddess when she gazes into the three-fold mirror, Woolf specifically links Isa to the maidenly *Korai* Persephone and Artemis, the maternal Demeter, and the crone Hecate. Throughout the novel, Isa feels split between flirtatious fantasies of the gentleman farmer, love for her children and allegiance to their father, and a desire for independence that leads her to shun fertility symbols. In this internal conflict, she embodies all aspects of the triple goddess: the virgin who may fall in love with a man but, not being a mother and wife, maintains an independent identity; the mother whose identity is tied to her children and to "the father of her children"; and the crone, again independent and now free of the concerns of sexuality and fertility.

The freedom and sense of possibilities that Isa experiences in her fantasies about the gentleman farmer suggest the sense of openness characteristic of the maiden. Despite featuring the gentleman farmer, her fantasies generally emphasize being free rather than tied down in marriage. Isa echoes this rejection of the binding ties of maternity and traditional femininity in her desire to look androgynous, thinking wistfully that she "never looked like Sappho, or one of the beautiful young men whose photographs adorned the weekly papers" (*BTA*, 11–12). William Dodge believes that Isa trusts him because their relationship is asexual. As William characterizes it, women "knew at once they had nothing to fear, nothing to hope. At first they resented—serving as statues in a greenhouse. Then they liked it" (78). In the first typescript of the novel, Woolf explicitly describes William as a "passionless" "eunuch" (*Pointz Hall* ETS, 120–22). Isa, who dwells on a newspaper description of a rape at an army barracks, is willing to "hand him ... a flower," a gesture that young Cam Ramsay refuses to make in *To the Lighthouse*, because she has "nothing to fear" and thus can maintain her spiritual virginity and independence (*BTA*, 78). William's reply to Isa's musing about why they could speak so plainly to each other suggests the *Kore* Artemis in particular. In an apparent non sequitur, he explains their immediate connection as due to "the doom of sudden death hanging over us" (79), alluding to Artemis's role in bringing sudden death to women. Woolf infuses this scene with allusions to Artemis and other virgin goddesses and *Korai*. Isa and William sit beneath "little grapes" that are "green buds." While the grapes are an overt reference to Dionysos, they also suggest the bud stage of the vegetation goddess embodied in Persephone, in contrast to the mature fruit stage embodied in Demeter (78). When she realizes that William does not present a sexual threat to her, Isa offers him a geranium, a flower associated with the virgin goddess Athena. The scene opens with Isa picking and playing with a plant identified in the novel as "Old Man's Beard" (77), which Cuddy-Keane identifies as *Artemisia abrotanum* (183n1). Isa picks this plant again as she strides toward her husband Giles and Manresa, aware of their liaison in the greenhouse, and "stripped the bitter leaf that grew, as it happened, outside the nursery window. Old Man's Beard. Shrivelling the shreds in lieu of words, for no words grow there" (141).

Despite repeated allusions to the maidenly Artemis, Athena, and Persephone in Isa's characterization, Woolf insists on undermining a symbolic system, even in early drafts of the novel. Like the subtle mythic inconsistency of the green buds of grapes that Isa and William sit beneath, the late scene in which William watches Isa pursue Giles and Mrs. Manresa undermines a straightforward system of mythic signification in the novel. As Isa shrivels the leaves of Artemisian Old Man's Beard in pursuit of her philandering husband, William translates Jean Racine's *Phèdre*, thinking that Isa is "like Venus . . . to her prey" (*BTA*, 141). Yet immediately after this reference to Venus, William ambiguously suggests Artemis when he wonders if Giles and Manresa "perceive the arrows about to strike them?," a question that may allude to both Artemis's hunting of humans with her bow or to Eros's arrows of love, but which in this context resonates with the Artemisian hunt.

Isa again expresses a desire for independence and a movement away from the bonds of fertility and maternity, this time indicating the chthonic crone, when she thinks of herself as wandering in a place where "there grows nothing for the eye" and emerges "in some harvestless dim field" (*BTA*, 105–6). In the published novel, Woolf composes an extended section in which Isa develops this crone aspect of her inner life, which becomes contrasted with audience members' patriarchal visions of the Victorian age; the section is missing or brief in the typescripts. In the "harvestless" space that Isa wanders, all things are equal, "Unblowing, ungrowing are the roses there. Change is not; nor the mutable and lovable; nor greetings nor partings; nor furtive findings and feelings" (106). Isa's poetry, emphasizing the absence of fertility, life, growth, and sexuality, derives its creative force from the isolation of the chthonic crone. This timeless, changeless dim field lies beyond human concerns of lovability and relation, marked by furtive findings and feelings, greetings and partings, a place where the roses neither grow nor blow in the breeze. The significance of this imagery emerges when contrasted with Mrs. Lynn Jones and Etty Springett's nostalgic recollections of the nineteenth century, especially of "the curtains blowing, and the men crying: 'All a blowing, all a growing,' as they came with geraniums, sweet william, in pots, down the street" (108). This description of men selling contained geraniums and sweet william follows Colonel Mayhew's complaint about the British Army being left out of the pageant of English history: "What's history without the Army, eh?" (107). This patriarchal vision of the glories of the nineteenth century contrasts with Isa's preference for picking the Athenenian wild geranium as a gift for the nonthreatening sweet William. Woolf creates a more direct contrast between flowers "all a blowing, all a growing" in the full flush of fertility and Isa's fantasy of wandering down into a place where roses are "unblowing, ungrowing." When considered in relation to LaTrobe's satiric framing of a nostalgic celebration of nineteenth century fertility, Isa's fantasy suggests a freedom from what she experiences as the patriarchal restrictions of fertility and maternity, a life that escapes the confines of marriage. In contrast to her maidenly fantasies of the gentleman farmer, which seem to offer freedom from her marriage through romantic liaison with a supposedly better man than Giles, this fantasy suggests a rejection of romantic attachments of any kind (greetings, partings, furtive findings, and feelings) and, instead, a movement into a spiritual realm of changelessness and immutability where nothing may be harvested by the hands of the fathers.

Woolf complicates this portrait of Isa's motives and values, a yearning for independence and a rejection of maternity and marriage, by having Isa repeatedly express allegiance to her husband as "the father of my children" (*BTA*, 10). She feels explicitly torn between the possibility of a different life that she associates with the gentleman farmer—her feeling of being "in love"—and her love for her child and husband. Isa, whose name suggests Isis, one of the most recognizable Mother goddesses, expresses both motherhood and the freedom and independence of the maiden and the crone.

Of all the female characters, Miss La Trobe most clearly embodies the isolation and spirituality of the crone figure. When the pageant has ended, La Trobe envisions her next play, the scenario "[rises] to the surface," high ground at midnight, a rock, two figures, but she cannot find the words with which to express her vision (*BTA*, 143). The words only come when she has escaped "the terror and horror of being alone" and has taken refuge in the "shelter; voices; oblivion" of the public house (143). There she performs a ritual that echoes the witchcraft associated with both the virgin goddess and the crone Hecate. In a scene replete with mythic images of Hecatean séances, she sinks into the smoky haze, lifts her drink to her lips, and listens to the buzz of voices, drowsing as she sits: "The mud became fertile. Words rose above the intolerably laden dumb oxen plodding through the mud. Words without meaning—wonderful words.... There was the high ground at midnight; there the rock; and two scarcely perceptible figures. Suddenly the tree was pelted with starlings. She set down her glass. She heard the first words" (144). The fertile mud from which La Trobe's words rise reintroduces the mud of the lily pool in which the carp, symbol of the Goddess, lives.[22] Anticipating La Trobe's ritual séance, Bart explicitly links La Trobe to the carp: "What she wanted, like that carp (something moved in the water) was darkness in the mud; a whisky and soda at the pub; and coarse words descending like maggots through the waters" (138). Woolf links La Trobe, like Lucy, "the old girl with a wisp of white hair flying, knobbed shoes as if she had claws corned like a canary's, and black stockings wrinkled over the ankles," to the figure of the Hecatean crone (19). While Lucy suggests the physicality of the witch, La Trobe employs her magical methods and tools in the service of her art. In the sole moment of connection between Lucy and La Trobe, Lucy struggles to find the words to thank La Trobe for showing her the many untapped facets of her potential as a woman. La Trobe intuits Lucy's message in a way suggestive of the Fates: "'You've twitched the invisible strings,' was what the old lady meant" (104–5). But, La Trobe continues, "Ah, she was not merely a twitcher of individual strings; she was one who seethes wandering bodies and floating voices in a cauldron, and makes rise from its amorphous mass a re-created world" (105).

However, La Trobe cannot be so easily read. While in many ways she embodies through her pageant the matrifocal and antipatriarchal value system that Cramer and other critics attribute to Woolf, her characterization inspires conflicting responses from readers. Steve Ellis argues that, while La Trobe is linked with the archaic, she is simultaneously a character with whom Woolf identifies and an antagonist to Woolf in her authoritarian tendencies, which Ellis finds embodied in her anonymity.[23] Likewise, Isa's characterization contains some of Woolf's most conflicting goddess imagery, suggesting the Demetrian mother, the maiden, and the crone. In this way, Woolf employs her mythic allusions to counteract falsely unified narratives both of the Goddess and of women's lives. This method continues with Manresa.

Of all the female characters, the mythic signification of Manresa creates the most challenge for readers due to its inconsistency. As Barrett notes, her name, "'man' plus *res*, the Latin for thing, emphasizes her allegiances and

---

22. Barrett, "Matriarchal Myth," 31.
23. Ellis, *British Writers*, 214–16.

establishes her as the image of the goddess in the male imagination."[24] In her drafts of the novel, Woolf frequently refers to Manresa as "the Manresa." The repetition of this unusual appellation suggests an uncanny monstrosity in the character and underscores the thingy-ness of her name. Interestingly, Woolf removes the article in *Between the Acts,* referring to her as Mrs. Manresa. In her public behavior, Manresa identifies with the male and supports male power.[25] But even the qualities in Mrs. Manresa that make her most obnoxious to the novel's other women and most distinct from them—her sexual energy and flirtations, her dismissal of demure feminine civilization, and her pursuit of earthly pleasure—suggest aspects of the goddess. In part, this inconsistency derives from a tension within the Great Goddess: the Vegetation Goddess, suggested by Isa and Lucy, and the Lady of the Beasts, suggested by Manresa. As Neumann summarizes, "The Lady of the Beasts is not a goddess of the cultural and agricultural cultural stage. . . . She is close to the wild, early nature of man, i.e., to the savage instinct-governed being who lived with the beasts and free-growing plants."[26] Manresa's most frequent epithet, a "wild child of nature," echoes Neumann's language very closely. Like the Lady of the Beasts and Harrison's vision of prepatriarchal religion, Manresa privileges instincts over rationality and shuns the culture and manners she sees embodied in the women around her. Woolf destabilizes Manresa's mythic identity by referencing the maiden Artemis in Manresa's perpetual adolescence and dogged refusal to grow up. Disagreeing with Lucy about the need for ghost stories, Manresa proclaims, "I'm nothing like so grown up as you are," then preens, "approving her adolescence" (*BTA,* 31). Woolf further undermines our ability to read Manresa through a mythic lens when, in this Artemisian moment, Manresa shifts to resembling Athena, becoming "solemn as an owl" (31). Bart praises Manresa for grounding Giles to the earth and fructifying it, both allusions to the earth mother Gaia (82). In the battle that plays out in the novel, especially between the rational, modern, and patriarchal, embodied in both Bartholomew and Giles, and the nonrational, ancient, and maternal, embodied in both Lucy and Isa, Manresa clearly emerges on the side of the nonrational ancient goddesses in this passage, despite her allegiance to men. Even her worship by men and her focus on her male worshippers coincides with ancient images of the Lady of the Beasts, most notably the Minoan Mountain Mother who appears, in Emile Gilliéron's reconstruction of a Cretan seal, flanked by lions and facing an adoring male worshipper. In both the typescripts and the published novel, Woolf links Manresa to the Great Goddess

---

24. Barrett, "Matriarchal Myth," 24.
25. For more on this, see Barrett, 19, 24.
26. Neumann, *Great Mother,* 277.

through her practice of keeping a male consort. Giles plays this role in the novel, while in the earliest draft William Dodge explicitly states that "women like the Manresa need a young man about the house" and that he "let the Manresa pat me and pet me; among her purple plush; among her odious ornaments; china dogs; that potpourri" (*Pointz Hall* ETS, 121, 90).

The convolutions of the mythic allusions in these four characters make it impossible to gain a clear message from them. Woolf links Manresa, the least likely character, with Isa and Lucy through references to Artemis, Athena, and Aphrodite. Likewise, she links La Trobe to Lucy and Isa through the figure of the crone. The paratactic nature of Woolf's mythic references and the resulting challenges to interpretation lie at the heart of Woolf's mythic project in the novel.[27] Whatever political message she conveys through mythic allusion, as well as her unwillingness to convey any particular message at all, emerges from and expresses her awareness of the roots of action in patterns of thought. Through this paratactic style of allusion, fragmented and destabilizing, Woolf extends the radical potential of a Harrison-inflected reading of archaic myth as nonrational, countering the dominance of rational materialism by drawing out the internal tensions and overlaps in archaic myth. Woolf expresses this paratactic aesthetic, the refusal to settle meaning in the text, in Isa's response to the question of whether people are essentially the same or different, "Yes, No. Yes, yes, yes, the tide rushed out embracing. No, no, no, it contracted" (*BTA*, 146).

Woolf's paratactic allusions to myth shift us away from the appearance of monolithic unity and toward a recognition of the richness and diversity of human experience and of our culturally received stories.[28] By splintering and reconstituting the human body in new patterns, La Trobe's mirror trick at the end of her pageant manifests a new vision. The choral passages that follow this moment demonstrate the shift in the audience members' consciousness effected by this liminal moment. The disruptive quality of the mirror trick follows a transition from a waltz to cacophonous music that "snapped; broke; jagged" (*BTA*, 124). The waltz suggests the unifying, whole-making tendency characteristic of fascism, "barred" as it is by temple martins, birds that signal conflict, fascist containment, and the drive to mechanistic unification. The martins "prevented what was fluid from overflowing," and "seemed to foretell" a mechanistic utopian promise: "Homes will be built. Each flat with its own refrigerator, in the crannied wall. Each of us a free man; plates washed

---

27. On Woolf's interest in the "*dis*orderly potential" of allusion, see Cuddy-Keane, Introduction to *Between the Acts*, viii.

28. On Woolf's use of the fragment to reveal new ways of seeing, see Cuddy-Keane, "Politics of Comic Modes," 283.

by machinery; not an aeroplane to vex us; all liberated; *made whole*" (124, emphasis mine). The shift from this traditional European—more specifically, Germanic and Austrian—music to contemporary cacophonous music suggestive of the Fox Trot and Jazz signals for LaTrobe's audience what they take to be her irreverent "game," to "disrupt . . . jog and trot . . . jerk and smirk . . . shiver into splinters the old vision; smash to atoms what was whole" (124). Set to this soundtrack, the "riff-raff . . . imps—elves—demons" appear holding any object bright enough to reflect the audience "as we are, here and now" (126). What they reflect is at first a shifting kaleidoscope as the audience's original unities of selves split into fragmented body parts and clothing, "Here a nose . . . There a skirt . . . Then trousers only . . . Now perhaps a face . . . Ourselves? But that's cruel" (125, ellipses in original). This fragments the unity of each discrete body and the blurred distinction between bodies reappears when the cows and dogs join in with "the jangle and the din, . . . and the barriers which should divide Man the Master from the Brute were dissolved" (125). Woolf suggests it again in the characters' random declamation of "some phrase or fragment from their parts" in the pageant, disordering the formerly linear presentation of English history (125).

By assaulting the audience in these ways, shaking loose the former logic of wholeness, La Trobe achieves a new vision of truth, however unsustainable, through fragmentation. And this moment of truthful seeing changes the audience's relation to the world, to themselves, and to language, at least temporarily. When Reverend Streatfield mounts the soapbox to decode the message of the pageant for them, the audience gazes at him; the narrator, perhaps speaking their collective thoughts, describes this village authority as "an intolerable constriction, contraction, and reduction to simplified absurdity" (*BTA*, 129). Woolf links this constricted feeling to language itself when the narrator steals the Reverend's religious language to invoke protection against it, proclaiming, "O Lord, protect and preserve us from words the defilers, from words the impure! What need have we of words to remind us? Must I be Thomas, you Jane?" (129). Against Streatfield's authoritative patriarchal message reminding them of the proper order of things, the audience demands an escape from the sexually generic Thomas and Jane, conventional linguistic and cultural designations, to remain diffuse in their identities. In short, under La Trobe's influence, they reject Streatfield's syntactic, or even hypotactic, construction of language and demand paratactic openness.

While Streatfield declares the meaning of the pageant to be the unity of the audience, that "each is part of the whole . . . we act different parts; but are the same" (*BTA*, 130), La Trobe has been clear to refuse such interpretive closure, vacillating between approbation and criticism of the crowd, who are simultaneously deplorable "orts, scraps, and fragments" and, in their moments of kindness and integrity, more than that (127–28). This shift can be felt in the return, after La Trobe's speech, to "Bach, Handel, Beethoven, Mozart or nobody famous, but merely a traditional tune" (128). While her initial transition from the waltz to the cacophony of the Fox Trot or Jazz seem to suggest a definitive message of disruption, her return to Germanic traditional music, especially after her dictatorial speech over the megaphone, resists such neat interpretation. This refusal to unify meaning infects the audience as well, which both diverges and draws together, controlled not by "the melody of surface sound alone . . . but also the warring battle-plumed warriors straining asunder: To part? No. . . . they crashed; solved; united" (128).

These musical alterations frame the mirror trick as a sacred and liminal experience, separate from ordinary reality. Like any ritual, this one effects a shift in perception. The role of music and later the fragmented choral structure in the creation of the sacred space indicate the potential of art to both promote and counteract fascism. Accordingly, Woolf does not advocate melody, the "surface sound alone," since the straining warriors beneath, pulling apart and together, suggest the harmony of the collective mind consisting of multiple unique parts in relation. The parting message of the gramophone reiterates the emphasis on harmony over the "simplified absurdity" of melody. The gramophone is "affirming in tones . . . triumphant yet valedictory: *Dispersed are we; who have come together. But,* the gramophone asserted, *let us retain whatever made that harmony*" (BTA, 133, emphasis in original). Instead of disbanding into solipsistic visions of individual melodies, an equally constricting and artificial image of the self, the gramophone urges the villagers to "keep together . . . in company," maintaining community without the appeal to sameness (133).

For Woolf, poetic drama is the genre that encourages this multivocal community through collaboration between playwright, actor, and audience. She argues in "Poetry, Fiction, and the Future" (later published by Leonard as "The Narrow Bridge of Art") that the genre is uniquely suited to the modern "atmosphere of doubt and conflict" in which "all bonds of union seem broken, yet some control must exist" (430). Woolf recreates the atmosphere she describes in this essay in *Between the Acts,* and she partly conceived of *Between the Acts* as a play, writing in her diary that "Pointz Hall [was] to become in the end a play" (May 9, 1938: *Diary* 5, 139). Writing about fifth-century Greek tragedy in her 1925 essay, "On Not Knowing Greek," Woolf stated that "to grasp the meaning of the play the chorus is of the utmost importance (46)."[29] Novelists lack this tool and so "are always devising some substitute for it" (46).

---

29. Page references are to the 1984 edition.

Since *Jacob's Room*, Woolf had invented ways to disrupt the novel's structure with substitutes for the tragic chorus. When writing *Mrs. Dalloway*, Woolf tried to incorporate the chorus, and on February 26, 1923, she wondered, "Could not the scenes be divided like acts of a play into five, say, or six?" ("Hours," 420). While Woolf eventually felt that her efforts with the chorus in that novel were not working, she continued experimenting with the form in later novels. In *Between the Acts*, her novel-play, Woolf adapts the tragic chorus as a means of expressing the shift in consciousness that La Trobe's pageant effects. The choral passages that follow La Trobe's mirror trick embody a harmonious image of collectivity characterized by disjointed fragments, counteracting Streatfield's "intolerable constriction, contraction, and reduction to simplified absurdity" (*BTA*, 129). Woolf's fragmentary version of the tragic chorus contributes to her larger undermining of fascistic thinking. In its merging of audience and stage character, by locating the audience both on and off stage, the novel resembles modern experimental theater by breaking the fourth wall, challenging the audience to critically examine themselves in the reflection.[30]

In Greek tragedy, the chorus effects this merging of the audience and the stage characters by representing the perspective of the audience on stage. Woolf's adaptation of the choral passage in *Between the Acts* moves it offstage; it arises out of the voices of the villagers and the novel thus mirrors the structure of experimental theater. Woolf's fragmentary choral passages, where a reader inspired by her essay on Greek tragedy might seek for the "meaning" of her novel, are paratactic, incorporating disconnected bits and pieces of political and social commentary, news and concerns, interspersed with gossip and formulaic daily chatter. At the end of the play, the audience discusses the need for "a centre. Something to bring us all together," a local family who has gone to Italy despite the war raging on the continent, whether the Christian faith can adapt itself to modern times, the lack of Church attendance, the way that the new science makes things more spiritual, the threat of war overhead in the form of low-flying airplanes, the unconscious, sex and savages, and the effects of technology and modern machinery on human culture (*BTA*, 134–36). This appears over the course of three pages with interruptions about the cars people drive, what shoes are made of, the weather, and salutations.

These seemingly random fragments, spliced up and reconstructed, form a new kaleidoscopic pattern that frustrates and disrupts logical consistency, exemplifying Woolf's paratactic method more intensely than nearly any of its other manifestations that we have examined. This endlessly changing structure continues Woolf's portrayal of thought throughout her fiction as

---

30. See Cuddy-Keane, Introduction to *Between the Acts*, lxi.

nonlinear and antisystematic. Here, she extends her treatment of decentered thought in novels like *Mrs. Dalloway,* going beyond the minds of individuals to demonstrate the disruptive quality of collective thought. This shift from the individual to the collective allows her to build on her critique of Western conceptions of knowledge and thinking to reimagine collectivity in ways other than fascistic idealizations of unity and order.

By refusing to use allusion as an ordering device, emphasizing instead its disordering, disruptive power, Woolf resists fascism and the structures of thought and perception that give rise to it. Her paratactic adaptation of ancient Greek material in *Between the Acts*—both archaic goddess imagery and the tragic chorus—is her final, and I believe most extreme, attempt to counteract rational materialist structures of thought that flatten the world. Yet, she counters exclusionary politics most effectively by combining this impulse to criticize and undo false unities with an optimistic, if fragile, vision of harmonious community, drawing strength from her liminal perspective, neither wholly supportive nor wholly critical of society. Her paratactic mythic method becomes one of her most powerful tools in this effort.

As I argue in the introduction, the mythic material that Woolf draws on—archaic, pre-Olympian myth—is inherently paratactic in both content and aesthetic. Dionysus, Persephone, Artemis, and the Sirens, the mythic figures that feature prominently in her novels, all embody simultaneously irreconcilable qualities. Harrison's influence on and compatibility with Woolf's interpretation of myth may be felt both in Woolf's preference for archaic traditions and in her emphasis on their paradoxical aspects. Her treatment of the Great Goddess in *To the Lighthouse* and of an Eleusinian community of women in *Mrs. Dalloway* draw attention to the attractions and difficulties of translating archaic values to the modern world. Whether through Septimus's Dionysian experiences or Peter Walsh's mythic visions of women, she avoids the temptation to idealize the delirious pleasures of leaving behind the confines of reason, acknowledging both the liberatory and destructive sides of the mythic. While Woolf often shows us the dangers of a romantic, antirational return to the mythic and the ways it may be absorbed into the very structures of rational modernity, she does offer a tentatively hopeful alternative. In Lily's hard-won inspiration, forged through tension with a myth-infused Mrs. Ramsay, and in La Trobe's creation of a potential harmonious community of *Between the Acts,* Woolf offers a vision of myth's potential to resist the hegemonic forces of rational modernity.

BIBLIOGRAPHY

Abel, Elizabeth. "Narrative Structure(s) and Female Development: The Case of Mrs. Dalloway." In *The Voyage In: Fictions of Female Development,* edited by Elizabeth Abel, Marianne Hirsch, and Elizabeth Langland, 161–85. Hanover, NH: University Press of New England, 1983.

———. *Virginia Woolf and the Frontiers of Psychoanalysis.* Chicago: University of Chicago Press, 1989.

Allan, Tuzyline. "The Death of Sex and the Soul in *Mrs. Dalloway* and Nella Larsen's *Passing.*" In *Virginia Woolf: Lesbian Readings,* edited by Eileen Barrett and Patricia Cramer, 167–95. New York: New York University Press, 1997.

Altieri, Charles. "Afterword: How the 'New Modernist Studies' Fails the Old Modernism." *Textual Practice* 26, no. 4 (2012): 763–82.

Athanassakis, Apostolos N., ed. and trans. "Homeric *Hymn to Aphrodite.*" In *The Homeric Hymns,* 47–55. Baltimore: Johns Hopkins University Press, 1976.

Auerbach, Erich. *Mimesis: The Representation of Reality in Western Literature.* Translated by Willard Trask. Princeton: Princeton University Press, 1953. Originally published in 1946 by Verlag.

Auerbach, Nina. *Woman and the Demon: The Life of a Victorian Myth.* Cambridge, MA: Harvard University Press, 1982.

Bachofen, J. J. *Das Mutterrecht: Eine Untersuchung über die Gynaikokratie der alten Welt nach Ihrer Religiösen und Rechtlichen Natur.* Stuttgart: Krais and Hoffmann, 1861.

———. *Myth, Religion, and Mother Right: Selected Writings of J. J. Bachofen.* Translated by Ralph Manheim. Bollingen Series 84. Princeton: Princeton University Press, 1967.

Bagley, Melissa. "Nature and the Nation in *Mrs. Dalloway.*" *Woolf Studies Annual* 14 (2008): 35–51.

Baldanza, Frank. "Clarissa Dalloway's 'Party Consciousness.'" *Modern Fiction Studies* 2, no. 1 (Feb. 1956): 24–30.

Banfield, Ann. *The Phantom Table: Woolf, Fry, Russell and the Epistemology of Modernism.* Cambridge and New York: Cambridge University Press, 2000.

Barr, Tina. "Divine Politics: Virginia Woolf's Journey toward Eleusis in *To the Lighthouse.*" *boundary 2: An International Journal of Literature and Culture* 20, no. 1 (Spring 1993): 125–45.

Barrett, Eileen. "Matriarchal Myth on a Patriarchal Stage: Virginia Woolf's *Between the Acts.*" *Twentieth Century Literature* 33, no. 1 (Spring 1987): 18–37.

———. "Septimus and Shadrack: Woolf and Morrison Envision the Madness of War." In *Virginia Woolf: Emerging Perspectives: Selected Papers from the Third Annual Conference on Virginia Woolf,* edited by Mark Hussey and Vara Neverow-Turk, 26–31. New York, Pace University Press, 1994.

———. "Unmasking Lesbian Passion: The Inverted World of *Mrs. Dalloway.*" In *Virginia Woolf: Lesbian Readings,* edited by Eileen Barrett and Patricia Cramer, 146–64. New York: New York University Press, 1997.

Baudelaire, Charles. "A Une Passante." In *Les Fleurs Du Mal.* Introduction by Théophile Gautier. Paris: Michel Levy Freres, 1968.

Baumann, Zygmunt. *Modernity and the Holocaust.* Ithaca: Cornell University Press, 1989.

Beck, Warren. "For Virginia Woolf." In *Forms of Modern Fiction,* edited by William Van O'Connor, 243–53. Minneapolis: University of Minnesota Press, 1948.

Beer, Gillian. *Virginia Woolf: The Common Ground.* Ann Arbor: University of Michigan Press, 1996.

———. *Wave, Atom, Dinosaur: Woolf's Science.* London: Virginia Woolf Society of Great Britain, 2000.

Bell, Michael. *Literature, Modernism and Myth: Belief and Responsibility in the Twentieth Century.* Cambridge: Cambridge University Press, 1997.

Bennett, Paula. "Critical Clitoridectomy: Female Sexual Imagery and Feminist Psychoanalytic Theory." *Signs* 18, no. 2 (Winter 1993): 235–59.

Benziman, Galia. "'Dispersed Are We': Mirroring and National Identity in Virginia Woolf's *Between the Acts.*" *Journal of Narrative Theory* 36, no. 1 (Winter 2006): 53–71.

Bishop, Edward L. "Mind the Gap: The Spaces in *Jacob's Room.*" In *Woolf Studies Annual* 10 (2004): 31–49.

———. "The Subject in Jacob's Room." *Modern Fiction Studies* 38, no. 1 (Spring 1992): 147–75.

Blodgett, Harriet. "The Nature of *Between the Acts.*" *Modern Language Studies* 13, no. 3 (Summer 1983): 27–37.

Blotner, Joseph. "Mythic Patterns in *To the Lighthouse.*" *PMLA* 71 (1956): 547–62. Reprinted in *Myth and Literature: Contemporary Theory and Practice,* edited by John Vickery, 243–56. Lincoln: University of Nebraska Press, 1966.

Bowlby, Rachel. *Feminist Destinations and Further Essays on Virginia Woolf.* Edinburgh: Edinburgh University Press, 1997.

Burrow, J. W. *The Crisis of Reason: European Thought, 1848–1914.* New Haven and London: Yale University Press, 2000.

Callan, Stephanie. "Exploring the Confluence of Primitive Ritual and Modern Longing in *Between the Acts.*" In *Woolf and the Art of Exploration: Selected Papers from the 15th International Conference on Virginia Woolf,* edited by Helen Southworth and Elisa Sparks, 225–31. Clemson, SC: Clemson University Digital Press, 2006.

Camarasana, Linda. "Trespassing the Nation: A Queer Reading of *Between the Acts.*" *Virginia Woolf Miscellany* 82 (Fall 2012): 9–11.

Carpentier, Martha C. *Ritual, Myth, and the Modernist Text: The Influence of Jane Ellen Harrison on Joyce, Eliot, and Woolf.* Amsterdam: Gordon and Breach, 1998.

Carr, Jamie. "Novel Possibilities: Re-Reading Sexuality and 'Madness' in *Mrs. Dalloway,* Beyond the Film." In *Virginia Woolf Out of Bounds: Selected Papers from the Tenth Annual Conference on Virginia Woolf,* edited by Jessica Berman and Jane Goldman, 19–25. New York: Pace University Press, 2001.

Carroll, Berenice. "'To Crush Him in Our Own Country': The Political Thought of Virginia Woolf." *Feminist Studies* 4, no. 1 (Feb. 1978): 99–132.

Caughie, Pamela L. *Virginia Woolf & Postmodernism: Literature in Quest & Question of Itself.* Urbana & Chicago: University of Illinois Press, 1991.

Cheng, Yuan-Jung. *Heralds of the Postmodern: Madness and Fiction in Conrad, Woolf, and Lessing.* New York: Peter Lang, 1999.

Clader, Linda Lee. *Helen: The Evolution from Divine to Heroic in Greek Epic Tradition.* Netherlands: Brill, 1976.

Cohen, Scott. "The Empire from the Street: Virginia Woolf, Wembley, and Imperial Monuments." *Modern Fiction Studies* 50, no. 1 (Spring 2004): 85–109.

Connelly, Frances S. *The Sleep of Reason: Primitivism in Modern European Art and Aesthetics, 1725–1907.* University Park: Pennsylvania State University Press, 1995.

Corsa, Helen. "*To The Lighthouse:* Death, Mourning, and Transfiguration." *Literature and Psychology* 21, no. 3 (1971): 115–31.

Cramer, Patricia. "Notes from Underground: Lesbian Ritual in the Writings of Virginia Woolf." In *Virginia Woolf Miscellanies: Proceedings of the First Annual Conference on Virginia Woolf,* edited by Mark Hussey and Vara Neverow-Turk, 177–88. New York: Pace University Press, 1992.

———. "Virginia Woolf's Matriarchal Family of Origins in *Between the Acts.*" *Twentieth Century Literature* 39, no. 2 (Summer 1993): 166–84.

Cramer, Patricia Morgne. "Virginia Woolf and Sexuality." In *The Cambridge Companion to Virginia Woolf.* 2nd ed, edited by Susan Sellers, 180–96. Cambridge: Cambridge University Press, 2010.

Crawford, Nicholas. "Orientalizing Elizabeth: Empire and Deviancy in *Mrs. Dalloway.*" *Virginia Woolf Miscellany* 70 (Fall 2006): 20 and 25–26.

Cuddy-Keane, Melba. Annotation to *Between the Acts,* by Virginia Woolf, xxxv–lxvi. Introduction and annotation by Melba Cuddy-Keane. Orlando: Harcourt, 2008.

———. Introduction to *Between the Acts,* by Virginia Woolf, xxxv–lxvi. Introduction and annotation by Melba Cuddy-Keane. Orlando: Harcourt, 2008.

———. "The Politics of Comic Modes in Virginia Woolf's *Between the Acts.*" *PMLA* 105 (Mar. 1990): 273–85.

Dalgarno, Emily. *Virginia Woolf and the Migrations of Language.* Cambridge and New York: Cambridge University Press, 2012.

———. *Virginia Woolf and the Visible World.* Cambridge and New York: Cambridge University Press, 2001.

Daniélou, Alain. *Shiva and Dionysus.* Translated by K. F. Hurry. London and the Hague: East-West Publications, 1982.

Dashu, Max. "Knocking Down Straw Dolls: A Critique of Cynthia Eller's *The Myth of Matriarchal Prehistory: Why an Invented Past Won't Give Women a Future.* The Suppressed History Archives. Last modified 2000. Accessed March 22, 2013. http://www.suppressedhistories.net/articles/eller.html. Republished in *Feminist Theology* 13, no. 2 (2005): 185–216.

Daugherty, Beth Rigel. "'There She Sat': The Power of the Feminist Imagination in *To the Lighthouse*." *Twentieth Century Literature* 37, no. 3 (Autumn 1991): 289–308.

de Lauretis, Teresa. *The Practice of Love: Lesbian Sexuality and Perverse Desire*. Bloomington and Indianapolis: Indiana University Press, 1994.

DeMeester, Karen. "Trauma, Post-Traumatic Stress Disorder, and Obstacles to Postwar Recovery in *Mrs. Dalloway*." In *Virginia Woolf and Trauma: Embodied Texts*, edited by Suzette Henke and David Eberly, 77–94. New York: Pace University Press, 2007.

Detloff, Madelyn. *The Persistence of Modernism: Loss and Mourning in the Twentieth Century*. Cambridge: Cambridge University Press, 2009.

Dodds, E. R. *The Greeks and the Irrational*. 1951. Reprint, Berkeley: University of California Press, 2004.

Douglas, Erin. "Queering Flowers, Queering Pleasures in 'Slater's Pins Have No Points.'" *Virginia Woolf Miscellany* 82 (Fall 2012): 13–15.

———. "'That was a terrible thing to do to a flower': Floral Pleasures and Changeable Bodies in Virginia Woolf's *Orlando* and Jeanette Winterson's *The PowerBook*." *Virginia Woolf Miscellany* 75 (Spring 2009): 13–15.

Dunlap, Sarah. "'One Must Be Scientific': Natural History and Ecology in *Mrs. Dalloway*." In *Interdisciplinary / Multidisciplinary Woolf: Selected Papers from the Twenty-Second Annual International Conference on Virginia Woolf*, edited by Kathryn Holland and Ann Martin, 127–31. Clemson, SC: Clemson University Digital Press, 2013.

Eisenberg, Nora. "Virginia Woolf's Last Words on Words: *Between the Acts* and 'Anon.'" In *New Feminist Essays on Virginia Woolf*, edited by Jane Marcus, 253–66. Lincoln: University of Nebraska Press, 1981.

Eisler, Riane. *The Chalice and the Blade: Our History, Our Future*. San Francisco: Harper Collins, 1987.

Elderkin, G. W. "The Bee of Artemis." *American Journal of Philology* 60, no. 2. (1939): 203–13.

Eliot, T. S. "Ulysses, Order, and Myth." *Dial* 75, no. 5 (Nov. 1923): 480–83.

———. "The Waste Land." In *The Waste Land and Other Writings*, 38–56. New York: Modern Library, 2002. Originally published in 1922.

Eller, Cynthia. *Gentlemen and Amazons: The Myth of Matriarchal Prehistory, 1861–1900*. Berkeley and Los Angeles: University of California Press, 2011.

———. *The Myth of Matriarchal Prehistory: Why an Invented Past Won't Give Women a Future*. Boston: Beacon Press, 2000.

Ellis, Steve. *British Writers and the Approach of World War II*. Cambridge and New York: Cambridge University Press, 2015.

———. *Virginia Woolf and the Victorians*. Cambridge and New York: Cambridge University Press, 2007.

Ellwood, Robert. *The Politics of Myth: A Study of C. G. Jung, Mircea Eliade, and Joseph Campbell*. Albany: State University of New York Press, 1999.

Engels, Frederick. *The Origin of the Family, Private Property, and the State*. Translated by Ernest Untermann. Chicago: Charles H. Kerr & Company, 1902. Originally published in 1884 and revised to the 4th edition in 1891.

Esty, Jed. *A Shrinking Island: Modernism and National Culture in England*. Princeton: Princeton University Press, 2004.

Eysteinnson, Astradur. *The Concept of Modernism*. Ithaca: Cornell University Press, 1990.

Felson, Nancy. *Regarding Penelope: From Character to Poetics*. Norman: University of Oklahoma Press, 1994.

Fernald, Anne, ed. *Mrs. Dalloway* by Virginia Woolf. The Cambridge Edition of the Works of Virginia Woolf. Cambridge: Cambridge University Press, 2015.

———. "*To the Lighthouse* in the Context of Woolf's Diaries and Life." In *The Cambridge Companion to* To the Lighthouse, edited by Allison Pease, 6–18. Cambridge: Cambridge University Press, 2014.

———. *Virginia Woolf: Feminism and the Reader*. New York: Palgrave Macmillan, 2006.

Flam, Jack and Miriam Deutch, eds. *Primitivism and Twentieth-Century Art: A Documentary History*. Berkeley: University of California Press, 2003.

Foley, Helene P., ed. *The Homeric* Hymn to Demeter: *Translation, Commentary, and Interpretive Essays*. Princeton: Princeton University Press, 1994.

Forbes, Shannon. "'When Sometimes She Imagined Herself Like Her Mother': The Contrasting Responses of Cam and Mrs. Ramsay to the Role of the Angel in the House." *Studies in the Novel* 32, no. 4 (Winter 2000): 464–87.

Foster, J. Ashley. "Writing in the 'White Light of Truth': History, Ethics, and Community in Virginia Woolf's *Between the Acts*." *Woolf Studies Annual* 22 (2016): 41–74.

Foucault, Michel. *Madness and Civilization: A History of Insanity in the Age of Reason*. Translated by Richard Howard. New York: Random House, 1965.

Fowler, Rowena. "Moments and Metamorphoses: Virginia Woolf's Greece." *Comparative Literature* 51, no. 3 (Summer 1999): 217–42.

Franks, Matt. "Mrs. Ramsay's Queer Generationality." *Virginia Woolf Miscellany* 82 (2012): 15–17.

Frazer, Sir James George. *The Golden Bough Part III: The Dying God*. 3rd ed. 1913. Reprint, London: Macmillan, 1980.

Freedman, Ralph. "The Form of Fact and Fiction: *Jacob's Room* as Paradigm." In *Virginia Woolf: Revaluation and Continuity*, edited by Ralph Freedman, 123–40. Berkeley: University of California Press, 1980.

Freud, Sigmund. *Three Essays on the Theory of Sexuality*. Rev'd ed. New York: Basic Books, 2000.

Friedman, Susan Stanford. "Definitional Excursions: The Meaning of Modern/Modernity/Modernism." *Modernism/modernity* 8, no. 3 (Sept. 2001): 493–513.

———. "Lyric Subversion of Narrative in Women's Writing: Virginia Woolf and the Tyranny of Plot." In *Reading Narrative: Form, Ethics, Ideology*, edited by James Phelan, 162–85. Columbus: The Ohio State University Press, 1989.

Froula, Christine. *Virginia Woolf and the Bloomsbury Avant-Garde: War, Civilization, Modernity*. New York: Columbia University Press, 2005.

Gaipa, Mark. "An Agnostic Daughter's Apology: Materialism, Spiritualism, and Ancestry in Woolf's *To the Lighthouse*." *Journal of Modern Literature* 26, no. 2 (Winter 2002–3): 1–41.

Gerhard, Eduard. *Greichische Mythologie*. Berlin: Reimer, 1854.

Gerzina, Gretchen Holbrook. "Bloomsbury and Empire." In *The Cambridge Companion to the Bloomsbury Group*, edited by Victoria Rosner, 112–28. Cambridge Companions to Literature. Cambridge: Cambridge University Press, 2014.

———. "Bushmen and Blackface: Bloomsbury and 'Race.'" *The South Carolina Review* 38, no. 2 (Spring 2006): 46–64.

Gilman, Sander. *Difference and Pathology: Stereotypes of Sexuality, Race, and Madness*. Ithaca and London: Cornell University Press, 1985.

Golden, Amanda. "Textbook Greek: Thoby Stephen in *Jacob's Room*." *Woolf Studies Annual* 23 (2017): 83–108.

Goldman, Jane. *The Feminist Aesthetics of Virginia Woolf: Modernism, Post-Impressionism, and the Politics of the Visual*. Cambridge: Cambridge University Press, 1998.

———. "Following Bradshaw and Bishop into *Jacob's Room*: British and Canadian Editing Strategies (Tunnelling the Textual Hotspots, Minding the Gaps)." *Feminist Modernist Studies* 3, no. 1 (2020): 32–50.

Goldwater, Robert. *Primitivism in Modern Art*. 1938. Enlarged ed. Cambridge, MA: Harvard University Press, 1986.

Gourd, Elizabeth. "Whose Idea of Tragedy? *Mrs. Dalloway* and the Ancient Greek Tradition." In *Virginia Woolf and Heritage: Selected Papers from the Twenty-Sixth Annual International Conference on Virginia Woolf*, edited by Jane DeGay, Tom Breckin, and Anne Reus, 96–101. Clemson, SC: Clemson University Press, 2017.

Gramsci, Antonio. *Prison Notebooks*. Vol. 1. Edited and with an introduction by Joseph A. Buttigieg. New York: Columbia University Press, 2011.

Gronow, Jukka. "The Element of Irrationality: Max Weber's Diagnosis of Modern Culture." *Acta Sociologica* 31, no. 4 (1988): 319–31.

Groover, Kristina. "Body and Soul: Virginia Woolf's *To the Lighthouse*." *Renascence: Essays on Values in Literature* 66, no. 3 (Summer 2014): 217–29.

———. "A God 'in Process of Change': Woolfian Theology and *Mrs. Dalloway*." In *Religion, Secularism, and the Spiritual Paths of Virginia Woolf*, edited by Kristina K. Groover, 33–50. Cham, Switzerland: Palgrave Macmillan, 2019.

Guth, Deborah. "Virginia Woolf: Myth and *To the Lighthouse*." *College Literature* 11, no. 3 (Fall 1984): 233–49.

Habermas, Jürgen. "The Entwinement of Myth and Enlightenment: Max Horkheimer and Theodor Adorno." In *The Philosophical Discourse of Modernity: Twelve Essays*, translated by Frederick G. Lawrence, 106–30. Cambridge, MA: MIT Press, 1990.

Hackett, Robin. *Sapphic Primitivism: Productions of Race, Class, and Sexuality in Key Works of Modern Fiction*. New Brunswick, NJ: Rutgers University Press, 2004.

Hagen, Ben. "A Car, A Plane, and a Tower: Interrogating Public Images in *Mrs. Dalloway*." *Modernism/Modernity* 16, no. 3 (Sept. 2009): 537–51.

Hale, Constance. *Sin and Syntax: How to Craft Wicked Good Prose*. New York: Broadway Books, 1999.

Haller, Evelyn. "Isis Unveiled: Virginia Woolf's Use of Egyptian Myth." In *Virginia Woolf: A Feminist Slant*, edited by Jane Marcus, 109–31. Lincoln: University of Nebraska Press, 1983.

Harmon, William. "T. S. Eliot, Anthropologist and Primitive." *American Anthropologist* 78, no. 4 (Dec. 1976): 797–811.

Harrison, Jane Ellen. *Aspects, Aorists, and the Classical Tripos*. Cambridge: Cambridge University Press, 1919.

———. *Mythology*. 1924. Reprint, Whitehead, MT: Kessinger, 2007.

———. *Prolegomena to the Study of Greek Religion*. Mythos Series. 1903. Reprint, Princeton: Princeton University Press, 1991.

———. *Themis: A Study of the Origins of Greek Religion*. Cambridge: Cambridge University Press, 1912.

Harrison, Peter. *The Territories of Science and Religion*. Chicago: University of Chicago Press, 2015.

Henderson, Diana E. *Collaborations with the Past: Reshaping Shakespeare Across Time and Media*. Ithaca: Cornell University Press, 2006.

Heney, Alison. "Kandinsky's 'On the Problem of Form' and the Fiction of Virginia Woolf." *Virginia Woolf Miscellany* 80 (Fall 2011): 18–19.

Henke, Suzette. "Modernism, Trauma, and Narrative Reformulation." In *Gender in Modernism: New Geographies, Complex Intersections*, edited by Bonnie Kime Scott, 555–87. Urbana: University of Illinois Press, 2007.

———. "'Mrs. Dalloway': The Communion of Saints." In *New Feminist Essays on Virginia Woolf*, edited by Jane Marcus, 125–46. Lincoln: University of Nebraska Press, 1981.

———. *Virginia Woolf and Madness: Trauma Narrative in* Mrs. Dalloway. The Virginia Clark Memorial Lecture. London: South Place Ethical Society, 2010.

Hinnov, Emily. "'Each is part of the whole: We act different parts; but are the same': From Fragment to Choran Community in the Late Work of Virginia Woolf." *Woolf Studies Annual* 13 (2007): 1–23.

Hirsch, Marianne. *The Mother / Daughter Plot: Narrative, Psychoanalysis, Feminism*. Bloomington: Indiana University Press, 1989.

Hite, Molly. *Woolf's Ambiguities: Tonal Modernism, Narrative Strategy, Feminist Precursors*. Ithaca: Cornell University Press, 2017.

Ho, Janice. *Nation and Citizenship in the Twentieth-Century British Novel*. Cambridge and New York: Cambridge University Press, 2015.

Hoff, Molly. "Peter Walsh and Women's Mysteries." *Virginia Woolf Miscellany* 82 (Fall 2012): 22–23.

———. "The Pseudo-Homeric World of Mrs. Dalloway." *Twentieth-Century Literature* 45, no. 2 (Summer 1999): 186–209.

———. *Virginia Woolf's Mrs. Dalloway: Invisible Presences*. Clemson, SC: Clemson University Digital Press, 2009.

Hoffman, Anne G. "Demeter and Poseidon: Fusion and Distance in *To the Lighthouse*." *Studies in the Novel* 16, no. 2 (Summer 1984): 182–96.

Högberg, Elsa. *Virginia Woolf and the Ethics of Intimacy*. London and New York: Bloomsbury Academic, 2020.

Homer. *Odyssey*. Translated by Robert Fitzgerald. New York: Vintage-Random House, 1990.

Horacki, Michael. "Apollonian Illusion and Dionysian Truth." In *Interdisciplinary / Multidisciplinary Woolf: Selected Papers from the Twenty-Second Annual International Conference on Virginia Woolf*, edited by Kathryn Holland and Ann Martin, 138–42. Clemson, SC: Clemson University Digital Press, 2013.

Horkheimer, Max, and Theodor W. Adorno. *Dialectic of Enlightenment: Philosophical Fragments*, edited by Gunzelin Schmid Noerr. Translated by Edmund Jephcott. Stanford, CA: Stanford University Press, 2002. Originally published in 1947.

Houghton, Walter. *The Victorian Frame of Mind, 1830–1870*. New Haven and London: Yale University Press, 1957.

Hussey, Mark. *Virginia Woolf A–Z: A Comprehensive Reference for Students, Teachers, and Common Readers to Her Life, Work, and Critical Reception*. New York: Oxford University Press, 1995.

———, ed. *Virginia Woolf and War: Fiction, Reality and Myth*. Syracuse, NY: Syracuse University Press, 1991.

Huxley, T. H. "On The Physical Basis of Life." 1868 lecture. New Haven, CT: Yale College Courant, 1869.

Jacobs, Karen. *The Eye's Mind: Literary Modernism and Visual Culture*. Ithaca and London: Cornell University Press, 2001.

Johnson, Buffie. *Lady of the Beasts: The Goddess and Her Sacred Animals*. Rochester, VT: Inner Traditions International, 1994.

Jones, Christine Kenyon, and Anna Snaith. "'Tilting at Universities': Woolf at King's College London." *Woolf Studies Annual* 16 (2010): 1–44.

Jones, Clara. *Virginia Woolf: Ambivalent Activist*. Edinburgh: Edinburgh University Press, 2016.

Joplin, Patricia Klindeinst. "The Authority of Illusion: Feminism and Fascism in Virginia Woolf's *Between the Acts*." *South Central Review* 6, no. 2 (Summer 1989): 88–104.

Josephson-Storm, Jason A. *The Myth of Disenchantment: Magic, Modernity, and the Birth of the Human Sciences*. Chicago: University of Chicago Press, 2017.

Jung, C. G., and Carl Kerényi. *Essays on a Science of Mythology*. Translated by R. F. C. Hull. Bollingen Series 22. Rev'd ed. Princeton: Princeton University Press, 1969.

Kerényi, Carl. *Eleusis: Archetypal Image of Mother and Daughter*. Translated by Ralph Manheim. Bollingen Series 65, vol. 4. New York: Pantheon-Random House, 1967.

———. *The Gods of the Greeks*. Translated by Norman Cameron. London: Thames and Hudson, 1951.

———. *Zeus and Hera: Archetypal Image of Father, Husband, and Wife*. Translated by Christopher Holme. Bollingen Series 65, vol. 5. Princeton: Princeton University Press, 1975.

Kermode, Frank. *The Sense of an Ending: Studies in the Theory of Fiction with a New Epilogue*. Rev'd ed. Oxford: Oxford University Press, 2000.

King, Amy. *Bloom: The Botanical Vernacular in the English Novel*. Oxford: Oxford University Press, 2004.

Kołakowski, Leszek. *The Presence of Myth*. Translated by Adam Czerniawski. Chicago and London: University of Chicago Press, 1989. Originally published as *Obecność Mitu* (Paris: Institut Literaire, 1972).

Kostkowska, Justyna. "'Scissors and Silks,' 'Flowers and Trees,' and 'Geraniums Ruined by the War': Virginia Woolf's Ecological Critique of Science in *Mrs. Dalloway*." *Women's Studies* 33: 183–98.

Koulouris, Theodore. *Hellenism and Loss in the Work of Virginia Woolf*. Burlington, VT: Ashgate, 2010.

———. "Virginia Woolf's 'Greek Notebook' (VS Greek and Latin Studies) An Annotated Transcription." *Woolf Studies Annual* 25 (2019): 1–72.

Koutsoudaki, Mary. "The 'Greek' Jacob: Greece in Virginia Woolf's *Jacob's Room*." *Papers in Romance* 2, no. 1 (Jul. 1980): 67–75.

Lackey, Michael. "Modernist Anti-Philosophicalism and Virginia Woolf's Critique of Philosophy." *Journal of Modern Literature* 29, no. 4 (Summer 2006): 76–98.

———. "Virginia Woolf and T. S. Eliot: An Atheist's Commentary on the Epistemology of Belief." *Woolf Studies Annual* 8 (2002): 63–91.

Lambert, Elizabeth G. "Proportion Is in the Mind of the Beholder: *Mrs. Dalloway*'s Critique of Science." In *Virginia Woolf: Emerging Perspectives. Selected Papers from the Third Annual Conference on Virginia Woolf*, edited by Mark Hussey and Vara Neverow-Turk, 278–82. New York: Pace University Press, 1993.

Lanser, Susan Sniader. *Fictions of Authority: Women Writers and Narrative Voice*. Ithaca: Cornell University Press, 1992.

Laurence, Patricia. "A Writing Couple: Shared Ideology in Virginia Woolf's *Three Guineas* and Leonard Woolf's *Quack, Quack!*" In *Women in the Milieu of Leonard and Virginia Woolf: Peace, Politics, and Education*, edited by Wayne Chapman and Janet Manson, 125–43. New York: Pace University Press, 1998.

Leaska, Mitchell. Introduction and preface to *Pointz Hall: The Earlier and Later Typescripts*. New York: New York University Press, 1983.

Lee, Hermione. *Virginia Woolf*. New York: Knopf, 1997.

Lerner, Gerda. *The Creation of Patriarchy*. New York: Oxford University Press, 1986.

Levenback, Karen L. *Virginia Woolf and the Great War*. Syracuse, NY: Syracuse University Press, 1999.

Levinas, Emmanuel. *Totality and Infinity: An Essay on Exteriority*. Translated by Alphonso Lingis. Pittsburgh, PA: Duquesne University Press, 1969. Original published as *Totaite et Infini* (The Hague, Netherlands: Martinus Nijhoff, 1961).

Lilienfeld, Jane. "'The Deceptiveness of Beauty': Mother Love and Mother Hate in *To the Lighthouse*." *Twentieth Century Literature* 23, no. 3 (Oct. 1977): 345–76.

———. "'Like a Lion Seeking Whom He Could Devour': Domestic Violence in *To the Lighthouse*." In *Virginia Woolf Miscellanies: Proceedings of the First Annual Conference on Virginia Woolf*, edited by Mark Hussey and Vara Neverow-Turk, 154–63. New York: Pace University Press, 1992.

Lindberg, David C. *The Beginnings of Western Science: The European Scientific Tradition in Philosophical, Religious, and Institutional Context, Prehistory to A. D. 1450*. 2nd ed. Chicago: University of Chicago Press, 2018.

Little, Judy. "Festive Comedy in Woolf's *Between the Acts*." *Women and Literature* 5 (Spring 1977): 26–37.

Lloyd, Genevieve. *The Man of Reason: 'Male' and 'Female' in Western Philosophy*. York, UK: Methuen, 1984.

Love, Jean O. *Worlds in Consciousness: Mythopoetic Thought in the Novels of Virginia Woolf*. Berkeley: University of California Press, 1970.

Lovejoy, Arthur O., and George Boas. *A Documentary History of Primitivism and Related Ideas*. Baltimore: Johns Hopkins University Press, 1935.

Lukács, Georg. *Theory of the Novel*. Translated by Anna Bostrock. Cambridge, MA: MIT Press, 1971. Originally published as *Theorie des Romans* (Berlin: Cassirer, 1920).

Lusin, Caroline. "Red Flowers and a Shabby Coat: Russian Literature and the Presentation of 'Madness' in Virginia Woolf's *Mrs. Dalloway*." *Comparative Critical Studies* 5, nos. 2–3 (2008): 289–300.

Mahaffey, Vicki. *Modernist Literature: Challenging Fictions*. Malden, MA: Blackwell, 2007.

Maika, Patricia. "Alpha Not Omega: The Politics of Allusion in Virginia Woolf's *Between the Acts*." Master's thesis. Simon Fraser University, 1984.

———. *Virginia Woolf's* Between the Acts *and Jane Harrison's Con/spiracy*. London: UMI Research Press, 1987.

Mao, Douglas, and Rebecca Walkowitz, eds. *Bad Modernisms*. Durham, NC: Duke University Press, 2006.

———. "The New Modernist Studies." *PMLA* 123 (3) (May 2008): 737–48.

Marcus, Jane. *Art and Anger: Reading Like a Woman*. Columbus: The Ohio State University Press, 1988.

———. "Britannia Rules *The Waves*." In *Decolonizing Tradition: New Views of Twentieth-Century 'British' Literary Canon*, edited by Karen R. Lawrence, 36–62. Urbana: University of Illinois Press, 1992.

———. Introduction to *Three Guineas*, by Virginia Woolf. Introduction and annotation by Jane Marcus, xxxv–lxxii. Orlando: Harcourt, 2006.

———. "Liberty, Sorority, Misogyny." In *The Representation of Women in Fiction: Selected Papers from the English Institute, 1981*, edited by Carolyn Heilbrun and Margaret Higonnet, 60–97. Baltimore: John Hopkins University Press, 1983.

———. "Some Sources for *Between the Acts*." *Virginia Woolf Miscellany* 6 (Winter 1977): 1–3.

———. "Thinking Back through Our Mothers." In *New Feminist Essays on Virginia Woolf*, edited by Jane Marcus, 1–30. Lincoln: University of Nebraska Press, 1981.

———. *Virginia Woolf and the Languages of Patriarchy*. Bloomington: Indiana University Press, 1987.

McGee, Patrick. "The Politics of Modernist Form; or, Who Rules *The Waves*?" *Modern Fiction Studies* 38, no. 3 (1992): 631–50.

McIntire, Gabrielle. "Feminism and Gender in *To the Lighthouse*." In *The Cambridge Companion to* To the Lighthouse, edited by Allison Pease. Cambridge: Cambridge University Press, 2015.

———. *Modernism, Memory, and Desire: T. S. Eliot and Virginia Woolf*. Cambridge: Cambridge University Press, 2007.

McLennan, John Ferguson. *Primitive Marriage: An Inquiry into the Origin of the Form of Capture in Marriage Ceremonies*. Edinburgh: Adam and Charles Black, 1865.

McNaron, Toni. "'The Albanians, or Was It the Armenians?': Virginia Woolf's Lesbianism as Gloss on Her Modernism." In *Virginia Woolf: Themes and Variations: Selected Papers from the Second Annual Conference on Virginia Woolf*, edited by Vara Neverow-Turk and Mark Hussey, 134–41. New York: Pace University Press, 1993.

McVicker, Jeanette. "'Six Essays on London Life': A History of Dispersal Part I." *Woolf Studies Annual* 9 (2003): 143–65.

———. "Woolf in the Context of Fascism: Ideology, Hegemony and the Public Sphere." In *Virginia Woolf: Texts and Contexts. Selected Papers from the Fifth Annual International Conference on Virginia Woolf*, edited by Beth Rigel Daugherty and Eileen Barrett, 30–35. New York: Pace University Press, 1996.

Mercatante, Anthony S. *The Magic Garden: Myth and Folklore of Flowers, Plants, Trees, and Herbs*. New York: Harper & Row, 1976.

Mezei, Kathy. "Free Indirect Discourse, Gender, and Authority in *Emma, Howards End,* and *Mrs. Dalloway*." In *Ambiguous Discourse: Feminist Narratology and British Women Writers*, edited by Kathy Mezei, 66–92. Chapel Hill and London: University of North Carolina Press, 1996.

Mignolo, Walter. *The Darker Side of Western Modernity: Global Futures, Decolonial Options*. Latin America Otherwise, edited by Walter Mignolo, Irene Silverblatt, and Sonia Saldivar-Hull. Durham and London: Duke University Press, 2011.

Miller, Marlow A. "Unveiling 'The Dialectic of Culture and Barbarism' in British Pageantry: Virginia Woolf's *Between the Acts*." *Papers on Language and Literature: A Journal for Scholars and Critics of Language and Literature* 34, no. 2 (Spring 1998): 134–61.

Mills, Jean. *Virginia Woolf, Jane Ellen Harrison, and the Spirit of Modernist Classicism*. Columbus: The Ohio State University Press, 2014.

Minow-Pinkney, Makiko. *Virginia Woolf & the Problem of the Subject: Feminine Writing in the Major Novels*. Brighton, UK: Harvester, 1987.

Monte, Steven. "Ancients and Moderns in *Mrs. Dalloway*." *Modern Language Quarterly* 61, no. 3. December 2000: 587–616.

Moody, A. D. "*Mrs. Dalloway* as Comedy." In *Critics on Virginia Woolf*, edited by Jacqueline E. M. Latham, 48–51. Readings in Literary Criticism 8. Coral Gables, FL: University of Miami Press, 1970. Originally published in *Virginia Woolf* (Edinburg: Oliver and Boyd, 1963).

Moore, Madeline. *The Short Season between Two Silences: The Mystical and the Political in the Novels of Virginia Woolf*. Boston: George Allen and Unwin, 1984.

———. "Some Female Versions of Pastoral: *The Voyage Out* and Matriarchal Mythologies." In *New Feminist Essays on Virginia Woolf*, edited by Jane Marcus, 82–104. Lincoln: University of Nebraska Press, 1981.

Morretti, Franco. *Modern Epic: The World System from Goethe to Garcia Marquez*. Translated by Quintin Hoare. London and New York: Verso, 1996. Originally published in 1994.

Muñoz Simonds, Peggy. *Myth, Emblem, and Music in Shakespeare's* Cymbeline: *An Iconographic Reconstruction*. London and Toronto: Associated University Presses, 1992.

Naremore, James. *The World Without a Self: Virginia Woolf and the Novel*. New Haven: Yale University Press, 1973.

Neumann, Erich. *The Great Mother: An Analysis of the Archetype*. Translated by Ralph Manheim. Bollingen Series 47. 1955. Reprint. Princeton: Princeton University Press, 1972.

———. *The Origins and History of Consciousness*. 2 vols. Translated by R. F. C. Hull. Bollingen Series 42. 1954. Reprint. New York: Torchbook-Harper, 1962.

Neverow, Vara. Annotation to *Jacob's Room*, by Virginia Woolf, xxxvii–xciv. Introduction and annotation by Vara Neverow. Orlando: Harcourt, 2008.

———. Introduction to *Jacob's Room*, by Virginia Woolf, xxxvii–xciv. Introduction and annotation by Vara Neverow. Orlando: Harcourt, 2008.

———. "The Return of the Great Goddess: Immortal Virginity, Sexual Autonomy and Lesbian Possibility in *Jacob's Room*." *Woolf Studies Annual* 10 (2004): 203–31.

Nietzsche, Friedrich. *Ecce Homo and The Birth of Tragedy*. Translated by Clifton P. Fadiman. New York: Modern Library, 1927.

Nikopolous, James. "The Wisdom of Myth: Eliot's 'Ulysses, Order, and Myth.'" In *Brill's Companion to the Reception of Classics in International Modernism and the Avante-Garde*, edited by Adam J. Goldwyn and James Nikopoulos, 292–311. Leiden and Boston: Brill, 2017.

Norris, Nanette. *Modernist Myth: Studies in H. D., D. H. Lawrence, and Virginia Woolf*. Fergus, Ontario: Dreamridge, 2010.

Norton, Robert E. "The Myth of the Counter-Enlightenment." *Journal of the History of Ideas* 68, no. 4 (Oct. 2007): 635–38.

Olano, Pamela. "'Women alone stir my imagination': Reading Virginia Woolf as a Lesbian." In *Virginia Woolf: Themes and Variations: Selected Papers from the Second Annual Conference on Virginia Woolf*, edited by Vara Neverow-Turk and Mark Hussey, 158–71. New York: Pace University Press, 1993.

Otto, Walter F. *Dionysus: Myth and Cult*. Translated by Robert B. Palmer. Bloomington: Indiana University Press, 1965.

Panken, Shirley. *Virginia Woolf and the Lust of Creation: A Psychoanalytic Exploration*. Albany: SUNY Press, 1987.

Patea, Viorica. "T. S. Eliot's *The Waste Land* and the Poetics of the Mythical Method." In *Modernism Revisited: Transgressing Boundaries and Strategies of Renewal in American Poetry*, edited by Viorica Patea and Paul Scott Derrick. Amsterdam and New York: Rodopi, 2007.

Pawlowski, Merry, ed. *Virginia Woolf and Fascism: Resisting the Dictators' Seduction*. Basingstokes, UK: Palgrave, 2001.

Perloff, Marjorie. "The Aura of Modernism." *Modernist Cultures* 1, no. 1 (Summer 2005): 1–14.

Petersen, Kristen Holst, and Anna Rutherford, eds. *A Double Colonization: Colonial and Post-Colonial Women's Writing*. Oxford: Dangaroo Press, 1986.

Phillips, Kathy. *Dying Gods in Twentieth-Century Fiction*. Lewisburg: Bucknell University Press, 1990.

———. *Virginia Woolf against Empire*. Knoxville: University of Tennessee Press, 1994.

Pratt, Annis. "Sexual Imagery in *To the Lighthouse*: A New Feminist Approach." *Modern Fiction Studies* 18 (1972): 417–31.

Pratt, Mary Louise. *Imperial Eyes: Travel Writing and Transculturation.* London and New York: Routledge, 1992.

Pridmore-Brown, Michele. "1939–40: Of Virginia Woolf, Gramophones, and Fascism." *PMLA* 113, no. 3 (May 1998): 408–21.

Pringle, Mary Beth. "Killing the House of the Angel: Spatial Poetics in Woolf's *To the Lighthouse.*" In *Virginia Woolf: Emerging Perspectives,* edited by Mark Hussey and Vara Neverow, 306–12. New York: Pace University Press, 1994.

Prins, Yopie. *Ladies' Greek: Victorian Translations of Tragedy.* Princeton: Princeton University Press, 2017.

Prudente, Teresa. *A Specially Tender Piece of Eternity: Virginia Woolf and the Experience of Time.* Lanham, MD: Lexington Books, 2009.

Rankine, Patrice D. *Ulysses in Black: Ralph Ellison, Classicism, and African American Literature.* Madison and London: University of Wisconsin Press, 2006.

Raschke, Debrah. *Modernism, Metaphysics, and Sexuality.* Selinsgrove, PA: Susquehanna University Press, 2006.

Reid, Susan. "Killing the Angel in the House: Virginia Woolf, D. H. Lawrence, and the Boundaries of Sex and Gender." In *Woolfian Boundaries: Selected Papers from the Sixteenth Annual International Conference on Virginia Woolf,* edited by Anna Burrells, Steve Ellis, Deborah L. Parsons, and Kathryn Simpson, 65–71. Clemson, SC: Clemson University Digital Press, 2007.

Richter, Harvena. *Virginia Woolf: The Inward Voyage.* Princeton: Princeton University Press, 1970.

Ritzer, George. *The McDonaldization of Society: An Investigation into the Changing Character of Contemporary Social Life.* Newbury Park, CA: Pine Forge Press, 1993.

Robinson, Annabel. "Something Odd at Work: The Influence of Jane Harrison on *A Room of One's Own.*" *Wascana Review* 22 (1987): 82–88.

Roller, Lynn E. *In Search of God the Mother: The Cult of Anatolian Cybele.* Berkeley: University of California Press, 1999.

Ronchetti, Ann. *The Artist, Society, and Sexuality in Virginia Woolf's Novels.* New York: Routledge, 2004.

Roof, Judith. "The Match in the Crocus: Representations of Lesbian Sexuality." In *Discontent Discourses: Feminism/Textual Intervention/Psychoanalysis,* edited by Marleen S. Barr and Richard Feldstein, 100–116. Urbana: University of Illinois Press, 1989.

Rosenfeld, Natania. "Monstrous Conjugations: Images of Dictatorship in the Anti-Fascist Writings of Virginia and Leonard Woolf." In *Virginia Woolf and Fascism: Resisting the Dictator's Seduction,* edited by Merry M. Pawlowski, 122–38. Basingstokes, UK: Palgrave, 2001.

———. *Outsiders Together: Virginia and Leonard Woolf.* Princeton: Princeton University Press, 2001.

Rosenman, Ellen Bayuk. *The Invisible Presence: Virginia Woolf and the Mother-Daughter Relationship.* Baton Rouge: Louisiana State University Press, 1986.

Ruotolo, Lucio. "*Mrs. Dalloway*: The Unguarded Moment." In *Virginia Woolf, Revaluation and Continuity: A Collection of Essays,* edited by Ralph Freedman, 141–60. Berkeley: University of California Press, 1980.

Said, Edward. *Orientalism: Western Representations of the Orient.* London: Routledge & Kagan Paul. 1978.

Sautter-Léger, Sabine. "Railed in by a Maddening Reason: A Reconsideration of Septimus Smith and His Role in Virginia Woolf's *Mrs. Dalloway.*" *Papers on Language and Literature: A Journal for Scholars and Critics of Language and Literature* 53, no. 1 (Dec. 2017): 3–31.

Schlack, Beverly Ann. *Continuing Presences: Virginia Woolf's Use of Literary Allusion.* University Park and London: Pennsylvania State University Press, 1979.

Schroder, Leena Kore. "*Mrs. Dalloway* and the Female Vagrant." *Essays in Criticism* 45, no. 4 (Oct. 1995): 324–46.

Scott, Bonnie Kime. Annotation to *Mrs. Dalloway,* by Virginia Woolf, 191–218. Introduction and annotation by Bonnie Kime Scott. Orlando: Harcourt, 2005.

———, ed. *The Gender of Modernism: A Critical Anthology.* Bloomington: Indiana University Press, 1990.

———. *In the Hollow of the Wave: Virginia Woolf and Modernist Uses of Nature.* Charlottesville and London: University of Virginia Press, 2012.

Seaford, Richard. *Dionysos. Gods and Heroes of the Ancient World,* edited by Susan Deacy. London and New York: Routledge, 2006.

Sedon, Katherine. "Moments of Aging: Revising Mother Nature in Virginia Woolf's *Mrs. Dalloway.*" In *Virginia Woolf and the Natural World: Selected Papers from the Twentieth Annual International Conference on Virginia Woolf,* edited by Kristin Czarnecki and Carrie Rohman, 163–68. Clemson, SC: Clemson University Digital Press, 2011.

Seshagiri, Urmila. "Orienting Virginia Woolf: Race, Aesthetics, and Politics in *To the Lighthouse.*" *Modern Fiction Studies* 50, no. 1 (Spring 2004): 58–84.

Shattuck, Sandra. "The Stage of Scholarship: Crossing the Bridge from Harrison to Woolf." In *Virginia Woolf and Bloomsbury: A Centenary Celebration,* edited by Jane Marcus, 278–98. London: Palgrave Macmillan, 1987.

Showalter, Elaine. *The Female Malady: Women, Madness and English Culture, 1830–1980.* New York: Pantheon, 1985. Reprint, London: Virago, 1987.

Silver, Brenda. *Virginia Woolf's Reading Notebooks.* Princeton: Princeton University Press, 1983.

Simpson, Kathryn. "'Lappin and Lapinova': A Woolf in Hare's Clothing?" In *Virginia Woolf and the Natural World,* edited by Kristin Czarnecki and Carrie Rohman, 151–56. Liverpool: Liverpool University Press, 2011.

Sjoo, Monica, and Barbara Mor. *The Great Cosmic Mother: Rediscovering the Religion of the Earth.* San Francisco: Harper & Row, 1987.

Slater, Philip E. *The Glory of Hera: Greek Mythology and the Greek Family.* Boston: Beacon Press, 1968.

Smith, Amy C. "Bad Religion: The Irrational in *Mrs. Dalloway.*" *Virginia Woolf Miscellany* 70 (Fall 2006): 17–18.

———. "Loving Maidens and Patriarchal Mothers: Revisions of the Homeric *Hymn to Demeter* and *Cymbeline* in *Mrs. Dalloway.*" *Woolf Studies Annual* 17 (2011): 151–72.

———. "Primitive Women and Divine Colonials in *Mrs. Dalloway.*" *Lamar Journal of the Humanities* 35, no. 1 (2010): 29–37.

———. "Virginia Woolf Reads 'Dover Beach': Romance and the Crisis of Faith in *To the Lighthouse.*" In *Religion, Secularism, and the Spiritual Paths of Virginia Woolf,* edited by Kristina K. Groover, 69–85. Cham, Switzerland: Palgrave Macmillan, 2019.

Snaith, Anna. "Leonard and Virginia Woolf: Writing against Empire." *Journal of Commonwealth Literature* 50, no. 1 (Fall 2014): 19–32.

———. *Virginia Woolf: Public and Private Negotiations.* New York: Palgrave Macmillan, 2000.

Sparks, Elisa Kay. "'Everything tended to set itself in a garden': Virginia Woolf's Literary and Quotidian Flowers: A Bar-Graphical Approach." In *Virginia Woolf and the Natural World: Selected Papers from the Twentieth Annual International Conference on Virginia Woolf,* edited by Kristin Czarnecki and Carrie Rohman, 42–60. Clemson, SC: Clemson University Digital Press, 2011.

———. "'A Match Burning in a Crocus': Modernism, Feminism, and Feminine Experience in Virginia Woolf and Georgia O'Keeffe." In *Virginia Woolf: Emerging Perspectives: Selected Papers from the Third Annual Conference on Virginia Woolf,* edited by Mark Hussey and Vara Neverow-Turk, 296–302. New York: Pace University Press, 1994.

Spiropoulou. Angeliki. "'On Not Knowing Greek': Virginia Woolf's Spatial Critique of Authority." *Interdisciplinary Literary Studies: A Journal of Criticism and Theory* 4, no. 1 (Fall 2002): 1–19.

———. *Virginia Woolf, Modernity and History: Constellations with Walter Benjamin.* London: Palgrave Macmillan, 2010.

Stephen, Leslie. "A Bad Five Minutes in the Alps." *Essays on Freethinking and Plainspeaking,* 125–57. London: Longmans, Green & Co., 1873.

———. *Mausoleum Book.* Oxford: Clarendon Press, 1977.

Stewart, Jack. "Lawrence and Gauguin." *Twentieth-Century Literature* 26, no. 4 (Winter 1980): 385–401.

Stone, Merlin. *When God Was a Woman.* New York: Harcourt Brace Jovanovich, 1978.

Strachey, Lytton. *Eminent Victorians: Cardinal Manning, Florence Nightingale, Dr. Arnold, General Gordon.* New York: Capricorn Books, 1963.

Suh, Judy. "Woolf and the Gendering of Fascism." In *Virginia Woolf and Communities: Selected Papers from the Eighth Annual International Conference on Virginia Woolf,* edited by Jeanette McVicker, Laura Davis, and Georgia Johnston, 141–46. New York: Pace University Press, 1999.

Sullivan, Margaret. "Let There Be Rose Leaves: Lesbian Subjectivity and Religious Discourse in *The Waves.*" *Virginia Woolf Miscellany* 80 (Fall 2011): 8–9.

Suter, Ann. *The Narcissus and the Pomegranate: An Archaeology of the Homeric Hymn to Demeter.* Ann Arbor: University of Michigan Press, 2002.

Tambling, Jeremy. "Repression in Mrs. Dalloway's London." *Essays in Criticism* 39, no. 2 (Apr. 1989): 137–55.

Tate, Trudi. "Mrs. Dalloway and the Armenian Question." *Textual Practice* 8, no 3. (Winter 1994): 467–86.

Tindall, William York. "D. H. Lawrence and the Primitive." *Sewanee Review* 45, no. 2 (Apr.–Jun. 1937): 198–211.

Torgovnick, Marianna. *Gone Primitive: Savage Intellects, Modern Lives.* Chicago: University of Chicago Press, 1991.

Tromanhauser, Vicki. "Eating Well with the Ramsays: The Spirituality of Meat in *To the Lighthouse.*" *Virginia Woolf Miscellany* 80 (Fall 2011): 14–16.

Tyler, Lisa. "The Loss of Roses: Mother-Daughter Myth and Relationships between Women in *Mrs. Dalloway.*" *West Virginia University Philological Papers* 52 (2005): 60–69.

———. "Mother-Daughter Passion and Rapture: the Demeter Myth in the Fiction of Virginia Woolf and Doris Lessing." In *Woolf and Lessing: Breaking the Mold,* edited by Ruth Saxton and Jean Tobin, 73–91. New York: St. Martin's Press, 1994.

Vanita, Ruth. "Bringing Buried Things to Light: Homoerotic Alliances in *To the Lighthouse.*" In *Virginia Woolf: Lesbian Readings,* edited by Eileen Barrett and Patricia Cramer, 165–79. New York: New York University Press, 1997.

Vernant, Jean Pierre. *Mortals and Immortals: Collected Essays.* Edited by Froma I. Zeitlin. Princeton: Princeton University Press, 1991.

Versnel, H. S. *Inconsistencies in Greek and Roman Religion I: Ter Unus.* Leiden, The Netherlands: E. J. Brill, 1990.

Vickery, John. "Myth and Ritual in the Short Fiction of D. H. Lawrence." *Modern Fiction Studies* 5, no. 1 (Spring 1959): 65–82.

Viola, André. "'Buds on the Tree of Life': A Recurrent Mythological Image in Virginia Woolf's *Mrs. Dalloway.*" *Journal of Modern Literature* 20, no. 2 (Winter 1996): 239–47.

Von Hendy, Andrew. *The Modern Construction of Myth*. Bloomington: Indiana University Press, 2002.

Walkowitz, Rebecca L. *Cosmopolitan Style: Modernism Beyond the Nation*. New York: Columbia University Press, 2006.

Watts, D. C. *Elsevier's Dictionary of Plant Lore*. London: Academic Press, 2007.

Weber, Max. "Science as a Vocation." In *From Max Weber: Essays in Sociology*, edited by Hans Gerth and Charles Wright Mills, 129–58. Oxford: Psychology Press, 1991.

Weil, Lise. "Entering a Lesbian Field of Vision: *To the Lighthouse* and *Between the Acts*." In *Virginia Woolf: Lesbian Readings*, edited by Eileen Barrett and Patricia Cramer, 241–58. New York: New York University Press, 1997.

Whitworth, Michael. "Porous Objects: Self, Community, and the Nature of Matter." In *Virginia Woolf Out of Bounds: Selected Papers from the Tenth Annual Conference on Virginia Woolf*, edited by Jessica Berman and Jane Goldman, 151–56. New York: Pace University Press, 2001.

———. "Virginia Woolf, Modernism and Modernity." In *The Cambridge Companion to Virginia Woolf*, edited by Sue Roe and Susan Sellers, 107–23. 2nd ed. Cambridge: Cambridge University Press, 2010.

Widmer, Kingsley. "The Primitivistic Aesthetic: D. H. Lawrence." *Journal of Aesthetics and Art Criticism* 17, no. 3 (Mar. 1959): 344–53.

Williams, Peter, and Laura Chrisman. *Colonial Discourse and Post-Colonial Theory*. New York: Columbia University Press, 1994.

Winterhalter, Teresa. "'What Else Can I Do But Write?' Discursive Disruption and the Ethics of Style in Virginia Woolf's *Three Guineas*." *Hypatia* 18, no. 4. (Fall/Winter 2003): 236–57.

Woolf, Leonard. *Downhill All the Way: An Autobiography of the Years 1919–1939*. New York: Harcourt, 1967.

———. *Quack, Quack!* Hogarth Press, 1935.

Woolf, Virginia. *Between the Acts*. 1941. Reprinted with introduction and annotation by Melba Cuddy-Keane. Orlando: Harvest-Harcourt, 2008.

———. *The Diary of Virginia Woolf, Volume Two: 1920–1924*, edited by Anne Olivier Bell, with the assistance of Andrew McNeillie. San Diego, New York, and London: Harcourt Harvest, 1978.

———. *The Diary of Virginia Woolf, Volume Three: 1925–1930*, edited by Anne Olivier Bell, with the assistance of Andrew McNeillie. San Diego, New York, and London: Harcourt Brace & Co., 1981.

———. *The Diary of Virginia Woolf, Volume Five: 1936–1941*, edited by Anne Olivier Bell, with the assistance of Andrew McNeillie. San Diego, New York, and London: Harcourt Brace & Co., 1985.

———. "The Greek Notebook." Monks House Papers, Ad. 41. University of Sussex Library, Brighton, UK.

———. "*The Hours*": *The British Museum Manuscript of* Mrs. Dalloway. Transcribed and edited by Helen M. Wussow. New York: Pace University Press, 1996.

———. *Jacob's Room*. 1922. Reprinted with introduction and annotation by Vara Neverow. Orlando: Houghton Mifflin Harcourt, 2008.

———. "Modern Fiction." In *The Common Reader*, 146–54. 1925. Reprinted with introduction and annotation by Andrew McNeillie. Orlando: Harvest-Harcourt, 1984.

———. *Moments of Being*, edited by Jeanne Schulkind. London: University of Sussex Press, 1976. 2nd rev'd ed. San Diego: Harcourt Brace, 1985.

———. *Mrs. Dalloway*. 1925. Reprinted with introduction and annotation by Bonnie Kime Scott. Orlando: Harvest-Harcourt, 2005.

———. "On Not Knowing Greek." In *The Common Reader*, 23–38. 1925. Reprinted with introduction and annotation by Andrew McNiellie. Orlando: Harvest-Harcourt, 1984.

———. "Poetry, Fiction, and the Future." In *The Essays of Virginia Woolf. Volume 4: 1925–1928*, edited by Andrew McNeillie. 428-40. London: Hogarth Press, 1984.

———. *Pointz Hall: The Earlier and Later Typescripts of Between the Acts*. Edited by and with introduction by Mitchell A. Leaska. New York: New York University Press, 1983.

———. "The Prime Minister." In *The Mrs. Dalloway Reader*, edited by Francine Prose, 65–76. New York: Harvest-Harcourt, 2003.

———. *A Room of One's Own*. 1929. Reprinted with introduction and annotation by Susan Gubar. Orlando: Harvest-Harcourt, 2005.

———. "Thoughts on Peace in an Air Raid." In *The Essays of Virginia Woolf. Volume 6: 1933–1941 and additional Essays 1906–1924*, edited by Stuart N. Clarke. 242–48. London: Hogarth Press, 2011.

———. *Three Guineas*. 1938. Reprinted with introduction and annotation by Jane Marcus. Orlando: Harcourt, 2006.

———. *To the Lighthouse*. 1927. Reprinted with introduction and annotation by Mark Hussey. Orlando: Harvest-Harcourt, 2005.

———. *To the Lighthouse: The Original Holograph Draft*. Transcribed and edited by Susan Dick. Toronto: University of Toronto Press, 1982.

———. "Thunder at Wembley." In *The Essays of Virginia Woolf, Vol. 3: 1919–1924*, edited by Andrew McNeillie, 410–14. New York: Harcourt Brace Jovanovich, 1986. Originally written in 1924.

Woolf, Virginia, Vanessa Bell, Thoby Stephen, and Gill Lowe. *Hyde Park Gate News: The Stephen Family Newspaper*. London: Hesperus Press, 2006.

Wright, T. R. *The Religion of Humanity: The Impact of Comtean Positivism on Victorian Britain*. Cambridge: Cambridge University Press, 1986.

Wyatt, Jean M. "The Celebration of Eros: Greek Concepts of Love and Beauty in *To the Lighthouse*." *Philosophy and Literature* 2, no. 2 (1978): 160–75.

———. "*Mrs. Dalloway*: Literary Allusion as Structural Metaphor." *PMLA* 88, no. 3 (1973): 440–51.

Young, Robert J. C. *Colonial Desire: Hybridity in Theory, Culture and Race*. London and New York: Routledge, 1995.

Zimmerman, Bonnie. "Is 'Chloe Liked Olivia' a Lesbian Plot?" *Women's Studies International Forum* 6, no. 2 (1983): 169–75.

Zwerdling, Alex. "*Between the Acts* and the Coming of War." *Novel* 10 (1977): 220–36.

———. *Virginia Woolf and the Real World*. Berkeley and Los Angeles: University of California Press, 1986.

INDEX

abstraction, 78, 80, 81, 84, 112–14

active reading, 4–5. *See also* participatory reading

Adorno, Theodor, 14, 19, 52n3, 53, 56, 59–60. *See also Dialectic of Enlightenment*; The Enlightenment; fascism; Max Horkheimer

Africa, 60, 71, 76–78, 82, 121–22. *See also* blackness; colonialism; primitivism; race; Hugo Ball

Allan, Tuzyline, 41–45

Altieri, Charles, 9

Angel in the House, 75, 95, 102, 114. *See also* modernity; Mrs. Ramsay; Leslie Stephen; *To the Lighthouse*

anthropomorphism: and primitivism, 78; flowers, 43–47; nonanthropomorphic, 79–81, 84, 103, 108–15. See also *Mrs. Dalloway*; *To the Lighthouse*; Peter Walsh; Clarissa Dalloway; Mrs. Ramsay; Lily Briscoe

anthropology, 18, 53–54, 78; E. B. Tylor, 18, 55, 78. *See also* Jane Ellen Harrison; J. G. Frazer; primitivism; premodern; Carl Kerényi

antirational, 15–18, 51–55, 67–68; antirationalism, 67; antirationalist, 16. *See also* modernity; primitivism

Aphrodite, 21, 91, 96–97, 99, 124, 131. *See also* Venus

Arnold, Matthew, 101. *See also* Victorian

Artemis, 20–22, 26–38, 43, 49–50, 91, 98–100, 108–12, 124–27; Artemisian community, 27, 34- 40, 45–50; Artemisian figure, 33–34, 98–99, 112, 124–27, 130; Atalanta, 33, 112; Britomartis (bee), 108. *See also* Diana; Eleusinian; Homeric *Hymn to Demeter*; Jane Ellen Harrison; Jean-Pierre Vernant

Athena, 20–21, 33, 91, 97, 99, 124, 127, 130–31

Bacchae, the (Euripides), 66. *See also* Dionysus; tragedy

Bachofen, J. J. 89, 92–93, 95. *See also* matriarchy; Victorian

Barrett, Eileen, 2n3, 3n4, 32–35, 51n1, 61, 123–25, 129–30

Ball, Hugo, 82. *See also* Africa; Dada; modernism; primitivism

Bataille, Georges, 85–86

• 153 •

Bennett, Paula, 39, 41, 46

Between the Acts, 2n3, 18, 20–23, 58, 119–35; Bart Oliver, 124, 129–30; Budge (Constable), 121–22; Giles Oliver, 126–28, 130–31; Reverend Streatfield, 132–34; William Dodge, 125–28, 130–31; pageant, 120–21, 128–29, 131–34. *See also Pointz Hall*; Isa Oliver; La Trobe; Lucy Swithin; Mrs. Manresa; fascism; tragedy

Birth of Tragedy (Nietzsche), 17, 18, 21, 55–56, 63–64. *See also* Dionysus; Jane Ellen Harrison

blackness, 74–78, 76n19, 81–82, 85–86; in Greek art, 81–82; Dreadnought Hoax, 82. *See also* Africa; colonialism; primitivism; Gretchen Holbrook Gerzina; Robert Young

Bowlby, Rachel, 72n6, 74, 83

British class system, 2, 11, 19, 26, 37, 39, 43, 49, 61, 71n5, 88–90

Burrow, J. W. 13, 101. *See also* rational materialism; modernity

Campbell, Joseph, 16, 123. *See also* Robert Ellwood

Carpentier, Martha C., 54, 97–98

civilization, 10, 18, 57, 67, 69–73, 85–89, 92n3, 95, 113–14, 130

Clarissa Dalloway, 14, 18–22, 25–50, 52–55, 67, 70–74, 87, 89–90, 107; as mature Mrs. Dalloway, 26, 37–39, 41–43, 49–50; as young Clarissa, 27, 30, 34–40, 42; as Persephone figure, 30–32, 36, 38, 43, 48–49; as Artemis figure, 32–35, 38, 43, 49; as patriarchal, 26, 38, 41–43; and lesbian desire, 26–27, 34, 38, 40–45, 45n34; and death, 29–33, 35–36, 39, 43, 48–49. *See also* Artemis; Eleusinian; flowers; Homeric *Hymn to Demeter*; *Mrs. Dalloway*; Persephone; "The Hours"

capitalism, 11, 14, 22, 24, 28, 38, 48–49, 61, 73, 83

classical, 2, 7, 15–18, 21, 66, 77, 96; classicism, 2, 2n2, 15; classicists, 18, 33. *See also* Olympian; Friedrich Nietzsche

coincidencia oppositorum, 81

colonialism, 69, 76–77, 86, 88, 95; colonial desire, 76–77, 81–82, 84, 86, 90. *See also* Africa; primitivism; Peter Walsh; Robert Young

community, 9, 20, 22–23, 25–27, 30, 33–34, 37–38, 40, 45, 47, 49, 50, 53–55, 62, 66–67, 96, 103, 108, 111–12, 121, 123, 133, 135; female community, 26–27, 33–34, 37–38, 40, 45, 47, 49, 50, 135; in Harrison's work, 9, 25, 27, 55, 67, 96, 103, 108; in Frazer's work, 54, 66; in Homeric *Hymn to Demeter*, 20, 22, 26–27, 34, 37–38, 40, 45, 50, 135. *See also* Eleusinian; isolation; Jane Ellen Harrison

complicity, 47, 77, 90, 92, 98n17. *See also* Clarissa Dalloway; Mrs. Ramsay; Peter Walsh

Comte, Auguste, 101

conservative: aspect of Artemis, 112; Eliot's view of history, 10; in Frazer's theory, 67; politics in *Mrs. Dalloway*, 30, 49. *See also* Richard Dalloway; Lady Bruton

Conversion and Proportion, 60–62, 67. *See also Mrs. Dalloway*; "The Hours"; Sir William Bradshaw; religion; nationalism

Cramer, Patricia Morgne, 27, 41, 121n8, 129

cubism, 4, 15, 78

Cuddy-Keane, Melba, 23, 127, 132n27, 132n28

Dada, 82. *See also* Africa; Hugo Ball; modernism; primitivism

Dalgarno, Emily, 8, 20n46, 51n1, 53, 58n15

Darwin, Charles, 57; Darwinian ethical theory, 13. *See also* Leslie Stephen; rational materialism; Victorian

Das Mutterrecht (Bachofen), 89, 92, 95. *See also* Bachofen; *Mother Right*; matriarchy

Demeter, 2n3, 8, 21, 27–29, 28n5, 34, 37, 39, 91, 96–99, 97n14, 98n17, 104n31, 124–27

destabilize: hegemony, 25, 90, 120, 123; narrative, 11, 23, 90, 91, 121; allusions, 11, 22, 130, 131. *See also* disruption; parataxis; fragment

Detloff, Madelyn, 120–22

Dialectic of Enlightenment (Horkheimer and Adorno), 14, 19, 52n3, 53, 56, 59–60

Diana, 83, 125. *See also* Artemis

Dionysus, 7, 20–22, 28, 52–53, 63, 65–68, 127, 135; as Prometheus, 65–67; Dionysian, 51, 55–56, 63–68, 69, 69n1, 135. *See also Bacchae* (Euripides); Nietzsche

disruption: narrative disruption, 4, 121, 122, 124, 134; allusion as disruptive, 135; of women's communion, 31, 40, 42–43;

mythic thinking as, 19, 86, 90; of social order, 74; in *Between the Acts*, 120, 132–135. *See also* La Trobe; destabilize

Eleusinian, 35n17, 38, 43, 44n31, 45, 48–50, 115, 135; Mysteries, 20, 21, 26, 28, 96, 125; Mother and *Kore*, 20, 22, 26, 28–29, 28n5, 39, 96; flowers in, 22, 26–27, 31, 33, 34, 36, 42, 83; Thesmophoria, 20, 21, 26–28, 37; Homeric *Hymn to Demeter*, 20, 22, 26–30, 33–35, 38–50, 53, 56, 84, 96, 125; Demeter, 2n3, 8, 21, 27–29, 28n5, 34, 37, 39, 91, 96–99, 97n14, 98n17, 104n31, 124–27; Artemis, 20–22, 26–38, 43, 49–50, 91, 98–100, 108–12, 124–27; Hecate, 20, 28–29, 28n5, 48, 96, 126, 128–29; in Harrison's work, 21, 26–28. *See also Prolegomena to the Study of Greek Religion*; Demeter; Persephone; Artemis; Hecate; flowers; Homeric *Hymn to Demeter*

Eliade, Mircea, 16, 123

Eliot, T. S., 1–4, 9–10, 16, 19, 25, 53–54, 57; "The Waste Land," 1, 9; "Ulysses, Order and Myth," 1–2, 2n2, 3n7, 9, 19, 53. *See also* mythical method; modernism

Ellwood, Robert, 16, 76, 123

empire, 2, 26, 28, 38, 56, 60, 62, 68, 72, 86, 88–90, 95, 115; British Empire, 60, 62, 70, 71, 71n5, 73, 77, 88, 113, 121–122; "Thunder at Wembley," 88; chow dogs, 71–72, 88; imperialism, 18–19, 22–24, 28, 37, 38, 42, 49, 51, 52–53, 55, 60–62, 67–68, 69–72, 74–77, 86–90, 95, 111, 113–14, 121–22

Enlightenment, The, 14, 14n31, 53, 54, 93, 101, 111, 117; reason, 9, 17, 19, 52n3, 59–60, 101–02; counter-Enlightenment, 75n13; Goddess of Reason, 113. *See also Dialectic of Enlightenment*

epistemology, 3–4, 9, 11–13, 15–16, 23, 29, 51, 58, 67, 100, 119

Erinyes/Eumenides, 8, 80–81, 86, 99. *See also* Great Goddess; Jane Ellen Harrison; matriarchy; pre-Olympian religion

Expressionism, 15. *See also* abstraction

Eysteinnson, Astradur, 4

fascism, 3, 14, 16, 23–24, 60, 119–123, 131–35. *See also Dialectic of Enlightenment*; Theodor Adorno; Max Horkheimer; *Between the Acts*; La Trobe

Fauvism, 15

Felson, Nancy, 5, 5n12, 70

feminism, 1, 2, 11, 20, 21, 23–24, 25–27, 38, 41, 47, 49–50, 55, 75, 91–95, 111–17, 123; feminist classicism, 33; maternalism, 16, 93, 93n4; liberal feminism, 93, 115–16; feminist theology, 93. *See also* matriarchy; Jane Ellen Harrison

Fernald, Anne, 8, 26n1, 100, 122

fertility: nonbiological, 22, 26, 27, 34, 49; and death, 22, 29–30, 48; floral imagery, 26, 54; matrifocal, 27, 49, 93–94, 103–105, 109–12, 114, 116; ritual, 27, 54, 56, 67; and race, 86; as repressive, 103, 110–14, 116, 126–128. *See also* feminism; Great Goddess; matriarchy

flowers, 5, 30–31, 36, 44n31, 46–47, 49; floral imagery, 38–47, 48; as female bodies, 39–43, 45, 48; clitoral symbolism, 39, 41, 44–46; "a match burning in a crocus," 26–27, 38, 40–47, 41n26, 42n28, 44n31, 45n34; Mulberry's flower shop, 27, 31, 40, 43–47; economy of, 26, 38–39, 46–48; red carnation, 43, 72, 83–84, 84n32; in Homeric *Hymn to Demeter*, 22, 26–27, 29, 31, 33–34, 36, 38, 42, 83. *See also* Eleusinian; lesbian; Paula Bennett

Foley, Helene, 33, 36, 37, 45, 96

Fowler, Rowena, 8, 8n22

fragment, 4, 8–9, 90, 119, 121–23, 131n28, 132, 134

Frazer, J. G., 9, 54–56, 66–67; *The Golden Bough*, 9, 54

free indirect discourse, 4, 20

Friedman, Susan Stanford, 8, 115

Fry, Roger, 75, 76n19

Gaipa, Mark, 13, 100, 101

Gauguin, Paul (*Oviri*), 78–79. *See also* modernism; abstraction; primitivism

Gerhard, Eduard, 92–93

Gerzina, Gretchen Holbrook, 76, 76n19, 82

Gramsci, Antonio, 69; civil and political society, 69–71, 73, 77, 87–90

Great Goddess, 2n3, 7, 20–23, 48, 78–81, 83–84, 91–99, 103–16, 123–24, 129–30, 135; in Jane Harrison's work, 7, 80–81, 96, 99, 103; Great Mother (Neumann), 20, 79, 97, 104, 106, 111, 130; Mistress of Wild Beasts (*Potnia therōn*), 29; appropriated by patriarchy, 23, 48, 93–94, 99, 103–04,

104n31, 113–14, 117, 124. *See also* feminism; Jane Ellen Harrison; matriarchy; premodern; pre-Olympian religion; vegetation deity

Greek, 2–5, 7–12, 3n5, 8n20, 8n22, 17–18, 21, 23–24, 25, 27, 32–33, 37, 41, 55–56, 63, 66, 70, 75, 78, 81, 83, 90, 91, 92, 95–96, 98–99, 108, 121, 124, 133–35; Greece, 8n22, 10, 21, 55–56, 66, 83. *See also* classical; Eleusinian; Hellenism; Homer; Jane Ellen Harrison; Olympian; preclassical oral literature

Hades, 20, 28–29, 31, 33, 38, 40, 42; The Underworld, 7, 29, 31, 33, 39, 48, 81. *See also* Eleusinian

Harrison, Jane Ellen, 3n5, 7–9, 16, 18, 27–29, 37, 45, 55–56, 67–68, 75, 80–81, 84, 86, 90, 92–96, 99, 102–04, 107–09, 111, 114, 116–17, 121n8, 131; *Mythology*, 29, 34, 94, 99, 114; *Prolegomena to the Study of Greek Religion*, 21, 26–28, 55, 63, 80, 93–94, 108; *Themis*, 16, 94, 104

Hecate, 20, 28–29, 28n5, 48, 96, 126, 128–29. *See also* Eleusinian

hegemony, 5, 23, 53, 60, 69, 87, 89–90, 119, 135; counterhegemonic, 11

Helen of Troy, 96–97

Hellenism (Victorian), 10, 18

Hera, 21, 44n31, 91, 97–99, 111; marriage with Zeus, 107–08. *See also hieros gamos*, Zeus

heroism, 9, 11, 81, 95, 102–03, 106–07, 114; exceptional individual, 11, 21, 102, 104; Olympian, 23, 94, 110; Homeric, 96, 102, 103; imperial, 84, 87. *See also* Homer

heterosexuality, 22, 26–27, 32–35, 38, 40, 42–47, 47n35, 49, 94, 103, 112, 115–16. *See also* Artemis; lesbian; sexuality

hieros gamos, 97–98, 108, 109. *See also* Hera; Zeus

Hite, Molly, 4, 5n12

Homer, 72, 83; *Odyssey*, 4–5, 22, 70, 81–82, 83; Odysseus, 22, 70, 81–82, 96, 102; Kirke, 81, 83; Sirens, 7, 20, 80–83, 86, 135; Homeric style, 70, 81–83, 96, 102; Homeric values, 94–96, 102; Homeric heroism, 96, 102. *See also* heroism; preclassical oral literature; Sirens

Homeric *Hymn to Aphrodite*, 96, 97

Homeric *Hymn to Demeter*, 20, 22, 26–30, 33–35, 38–50, 53, 56, 84, 96, 125

Horkheimer, Max, 14, 19, 52n3, 53, 56, 59–60. *See also* Theodor Adorno; *Dialectic of Enlightenment*; the Enlightenment; fascism

"Hours, The," 30–31, 34–35, 43–44, 52, 61–62, 65, 67, 134. See also *Mrs. Dalloway*

Huxley, T. H., 57, 101

indeterminacy: in Woolf's mythic method, 28, 44, 50, 52, 114–15, 116; narration, 91, 116; oral literature, 2, 5, 5n12, 70; pre-Olympian myth, 2, 7–8, 29, 30, 52, 81. *See also* parataxis

insanity, 51, 57, 59; Septimus, 22, 51–53, 51n1, 57–60; and Dionysus, 7, 51–53, 62–67; produced by instrumental reason, 52–53, 57–60, 67; and science, 57–60; and religion, 51–52, 57, 62, 67–68; as mystical vision, 53, 57–58, 67–68. *See also Dialectic of Enlightenment*; instrumental reason; modernity; mythic vision; rational materialism; religion; Septimus Warren Smith; *Mrs. Dalloway*; "The Hours"

instrumental reason, 4, 52, 52n3, 60, 67, 110. *See also Dialectic of Enlightenment*; rational materialism

Isa Oliver, 122–24, 126–31. *See also Between the Acts*

isolation, 11; Persephone in heterosexual marriage, 30, 40, 45, 47; of Septimus, 65; Goddess as unifier of, 111; Crone, 127–28. *See also* community; heterosexuality; patriarchy

Jacob's Room, 6–7, 10–11, 18, 21, 122, 134

Joyce, James, 1, 4, 54; as paratactic, 4n8; Eliot on, 1, 10. *See also* T. S. Eliot

Jung, Carl, 16, 123; Jungian psychology, 76, 78, 104; archetypes, 62, 91n1, 92, 97, 113n41. *See also* Erich Neumann; Carl Kerényi; Great Goddess

Kerényi, Carl, 17, 39, 45, 83, 96, 98

Keres, 81, 86

Kołakowski, Leszek, 14, 19, 67, 95

Koulouris, Theodore, 8, 16n39

Index

La Trobe, 2n3, 120, 124, 128–29, 131–32, 135; as crone, 128–29, 131; La Trobe's pageant, 2n3, 120–21, 128–29, 131–34; mirror trick, 120, 131–34; gramophone, 120, 133. See also *Between the Acts*; fascism

Lady Bruton, 30, 31, 47, 70, 71n5, 72n6, 83–84; and imperialism, 62, 70–73, 71n5, 90; and religion as deceptive ideology, 72–73, 84; and Peter Walsh, 47, 70–73, 83. See also *Mrs. Dalloway*; "The Hours"; *Odyssey*; Peter Walsh; Empire

Lawrence, D. H., 16, 16n38, 54, 75

Leaska, Mitchell, 122–123. See also *Pointz Hall*

lesbian, 22, 26–28, 34–47, 41n26, 45n34, 115; Doris Kilman as lesbian, 46–47; "a match burning in a crocus," 26–27, 38, 40–47, 41n26, 42n28, 44n31, 45n34; patriarchal domination, 38–44. See also Artemis; Eileen Barrett; flowers; Judith Roof; Patricia Morgne Cramer; Tuzyline Allan

Lilienfeld, Jane, 92n2, 97, 100, 106

Lily Briscoe, 14, 18–20, 23, 64, 92–93, 97–98, 97n14, 100, 103, 106–17, 135. See also *To the Lighthouse*; *To the Lighthouse Holograph Draft*

liminality, 33, 35, 78, 131, 133, 135

Lucy Swithin, 123–126, 129–31. See also *Between the Acts*; *Pointz Hall*

Lukács, Georg, 14n31, 19, 52n3, 75, 105–06

madness. See insanity

Mahaffey, Vicki, 4, 5, 23

Maika, Patricia, 123–24

Marcus, Jane, 2n1, 24, 124

Marx, Karl, 17, 73, 90

materialism, 12–13, 15–17, 19, 23, 28, 51, 56–57, 58, 68, 75, 77, 92, 100–101, 104, 110–11, 113–15, 119, 131, 135; in "Modern Fiction," 15; antimaterialism, 58. See also rational materialism; rationalism; modernity; Leslie Stephen; Mark Gaipa

matriarchy, 2n3, 16, 45, 50, 91–96, 103–04, 108, 111–14, 123, 129; theories of matriarchy, 23, 89, 92n3, 93–95; Harrison's theory of, 27, 95, 103–04, 109, 111–14, 116–17; critiques of theory of matriarchy, 93; matriarchal (matrifocal) religion, 16, 21–22, 26–29, 45–50, 60–61, 75, 104, 108–09. See also J. G. Bachofen; Eileen Barrett; Patricia Morgne Cramer; *Das Mutterrecht*; Eduard Gerhard; Jane Ellen Harrison; feminism; Great Goddess; *Homeric Hymn to Demeter*

Medusa, 20, 99

mental illness. See insanity

metaphysics, 3, 11, 12–13, 100, 102

Mills, Jean, 1, 8, 17, 18, 27, 34n15, 75n11

modernism, 1, 4, 8–9, 12, 15, 16, 54, 75, 115; myth and modernism, 3, 4; modernist studies, 1, 3–4, 9; modernist 'mythical method,' 1–4, 3n7; primitivism, 15, 15n36, 74–75, 78, 84–86. See also Georges Bataille; Cubism; Dada; Expressionism; D. H. Lawrence; Fauvism; Hugo Ball; Paul Gauguin; Pablo Picasso; T. S. Eliot

modernity, 3n7, 10n25, 13–16, 14n31, 14n32, 19, 22–23, 28, 51-, 52n3, 55, 58–60, 67–68, 74–75, 84, 86, 90, 94, 105, 114, 122–23, 135; disenchantment, 13–14, 105; nostalgia for premodern, 15–16, 22–23, 28, 53, 74–76, 75n13, 114, 123. See also *Dialectic of Enlightenment*; Friedrich Nietzsche; instrumental reason; materialism; Max Weber; primitivism; rationalization; rational materialism; secularism

Moore, Madeline, 2n3, 104n31, 105, 115

Mother Right (Bachofen), 89, 92, 95. See also Bachofen; matriarchy; *Das Mutterrecht*

Mr. Ramsay, 11, 23, 94–96, 100–115. See also *To the Lighthouse*; *To the Lighthouse Holograph Draft*

Mrs. Dalloway, 5, 7, 11, 18, 21, 25–50, 51–68, 69–90, 107, 123, 134–35; Elizabeth Dalloway, 50, 50n36; Richard Dalloway, 29–30, 32, 47, 51, 62, 70–71, 89; Sally Seton, 26–28, 31, 34–50; Mrs. (Carrie) Dempster, 29, 39, 48–49; Maisie Johnson, 29, 39, 48–49; Miss Pym, 31, 39, 43, 44–45, 46; Doris Kilman, 29, 46–47; Hugh Whitbread, 41, 43, 62, 71, 83; Lady Bradshaw, 35, 61; Rezia (Lucrezia) Smith, 29, 48, 59, 61, 64–65, 65n29, 73. See also Clarissa Dalloway; Peter Walsh; Septimus Warren Smith; Sir William Bradshaw; "The Hours"

Mrs. Manresa, 124, 127, 129–31. See also *Between the Acts*; *Pointz Hall*

Mrs. Ramsay, 8, 13, 14, 23, 91–117, 135. See also Angel in the House; matriarchy; rational materialism; *To the Lighthouse*; *To the Lighthouse Holograph Draft* mythic vision, 19, 22–23, 28, 53, 69, 78, 90, 91–92, 135. *See also* Leszek Kołakowski

mythical method (T. S. Eliot), 1, 2n2, 3n7, 9, 19, 53–54. *See also* T. S. Eliot

nationalism, 9, 14, 25, 60, 62, 67, 120–21

Neumann, Erich, 76–79, 84–85, 89, 104–07, 107n36, 111, 130; Great Mother, 20, 79, 97, 104, 106, 111, 130; uroboric incest, 76–81, 84–86, 89–90. *See also* psychology; primitivism; Great Goddess

Nietzsche, Friedrich, 55–56, 63–67; Dionysian, 51, 55–56, 63–68, 69, 69n1, 135. *See also* *Birth of Tragedy*; Dionysus

Odyssey, 4–5, 22, 70, 81–82, 83. *See also* Homer; heroism; Lady Bruton; Peter Walsh; preclassical oral literature; Sirens

Olympian, 30, 55, 95–96, 104, 109, 117; religion, 16, 21, 94, 102, 104, 108; heroism, 23, 94, 102–03, 110. *See also* Jane Ellen Harrison; patriarchy; heroism

Origin of the Species (Darwin), 57. *See also* Darwin

parataxis, 4–7, 9, 12, 122, 123; hypotaxis, 5, 6; syntaxis, 5

participatory reading, 4–5. *See also* active reading

patriarchy, 8, 19, 22, 25–28, 37–38, 40–43, 47, 49–50, 60–62, 67, 86, 90, 92–95, 99, 103–05, 113–14, 115–16, 124, 127–28, 130, 132; Olympian, 9, 11, 16, 23, 38, 55, 94, 95, 104, 107–09; within women's relationships, 20, 27–28, 37–38, 40–43, 49; version of goddess, 23, 48, 92, 94, 103–105, 110–11, 114, 116, 124

Persephone, 2n3, 7, 20–22, 26–40, 28n5, 42–43, 45, 48–49, 81, 83, 91, 96, 98n17, 99, 124, 125, 126–27, 135. *See also* Artemis; Demeter; Eleusinian; Homeric *Hymn to Demeter*; Hades; Hecate; Helene Foley; Jane Ellen Harrison; matriarchy; Ann Suter

Peter Walsh, 5–6, 14, 18–19, 22–23, 28–29, 30, 31–32, 34, 36, 36n18, 42, 43, 47, 53, 69–90, 135; as critique of modernist primitivism, 70, 74–90; uroboric incest, 76–81, 84–86, 89–90; colonial desire, 76–78, 81, 84–86, 90. *See also* Antonio Gramsci; Empire; Erich Neumann; Homer; *Mrs. Dalloway*; *Odyssey*; primitivism; psychology; Robert Young; Sirens; "The Hours"

Phillips, Kathy, 7n5, 85, 86, 92n2, 95, 98n17

Picasso, Pablo (Les Desmoiselles d'Avignon), 78–79. *See also* modernism; abstraction; primitivism

Pointz Hall, 121–22, 125, 126, 131, 133. *See also* *Between the Acts*; Leaska

Poseidon, 39

preclassical oral literature, 4, 7; epic poetry, 5, 6, 70. *See also* active reading; Great Goddess; Homer; Jane Ellen Harrison; matriarchy; *Odyssey*; parataxis; participatory reading

premodern, 15, 52, 53–54, 63, 75, 78–79, 95, 123; as imagined utopia, 22–23, 28, 53, 74–76, 95, 123. *See also* anthropology; modernity; primitivism

pre-Olympian religion, 7, 11, 16–20, 25, 27, 45, 78, 89, 96, 130, 135. *See also* Artemis; Demeter; Dionysus; Eleusinian; Great Goddess; Hecate; Homeric *Hymn to Demeter*; Jane Ellen Harrison; matriarchy; patriarchy; Persephone

Pridmore-Brown, Michele, 120

primitivism, 10–11, 15–16, 15n36, 22–23, 28, 69–70, 74–90, 95, 106; "primitive" culture, 17–18, 78, 82, 92n3, 106; Erich Neumann, 76; Dreadnought Hoax, 82. *See also* abstraction; colonialism; Dada; Hugo Ball; Georges Bataille; D. H. Lawrence; Pablo Picasso; Paul Gauguin; Peter Walsh; Roger Fry

Procne and Philomela, 124. *See also* *Between the Acts*; Isa Oliver

Prometheus, 65–67. *See also* Dionysus; Friedrich Nietzsche; Septimus Warren Smith

psychology, 17, 76–77; jouissance, 44–45; Oedipal desire, 2, 37, 107; phallic symbolism, 44–45, 107, 107n36, 126; the unconscious, 17, 19, 76–77, 85, 134; uroboric incest, 76–81, 84–86, 89–90; Sigmund Freud, 76; Carl Jung, 16, 76, 78, 123; Erich Neumann, 76–79, 84–85, 89, 104–07, 107n36, 111, 130

queen, 30, 96; of the Underworld, 7, 29, 31, 32, 39–40, 81; of England, 31–32. *See also* Clarissa Dalloway; Persephone

race, 2–3, 76–79, 76n19, 81–83, 85–86, 121–22. *See also* Africa; blackness; colonialism; primitivism

rational materialism, 12–13, 15–17, 19, 23, 28, 51, 56–57, 68, 75, 77, 92, 100, 104, 111–14, 119, 135. *See also* epistemology; the Enlightenment; instrumental reason; J. W. Burrow; Leslie Stephen; materialism; modernity

rationalism, 12–13, 14, 15–16, 19, 22–23, 28, 53, 55–59, 67, 73, 75, 86, 90, 95, 102, 104, 106, 110, 113–14, 119; and Olympian religion, 104, 107. *See also* epistemology; the Enlightenment; instrumental reason; Leslie Stephen; materialism; modernity; rational materialism

rationalization, 13–14, 14n32, 113. *See also* modernity; Max Weber; Max Horkheimer; Theodor Adorno; secularism

reason. *See* the Enlightenment; instrumental reason; modernity; rational materialism; rationalism; rationalization

religion, 12–13, 26, 36–37, 42, 42n28, 44–45, 52, 55, 56–57, 60–62, 67–68, 73, 84, 92, 94, 100–103, 116, 121; Greek religion, 7, 11–12, 16, 18, 21, 27, 54–55, 78, 80, 92, 94, 97–98, 102, 104, 107–08, 130; Christianity, 52, 60–62, 67; eschatology, 79–80; soteriology, 84–85; theophany, 91–92, 114, 125–126. *See also* Angel in the House; Conversion and Proportion; Great Goddess; Jane Ellen Harrison; matriarchy; mythic vision; Olympian; pre-Olympian religion; spirituality

Romanticism, 10–11, 17, 51, 68, 75, 101, 135. *See also* modernity

Roof, Judith, 41, 44–45, 45n34

sacrifice, 9, 21–22, 48–49, 51, 54–56, 61, 62, 66–67. *See also* Dionysus; Emily Dalgarno; Friedrich Nietzsche; J. G. Frazer; *Mrs. Dalloway*; Septimus Warren Smith; "The Hours"; vegetation deity

Sautter-Léger, Sabine, 53

secularism, 14n32, 19, 102–03, 105, 113. *See also* the Enlightenment; Leslie Stephen; Max Weber; modernity; rationalization; religion

Septimus Warren Smith, 8, 14, 18–19, 20, 22, 28, 48, 49, 51–68, 69, 73–74, 86, 90, 135; death of, 48, 52–55, 57, 62–63, 64, 67; and Evans, 8, 58, 66; as inappropriately scientific, 57–60; and Leslie Stephen, 57; as mad, 22, 51–53, 51n1, 57–61, 68; and mystical vision, 22, 51–53, 57–60, 67–68; as Nietzschean Dionysian, 51–53, 56, 63–68. *See also Dialectic of Enlightenment*; Dionysus; Emily Dalgarno; Friedrich Nietzsche; insanity; J. G. Frazer; Jane Ellen Harrison; *Mrs. Dalloway*; Prometheus; "The Hours"; sacrifice; vegetation deity; sexuality; war; World War I

sexuality, 32–33, 38–39, 40, 41n26, 44–46, 47, 106–08, 121–22, 121n9, 126–28; asexuality, 32, 126–28; economy of female, 38–39, 48–49; genital, 41–42, 44–45; non-heterosexual fertility, 22, 26–28, 34, 49; sexual violence, 2n3, 39, 106–08, 112, 124, 126–27. *See also* Artemis; Eleusinian; fertility; flowers; heterosexuality; lesbian; patriarchy; Paula Bennett; psychology; spirituality; virgin goddesses

shell shock. *See* insanity, *Mrs. Dalloway*; Septimus Warren Smith

Sir William Bradshaw, 8, 60–62, 61n21, 65–68. *See also Mrs. Dalloway*; "The Hours"; Conversion and Proportion; Zeus

Sirens, 7, 20, 80–83, 86, 135. *See also* blackness; Great Goddess; Jane Ellen Harrison; Peter Walsh; pre-Olympian religion

spirituality, 12, 19, 22, 58–59, 65n29, 67–68, 75, 85, 102–103, 106, 109, 113–14, 117, 128, 134; ecstasy (*ecstasis*), 42n27, 63–64, 77, 84–85, 89, 92, 109, 114–16; lesbianism and, 26–27, 36–37, 42–45; and sexual inversion, 61; spiritual female community, 26–27, 37, 50; spiritual renewal, 26–27, 49, 50, 104; spiritual emptiness, 30–31, 102–106, 113–14, 117; spiritualism, 13. *See also* Georg Lukács; Jane Ellen Harrison; *Mrs. Dalloway*; *To the Lighthouse*; modernity; religion; secularism; sexuality

Stephen, Julia Duckworth, 13, 102. *See also* Leslie Stephen; Mark Gaipa; rational materialism

Stephen, Leslie, 13, 57, 100–102; marriage with Julia, 13, 102; *The Science of Ethics*, 13, 57; "An Agnostic's Apology," 57; *Mausoleum Book*, 102–03; in *Mrs. Dalloway*, 57; in *To the Lighthouse*, 100–02. *See also* Julia Duckworth Stephen; Mark Gaipa; rational materialism; T. H. Huxley

stream of consciousness. *See* free indirect discourse

Suter, Ann, 28n5, 34, 36, 45. *See also* Eleusinian; Homeric *Hymn to Demeter*; Persephone

Tennyson, Alfred Lord, 95, 101–02, 106

Three Guineas, 11, 25, 61, 70–71, 72, 120

To the Lighthouse, 2, 13, 18, 20, 21, 23, 57, 64, 91–117, 123, 125, 135; Andrew Ramsay, 99, 111; James Ramsay, 100, 107, 109–10, 112; Prue Ramsay, 98n17, 99, 111; Paul and Minta, 98, 104, 111; Mrs. McNab, 97; William Bankes, 97, 100, 104, 112–13. *See also* Lily Briscoe; Mrs. Ramsay; Mr. Ramsay; *To the Lighthouse Holograph Draft*

To the Lighthouse Holograph Draft, 96, 100, 105–07. *See also To the Lighthouse*

Torgovnick, Marianna, 15–16n36, 85–86. *See also* primitivism; Georges Bataille

tragedy, 2, 7–8, 23, 35–36, 66–67, 102, 121, 133–35; tragic chorus, 23, 121, 131–35. *See also The Bacchae*

Triple Goddess. *See* Eleusinian; Great Goddess; Homeric *Hymn to Demeter*; Jane Ellen Harrison

Tyler, Lisa, 2n3, 29, 35n17, 37, 47n35, 97n14

Tylor, E. B., 17, 18, 55, 78. *See also* anthropology

unconscious, the. *See* psychology; Carl Jung; Erich Neumann

vegetation deity, 20–22, 28, 39, 48, 51–52, 53–56, 62–63, 66–67, 111, 124, 127, 130. *See* Demeter; Dionysus; Eleusinian; Friedrich Nietzsche; Homeric *Hymn to Demeter*; J. G. Frazer; Jane Ellen Harrison; Persephone; pre-Olympian religion; sacrifice

Venus, 77, 124, 127. *See also* Aphrodite

Vernant, Jean-Pierre, 33, 81, 83, 98–99. *See also* Artemis; Keres; Sirens; flowers

Victorian, 73, 76, 93–95, 102–04, 110, 113, 114–15, 121–22, 127; Hellenism, 10, 17–18, 55; rational materialism, 13, 23, 55, 57–58, 67, 94, 100–03; sexology, 51n1, 61; theories of matriarchy, 92–95. *See also* Alfred Lord Tennyson; Angel in the House; epistemology; Hellenism; Leslie Stephen; Mark Gaipa; materialism; Matthew Arnold; rational materialism; secularism

war, 2–3, 11–12, 16, 24, 25–31, 49–50, 58–60, 66–68, 70, 71–72, 73–74, 95, 111–12, 114, 133, 134; militarism, 8, 22–23, 69–73, 87–89, 114; pacifism, 111. *See also Mrs. Dalloway*; Septimus Warren Smith; *To the Lighthouse*; World War I; World War II

Weber, Max, 13–14, 14n31, 14n32, 19, 52n3. *See also* modernity; rationalization; secularism

Weil, Lise, 97, 97n14, 115

White Hare (English folklore), 98

Whitworth, Michael, 10n25, 58, 75

Woolf, Leonard, 17, 119–20, 122, 133. *See also* fascism

Woolf, Virginia: *Diary*, 6, 11, 51, 57, 98n16, 99–100, 122, 133; "The Hours," 30–31, 34–35, 43–44, 52, 61–62, 65, 67, 134; "Hyde Park Gate News," 100; *Jacob's Room*, 6–7, 10–11, 18, 21, 122, 134; "Modern Fiction," 15; *Mrs. Dalloway*, 5, 7, 11, 18, 21, 25–50, 51–68, 69–90, 107, 123, 134–135; "Lappin and Lapinova," 98; "Mrs. Dalloway in Bond Street," 25; "On Not Knowing Greek," 8n22, 10, 24, 133; "A Sketch of the Past," 42n28, 44, 44n31; "The Prime Minister," 26–27, 134; "Thunder at Wembley," 88; *Three Guineas*, 11, 25, 61, 70–71, 72, 120; *To the Lighthouse*, 2, 13, 18, 20, 21, 23, 57, 64, 91–117, 123, 125, 135; *To the Lighthouse: The Original Holograph Draft*, 96, 100, 105–07

World War I, 1–2, 9, 21–22, 25–31, 49–50, 52, 58–60, 66–67, 69, 73–74, 87, 99, 111–12; Cenotaph, 87. *See also Mrs. Dalloway*; Peter Walsh; Septimus Warren Smith; *To the Lighthouse*

World War II, 134. *See also Between the Acts*; fascism

Young, Robert, 76–77, 76n19, 82, 84, 86, 90. *See also* Africa; blackness; colonialism; Peter Walsh; primitivism; psychology; race

Zeus, 20, 38, 65, 97–98, 104, 104n31, 107–08, 112; as Father God, 65; and Hera, 97–98, 107–08; and Prometheus, 65–66. *See also* Eleusinian; Hera; *hieros gamos*; Jane Ellen Harrison; Prometheus; Sir William Bradshaw

CLASSICAL MEMORIES/MODERN IDENTITIES
Paul Allen Miller and Richard H. Armstrong, Series Editors

Classical antiquity has bequeathed a body of values and a "cultural koine" that later Western cultures have appropriated and adapted as their own. However, the transmission of ancient culture was and remains a malleable and contested process. This series explores how the classical world has been variously interpreted, transformed, and appropriated to forge a usable past and a livable present. Books published in this series detail both the positive and negative aspects of classical reception and take an expansive view of the topic. Thus it includes works that examine the function of translations, adaptations, invocations, and classical scholarship in the formation of personal, cultural, national, sexual, and racial formations.

Virginia Woolf's Mythic Method
AMY C. SMITH

Shadows of the Enlightenment: Tragic Drama during Europe's Age of Reason
EDITED BY BLAIR HOXBY

Modern Odysseys: Cavafy, Woolf, Césaire, and a Poetics of Indirection
MICHELLE ZERBA

Archive Feelings: A Theory of Greek Tragedy
MARIO TELÒ

The Ethics of Persuasion: Derrida's Rhetorical Legacies
BROOKE ROLLINS

Arms and the Woman: Classical Tradition and Women Writers in the Venetian Renaissance
FRANCESCA D'ALESSANDRO BEHR

Hip Sublime: Beat Writers and the Classical Tradition
EDITED BY SHEILA MURNAGHAN AND RALPH M. ROSEN

Ancient Sex: New Essays
EDITED BY RUBY BLONDELL AND KIRK ORMAND

Odyssean Identities in Modern Cultures: The Journey Home
EDITED BY HUNTER GARDNER AND SHEILA MURNAGHAN

Virginia Woolf, Jane Ellen Harrison, and the Spirit of Modernist Classicism
JEAN MILLS

Humanism and Classical Crisis: Anxiety, Intertexts, and the Miltonic Memory
JACOB BLEVINS

Tragic Effects: Ethics and Tragedy in the Age of Translation
THERESE AUGST

Reflections of Romanity: Discourses of Subjectivity in Imperial Rome
RICHARD ALSTON AND EFROSSINI SPENTZOU

Philology and Its Histories
EDITED BY SEAN GURD

Postmodern Spiritual Practices: The Construction of the Subject and the Reception of Plato in Lacan, Derrida, and Foucault
PAUL ALLEN MILLER

www.ingramcontent.com/pod-product-compliance
Lightning Source LLC
Chambersburg PA
CBHW030113010526
44116CB00005B/235